Book Three
Communism

Second Edition

By K Kobayashi

In this book the author dissects the communist theories in relevance to the 20th century economy.

Strictly Literary™,
PO Box 242,
Scarborough, Queensland, Australia, 4020.
www.strictlyliterary.com
Phone: 0413 004 138
First published by Strictly Literary, Australia, in 2016

First Published 2016

Second Edition 2020

ISBN: 978-0-9924249-0-9

The author K Kobayashi is issuing the following series of books:

Book One *Idealism and Materialism*
Book Two *Religion*
Book Three *Communism*
Book Four *The Third Prophecy*
Book Five *The Sexual Laws*

Though the series is a coherent unit with the unified purpose, each book is designed to be read independently from the others. The first three books are preparing for the proposal and the last book is augmenting the proposal. His core proposition is in Book Four *The Third Prophecy*; in fact it can be expressed in one simple sentence 'To love a child is not to make one'.

He proposes the love which is the most beautiful and the strongest the humans will ever know; and unless this love is stronger than the love between the sexes the proposal does not make any sense. People imbued with this love gladly discard everything else including their sweethearts. As the concession to an idealised state of being single the sweethearts, unmarried, may remain friends to have sex with precaution against pregnancy. Buddhists and Christians have always taught their adherents to be single all their life. The author firmly believes that marriage has been the greatest curse of the human race. Men and women suffered tremendously through marriage all these millenniums still they could not work out the way out. Only the love of the Third Prophecy leads the ordinary people to stay out of marriage with the unwavering conviction.

This love when adopted by an individual will fulfil what the first (idealism; and religion as crystallisation of idealism) and second (materialism; and communism as an extreme form of materialism) prophecies promised but did not deliver in full to the humans and human societies. This love when adopted by a society as a whole will fulfil not only the first and second prophecies to the full but also will solve many serious problems the humans have had all these millenniums as well as the humans may have in the future. The acceptance of this new way of life by the bulk of the population will result in hugely reduced population with the predominantly beneficial results to the humans. This leaves one serious problem for the ordinary single men and women, that is, how to solve their sexual problem. The author proposes the solution of this problem mainly addressed to single men in Book Five *The Sexual Laws*. He expounds the solution getting the idea from 'mind only' developed by the Buddha; the mind only concept is explained in Book Two *Religion*.

The author wants to prove beyond reasonable doubt that the arrival of the societies dominated by this new way of life is inevitable in the future provided the humans act according to the survival instinct as they have done all these millenniums. Since his message is contrary to the people's way of thinking in the past and present, he thinks that the ordinary people at present do not comprehend the message of the Third Prophecy, and it will take one century for the general public to fully appreciate its teaching and live according to its creed.

Contents

Chapter 1 Communism Appraised

Preface

Karl Marx left voluminous written records of his understanding of political economy, and my cursory research into his works revealed the following findings:

In comparison with a large volume of documents concerning the capitalist economy, which he mostly criticised, he left only scant information as to how to build a communist society. This fact is surprising since we associate him with communism and expect that he must have formulated his communist theories thoroughly. Even his core theories on capitalism are limited in number and much more so on communism, and both appear piecemeal scattered in his vast writings. The passages of the same messages dotted his voluminous papers. *Capital* repeats the same arguments to the point to weary the readers. However, we have to appreciate, as Marx might have been aware, that if readers want to pick up quickly a few aspects of communism, then the repetitions are indispensable. Marx's followers also wrote about the communist theories; however, they mostly repeated the fundamental theories of Marxism and furthered only the practical aspects of the doctrines.

I am to rate truism of his political economy and not his literary competence. I collected only his thrust of the arguments and ignored his unimportant theories. Many of the theories Marx put up have no values as economic theories and some are even ludicrous; this book does not deal with these peculiarities. I am not the only person who dismissed some of his claims as nonsense and many economists voiced the view if Marx had actually believed in these propositions. For example, Marx made a point that the objective conditions of labour—raw materials and working instruments—are not the means employed by labour but they are the means of employing labour (Marx 1971, p. 115). This is a mere play of words and has no economic sense. Also Marx wrote that Egyptian pharaohs had absolute power and only one man was free in their society. This is true provided that he qualified the statement by the eras during the long history of Egypt. As a matter of fact he did not.

Also Engels inserted a comment now and again in his writings that Marx put more importance on a particular theory than it deserved. For example, he wrote, towards the end of Chapter XV Effect of the Time of Turnover on the Magnitude of Advanced Capital, *Capital* Volume II, the following comment:

> The uncertain results of these painstaking calculations led Marx to attach unwarranted importance to a circumstance, which, in my opinion, has actually little significance (Marx 1956, p. 288).

Lenin similarly commented in his works that Marx's theory on a particular subject was no longer valid. They both used extreme circumlocutions in expressing their opinions. I want to assess the merits rather than the demerits of Marxism, as the interviewers normally do during the job interviews: the interviewers look for the merits rather the demerits of the interviewees. This attitude comes about in part from the employer's desperate need to fill the vacancies. I use the similar approach when referring to Buddhism and Christianity in this series of books: I assess only the important teachings, discarding the rather dubious theories.

In developing his ideology, Marx naturally used the plights of the contemporary workers, which were quite different from those of today's economically advanced countries. Also I read some criticism that in fact his data were as much as 20 years behind his time, which was as a matter of fact advantageous to his line of argument. In dissecting his theories I use mainly the prevailing conditions of today's capitalist economy. There are a few good reasons for doing this:

- I have scanty information about the economic plights of Marx's contemporary society.
- Marx insisted that the working conditions of the workers would be worse off as the capitalism progressed. Hence analysing the current conditions would give a fair assessment of his doctrines.
- We all know that the industrial workers in Britain during the Industrial Revolution led appalling life—at work and at home, which led to the birth of scientific communism in the first place. This is a historical fact but should not be the criteria to adopt communism today. For us, only the economic analyses of today's working conditions make sense. It is illogical for us to assess Marxism on the 19th century European contexts. In the same way the Buddhist or Christian or any other religious doctrines must have relevance to our present life to be any value for us.

Section 1 Background of Communism

The Industrial Revolution is an imprecise term without any breaks but I apply it in this book in the sense Arnold Toynbee used to describe England's economic development from 1760 to 1840, whose major achievement was developments of steam engines, cotton-textile industry and steel making. Historians call this phase the First Industrial Revolution, sometimes referring also to that of a few other countries in Western Europe and North America. It is differentiated with the Second Industrial Revolution, which widely spread on such developments as in electricity, mechanical engineering, chemical engineering and internal combustion engines in the subsequent years. The steam proved to be a wasteful source of energy and active quest to replace it was succeeded by the development of electricity. During the late 19th century, electricity began to replace steam power. Germany and USA took the lead in this new Industrial Revolution, and Britain lost its lead. (Davison 1993, pp. 182-3) Continental Western Europe and North America took the initiatives of the Second Industrial Revolution in the latter part of the 19th century, and 20th century. Science and engineering are progressing rapidly at present, and the industrial revolution is still said to be in progress today and there is no end in sight.

As a matter of fact the industrial revolution is not a unique phenomenon as described above but is a general term indicating a rapid progress in the method of manufacturing commodities. We can find an instance of industrial revolution in the Chinese history. A commercial and industrial revolutions happened in China between the eighth and twelfth centuries. China exhibited widespread use of money, establishment of institutions for handling and advancing credits, increased trade regional and international, and cultivation of hitherto uncultivated land. The growths of mining and large scale manufacturing of iron goods and textiles carried China to the stage aptly called an early industrial revolution. The Chinese economy of the 12th and 13th centuries was by far the most advanced in the world. In conjunction with steelmaking they devised various innovations. They achieved high temperature using coke. They invented the predecessors of Bessemer steel process and Siemens-Martin process. China's steel production was enormous by the mid-11th century and made as much steel as Western Europe in 1700. There was a clear separation of workers and capitalists. The Chinese also built the predecessors of steam engines and textile machines. (Milston 1978, pp. 175-6) Producer goods operated on the different principles, and as far as consumer goods were concerned the following mechanism operated in China at the time. The machine production could not compete with the quality products by the craftsmen, and could not beat the price made by the domestic mass produce of the peasantry, so there was no gain in further mechanising the production.

Karl Marx developed his theories observing the First Industrial Revolution of Western Europe, particularly of England. He moved to England in 1849—just after the First Industrial Revolution of England, and wrote his books researching on the appalling working and living conditions of the workers. Adam Smith earlier wrote on political economy and advanced the concept of industrial capitalism; however, his major work published in 1776 centres on the fundamentals of pure capitalism encouraging the policy of laissez faire, and does not answer the problems of later years such as recessions and monopolies. Hence the governments of later industrialised economy moved away from his simple policies to more complex policies matching complex industrial societies. However, even today many economists highly regard his theories, saying that his fundamentals are correct. Similarly I have come to believe that Marx' theories are applicable only to the First Industrial Revolution and do not answer the later problems of capitalism. The communist governments after 1970s increasingly realised that communism was obsolete in their societies and moved away from the communist policies. People of the world in general discarded Marx' doctrines in the late 20th century.

The communists did not deviate from the production-oriented economy practised by the newly set-up industries during the First Industrial Revolution. Fundamentally the demand exceeded the supply well into the revolution and consequently the producers concentrated on manufacturing the commodities which sold themselves. Also during the First Industrial Revolution in Britain the capitalists could obtain the cheap labour without restrictions. The difficulty securing cheap labour in the middle of the 19th century contributed to end the revolution. Also the capitalist economists in the various countries as the capitalism progressed had to change from the production-oriented to the consumer-oriented economic thinking. As the huge number of the commodities flooded the market the producers found them hard to sell. This placed the importance on the consumers who could afford to buy more as their disposal income arose after the middle of the 19th century. The capitalists and workers purchased a large amount of consumer goods in their household, and even the firms purchased for their production and distribution a large amount of producer (capital) goods as well as some consumer goods.

For Marx and his contemporary people how to sell the manufactured commodities was not a serious concern. As capitalism progressed the makers of commodities had to find the buyers, which became harder and harder. The emphasis of the advanced capitalism shifted from manufacturing to consumption. The consumption-oriented meant that the manufacturers had to make and improve the commodities of the kinds the consumers want, and the manufacturers had to devote their efforts and finance to meet the demands on price, quality and variety. The communists till the end of the 20th century did not see the trend or more precisely they could not change, because many of the communist theories were based on erroneous premises placing the undue emphasis on production, in the same way Spain and Portugal in the earlier centuries placed too much emphasis on acquisition of gold and silver, which turned out to be an erroneous concept in the long run.

The consumers (general public and manufacturers) had no choice but to purchase what were in the markets under the production-oriented system. As the disposal incomes for the consumers increased they naturally wanted more varieties on quality and price; in fact this was the general trend under the advanced capitalist societies of the world.

As mentioned above, the manufacturing changed from production-oriented to consumer-oriented in the capitalist societies. The command economy of the communist countries is production (or producer) oriented. I am to cite an example about book writings. In the long past it was possible to write books from the view point of writers: the elite writers wrote the books for the elite of the society where the bulk of the population were illiterate. However today if the writers want to make a large sum of money, they must have readers in mind. In fact, this trend matches with the communists' assertion that the world affairs were decided by the masses rather than by the elite. The communists should have changed to consumption-based economy since they theorised that the masses decided, among the various ramifications, the economic matters, which resulted in the importance of consumers and marketing of the commodities. In this instance we can see the communists did not relate the theories to practice. In one sense the human greed of masses triumphed over the command economy of the communist government.

It is said that consumer spending account for two-third of capitalist economy today. This resulted from the past overall economic forces, some were perceived and acted upon and some unrecognised, and resulted in the survival of the capitalist economy. However it has brought one predicament of recession which no countries have managed to avoid all these years. The recessions were caused by the overproduction exceeding the willingness of spending on the part of the consumers. The communist countries did not have the recession through their life from the nature of the setup, that is, the production-oriented planning economy.

The communist theories were fossilised all these years in the form Karl Marx presented: they give us the impression that he fixed his theories so as not to allow any changes. The communists did not see any need to change. For example, they asserted correctly the communist societies did not have the problem of boom and bust as the capitalist societies had. However, the fundamental problem, as I see, is that Marxist theories were critically flawed, and the world outlook to see the world as being based on material did not give impetus for change. Materialism alone does not explain the humans and human behaviours. I set out this series of books on the premise that the humans are led by the following ideological means of survival: necessities of life, sex, religion, idealism, materialism, racism, nationalism, sexism and arts. The incorrect economic theories naturally lead to incorrect policies. One wrong theory may not produce a wrong policy since a policy is normally born from the assessments of the society and the common sense built on the various theories. However, it is absolutely imperative that we have to strive for the correctness of every economic theory, rather every theory in any human activities. Idealism did not make any progress since the early classical era simply because of its nature.

The elite of the communist party who controlled the government and society did not allow any deviations in their community, being afraid that the theoretical changes might jeopardise their prestige. Also the Communist Parties of Russia and China did not embrace the intellectuals as their comrades and the intellectuals did not form the core of the parties. The theoreticians with higher education could have developed the communist doctrines to suit as the capitalist counterparts have developed the capitalist doctrines as the problems arose. These flaws in the communist countries resulted in their poor rhetoric and policies.

The industrial capitalism was at an initial stage, and the depletion of natural resources and environmental damages were not the issues for Adam Smith and Karl Marx and their contemporary literati. Though Marx made a few references to consumption and recessions, his main focus was on production. Today we do not have any problems in producing various consumer and producer goods thanks for the consumers' desire for a variety of commodities and the producers' desire for profits assisted by a large number of economic and technical experts.

Since Marx's main concern was the First Industrial Revolution and communism, this book centres on these topics and briefly refers to the subsequent advancement of industries and also to communism in Russia and China.

The feudal system in Europe started to disintegrate at the end of the 15th century and people around the manors left their jobs to be absorbed by the capitalist mode of agricultural production and commodity manufacture. This process was completed by the middle of the sixteenth century.

The Industrial Revolution was not an accident and came about inevitably through the progress of Western Europe, particularly of Britain, as I expound in Chapter 4 Book One *Idealism and Materialism.*

Europe went through:

the Renaissance (14th-16th centuries)
Discovery of New World (14th-16th centuries)
Reformation (1517-1648)
European Expansion (15th century onwards)
Enlightenment (17th-18th centuries)
Industrial Revolution (18th century onwards)

The intellectual movement of Enlightenment produced, among others, political thoughts and scientific developments, both of which crucially contributed--possibly all the above events were indispensable--to the birth of the Industrial Revolution in Europe. The fundamental drive of the movement was the reasoned approach to life.

China's social settings in the eighth to twelfth centuries were entirely different from those of the European fourteenth to eighteenth centuries. We may posit that China could have developed the full industrial revolution provided it satisfied its own requirements different from those of Europe. However in view of the Third Prophecy expounded in Book Four of this series, this conjecture may not be valid. China could not have satisfied the requirements in the absence of the diffusion of idealism in their society as much as Europe could not have if idealism had not diffused in their society. These views may be contrasted with explaining the events from spiritual or temporal viewpoint. The Bible explains the events, personal and social, from the spiritual viewpoint; and the historians, history from the temporal (social, political and racial) viewpoint. I would rather not go into the debate such as if the two views should match, or if they do not match some of the assumptions are wrong.

> The 17th century was notable for the foundation of a number of national academies of science, through which the new generation of natural philosophers could exchange views. Outstanding among them were Royal Society of London (1660) and Paris Academy of Science (1666). (Williams 1987, p. 143)
>
> In the present century [18th], technology has become almost synonymous with applied science and the whole edifice of science is built on foundations laid in the 17th and 18th centuries. Nevertheless, the men who brought about the Industrial Revolution were in the main not scientists, but practical men of affairs with an eye for profit and little or no formal education. (p. 143)
>
> Prior to the Industrial Revolution, the only driving power available was humans, animals or winds (Wells 1925, p. 603).

Just before the Industrial Revolution, only 10% of the Europeans lived in cities. Majority of people lived in the rural areas and engaged in farming: they were virtually self-sufficient making clothing, furniture and tools. There were small guild shops in the towns offering various products such as cloths, hardware, jewellery and weapons. However, the entrepreneurs who distributed the raw materials to the homes and collected the finished products to sell commercially organised most of the manufacturing. Smelting of iron was carried out for thousands of years, using charcoal as an agent. Charcoal was used not only for smelting of iron but for many other purposes, and Britain almost exhausted the hardwood forests by the early 1700s. Because of high expense of charcoal smelting became increasingly unprofitable in Britain.

Enclosure movement in England started in the 12th century, progressed rapidly from 1450 to 1640, and completed by the end of the 19th century. In the rest of Europe the movement made little progress until the 19th century. People erected barriers or fences in the common land to appropriate the thus enclosed land for the individual cultivators, excluding the rights of the other people. This movement became the prelude of Agricultural Revolution (1750-1850) of Britain. The revolution produced more food, cotton and wool with efficiency and less labour. The forced-out labourers got employment in cottage industries and factories as the Industrial Revolution progressed. The increased food production was to feed the increased population, and cotton and wool became the raw material of the textile industries. The Agricultural Revolution entailed introduction of new machinery and new crops, better drainage and scientific methods of breeding among others.

By the mid-1700s Britain became the leading colonial power. She could obtain huge amount of raw material for textiles from her colonies and at the same time her colonies became the ready markets for the manufactured products especially of textiles and steel. She had enough wool within the country to supply the industries. She obtained silk from China, though China was not a colony at this time. She obtained cotton from the West Indies, Africa and the southern United States, though the United States soon became independent. She also had the large deposits of coal and iron ores to carry on the industrial production. Towards the end of the 18th century, iron-making process has improved tremendously; and coke, product of coal, replaced the charcoal for making steel. From then on Britain produced unfettered amount of steel.

The Industrial Revolution encompassed only the radical use of power and machinery and there was no comparable change in the chemical processes (Williams 1987, p. 117). The Mechanical Revolution may be the proper term instead of the Industrial Revolution used in this section since the mechanical power marked the revolution, uniquely describing the revolution. The industrial revolutions have occurred in many parts and eras of the human history. (Wells 1925, p. 602)

Though the revolutionary change to make the industrial products brought wealth to a small number of capitalists, it brought horrible working and living conditions to a large number of working people. The latter was so-called industrial proletariat who did not have any sizable property or education and hence had to earn a living by physical works. This resulted in part from the fact that capital available for the industries was scarce at the time and people expected high return for the capital.

Britain as a nation accumulated wealth through the overseas trade and the exploitations of her colonies from the 16th century onwards. Hence Britain had capital to do the trade and to proceed with agricultural and industrial revolutions. British banks had ample supply of capital seeking opportunities for investments in various ventures. From these facts many people concluded that commercial capital, as we may broadly class the above accumulated money, fed the Industrial Revolution. It seems that was not the case according to Francois Crouzet (1922-2010). In the following analyses of his we must remember that the overall statistics backing the assertions were simply not available, and he made his own conclusions from the available evidence which were the actual figures of the case studies.

It is impossible to describe the broad assessment how the revolution started and capital flowed to the industries. However, the following scenario may be typical. In the early 18th century, the small manufactures (middle class) saw the opportunity to make money and rise up the social ladder by setting up the textile machine shops. Free British political system among the other reasons encouraged them. Initial outlay for the small workshop was small and it seems many manufactures could afford it. Capital was spent for what we call the fixed capital, that is, equipment and machinery. Rapid capital accumulation with the success of the manufacturing allowed the rapid expansion of the factories. Of course capital for expansion also came from the merchants-manufacturers and the outside the industries such as the wealthy people and the merchants who might have the dealings with the selling of the products. However, the research indicated that the major capital utilised was the accumulation within the industries. The successful small manufacturers became industrialists and capitalists.

Industries were urban and capital intensive. Personal relationship was at the bottom of most investment. Capital of the great landowners played a minor role in financing the revolution with the exception of coal mining. The capital markets were badly organised compared with today's standard. Banks regarded factories as bad risk and many had the policy not to give long-term credits to the industrialists. The industrialists at the time had a low social standing and were not the profession of gentlemen. The industrialists acquired social respectability only after the Industrial Revolution was well under way, possibly in the middle of the 19th century. However, they often bought raw materials with the bank credits (short-term). The English banking system did not play any major role in financing the revolution. The industrialists needed money for expansion and incessantly complained about the scarcity of money. The above information comes from *Capital Formation in Great Britain during the Industrial Revolution* (1972) by Francois Crouzet.

The purpose of production originates in the anticipated strong desire for consumption on the part of the consumers. This strong desire is matched by the strong desire to make money on the part of the producers.

The Industrial Revolution in Britain came about by the huge demand for the products from her colonies. Britain also imported raw material for the industries not only from her colonies but from the non-colonial overseas suppliers using her extensive shipping networks.

In the first half of the 18th century, the large scale industry simply did not exist, and only the limited number of the factories in England operated on the division of labour. In the second half, the industry adopted a large number of machines resulting in the division of labour; and the wages fell sharply as a consequence.

The division of labour led to the increase of the production outputs by the same number of the workers. The reasons may be by:

- the increase of the dexterity of a worker by specialisation,
- the saving of time lost passing from one job to another,
- the benefit of the bulk purchase of raw material,
- the development of the specialised machine.

(Smith 1991, p. 13)

Though the capitalists introduced the machinery primarily to increase the amount of products and to lower the production costs, it is also true that the capitalists introduced it as a competitor to the workmen who subsequently felt threatened to lose their jobs, being made superfluous by its introduction (Marx 1954, p. 410). This feature is still observed today and it's been reported through the history of industries of the world that the workers tried to prevent the introduction of the latest machines and even to wreck the installed machines.

Britain, ahead of other nations, went through the Industrial Revolution from 1760 to 1840 though the historians have divergent opinions when it started and ended. This revolution in Britain occurred spontaneously, not being the result of conscious government policy which encouraged industrialisation as happened later in many other nations. (Mathias 1969, 4) Western Europe and north-eastern United States had widespread industries as the result of supply and demand using the new technologies by the mid-1800s.

The steam engine developed by the engineer James Watt became the driving force of the Industrial Revolution. James Watt of Scotland made the improved versions of the steam engine on the earlier models developed by Thomas Savery and Thomas Newcomen, and completed the Watt engine by 1790. The steam engine powered the spinning and weaving machines. The use of steam industrialised the cotton industry and then the other branches of manufacture. Steam-powered locomotion revolutionised the transport of land and sea.

> Apart from adopting steam as a new source of power, the Industrial Revolution was characterised by the increasing use of machinery--often of a quite novel kind--to carry out the work once done manually (Williams 1987, p. 151).

The Industrial Revolution resulted in the massive increase in productivity, especially in the textile industries. The factory system manifested the high productivity resulting from the division of labour and in the use of machines among other innovations. This high productivity stimulated a demand for more machines and more raw material, better communication and better transport. (Kennedy 1987, p. 145)

Between the 1750s and the 1830s the mechanisation of spinning in Britain had increased productivity by a factor of 300 to 400. As the other European nations and the United States gradually industrialised the production, the underdeveloped countries such as China and India could not compete and their fabric production fell sharply relying on the cheap imports. (p. 148)

Spinning and weaving processes were mechanised in Britain to meet the growing demands. Spinning is the process of making threads from raw material such as cotton or wool fibres and had been done traditionally on a spinning wheel. The various improvements were made on the traditional spinning wheels: roller-spinning machine (1738), spinning jenny (1760s), water frame (1760s) and spinning mule (1774-9). Weaving is the process of making cloth from threads, and had been done traditionally by a handloom. To speed up the process, the various improvements were made on the traditional handlooms: flying shuttle (1733), steam-powered loom (1780s), and further improvements in the early 1800s.

Also the machine tools such as boring machines and planers were in general use in Britain by 1830. The steam locomotives on the railroads came into general use to facilitate the transport of passengers and freight by the late 1830s. By the mid-1800s the steam boats carried raw materials and finished products as well as passengers across the oceans.

The machines powered by steam engines necessitated the establishment of the factory. The factory system was the concentrations of capital and labour. The capitalists (the industrialists) wanted high return for the capital which was scarce for them at the time. Many capitalists made fortunes through the ventures.

Division of labour had to come into effect for efficient running of the factory. Division of labour also meant that many jobs did not require strong physique or high skills, and women and children could perform the jobs. The hourly rate for the workers (women, children and even men), many of whom could not read or write, were quite low. They had to work long hours for little gains. They worked 12 to 14 hours a day for six days a week, though people in the domestic system worked just as long.

The parliaments made the factory laws favourable for the capitalists. The government were also on the side of the capitalists without any reservations. The capitalists, landowners and aristocrats controlled the parliaments and the government in Britain at the time. The workers did not have the right to vote and the British law forbade the formation of a union. The middle class, which consisted of business and professional people, became well off and gained political and educational benefits. By the mid-1800s the business interests largely controlled the parliaments. The workers must have wanted any institution which gave unqualified support for their cause; communism answered the desperate call.

In 1822 a Tory government was formed, and the Duke of Wellington, who had commanded the Allied army at the Battle of Waterloo (1815) to win over Napoleon, became Prime Minister from 1828 to 1830. He was determined not to change the electoral system and lost his office for opposing parliamentary reforms. In 1830 the Whigs formed the government. The parliament passed the Great Reform Bill in 1832, and as a consequence the franchise was extended and the new industrialised towns were represented in parliament. Before this an oligarchy of landowners ruled Britain, and after the passing of the bill the urban middle class had an increasing say. The working class still did not have the voting rights and the Chartists, thus formed, pressed for the voting rights for all men. This movement fizzled out for lack of support. However, the reforms followed. Most workers in the towns were given the vote in 1867. The Trade-Union Act of 1871 and 1875 gave British unionism its legal foundation. Before these acts became laws unions and unionists were regularly persecuted by the government, not to mention the hostility of the employers. Farm labourers were given the vote in 1884. Women did not have the franchise until 1894 when the women who owned the property could vote in local elections. Britain introduced the universal suffrage in the early 20th century.

Belgium was the second country to industrialise in Europe. With the financial support from the government, Belgium developed heavy and textile industries from 1830 onwards. France started to industrialise in the mid-1700s but Napoleonic wars hampered its progress. Industrialisation remained problematic and France remained largely a country of farms and small businesses for much of the 19th century. Though Germany had natural resources for industrialisation, the political and social obstacles delayed its industrialisation. Germany made good progress in producing coal and steel by the end of the 19th century. Even before the declaration of independence in 1776, the United States had many sizable industries. After the independence they were successful particularly in developing shipbuilding and steel making and became the most industrialised nation on earth at the turn to the 20th century. (*Encyclopedia World Book* 1999, sv, Industrial Revolution.)

The nations whose people valued liberty and equality of opportunity accepted easily the political philosophy of laissez faire and its economic corollary (Dye, Moore & Holly 1966, p. 65).

Adam Smith postulated that the key to national prosperity is self-interest of the industrialists who compete with each other for profits, and nothing much to do with hard work or people's concern for each other's welfare. He expressed the above postulate in *An Inquiry into the Nature and Causes of the Wealth of Nations* (1776) in a systematic manner and he is often called a founder of economics, though a few thinkers and writers had offered economic theories before him. He set out to write the above book in 1766 and finished in the next ten years, and it became an instance success when published. In the above argument he reasoned that invisible hand is at work such that self-interest works for the welfare of the nation. (Hodgetts & Smart 1988, p. 9) William Pitt made a speech in 1792 that machines and credits etc. were the causes of England's commercial supremacy but the most enduring cause was accumulation (Marx 1959, p. 396).

Adam Smith advocated the abolition of the trade restrictions en masse, which was in fact the basic mercantilist philosophy. However, the government were not so quick to adopt the free trade policy. (Dye, Moore & Holly 1966, p. 563)

The government can protect the domestic industries by:

- tariffs or quotas on the imported goods,
- bounties for the export,
- subsidies for the home industries,
- manipulation of the exchange rate for the natural equilibrium.

(p. 569)

Adam Smith justified the discouragement for exporting the manufacturing materials by absolute prohibition or higher duties (Smith 1991, p. 429).

He was also against the perfect freedom of trade in the following particulars:

- Defence,
- When tax is levied at home, the equivalent foreign commodities should be taxed upon entry into the home market.

(p. 361)

For fifty years or more following 1815 the armed services consumed only 2-3 per cent of GNP in Britain, and the central government expenditures as a whole took much less than 10% (Kennedy 1987, p. 153).

Money is necessary to fuel the industrial and commercial progress and more money is generated in the form of returns upon capital invested (p. 155).

The prosperity of the mid-Victoria era in Britain--Victoria was queen of the United Kingdom from 1837 to 1901--was based on the principles of classical political economy and majority of British people except for Tory protectionists and socialists did not doubt the validity of laissez-faire economics (p. 156).

By the middle decades of the nineteenth century, as Britain changed from being predominantly agricultural to being predominantly industrial, it became increasingly dependent on the international trade, and more importantly on the international finance. Exports composed as much as one-fifth of total national income. In the fastest-growing sector of all, the invisible services of banking, insurance, commodity dealing and overseas investment, the reliance upon a world market was even more critical. (p. 157)

Already by the mid-18th century, the American colonies occupied a significant place in the pattern of maritime commerce and were beginning the first hesitant stages of industrialisation. By 1830 the country became the 6th industrial power. (p. 94)

The manufacturing sectors of the United States developed slowly in the first half of the 19th century, and only in the second half of the century the United States felt the impact of the Industrial Revolution; there was a tremendous increase in capital generated, in turn to introduce new technology. (Dye, Moore & Holly 1966, p. 68) The founders of America believed in the policy of laissez faire in the economic field. However, since the 1880s federal, state and local governments passed the legislations to regulate economic activities and America became modified capitalism. (Hodgetts & Smart 1988, p. 28)

In spite of the above legislations, the American people in general accepted the philosophy of laissez faire without reservation until the depression of 1930s. During and after the depression the people wanted the government to play roles in eventuating a sound and stable economy. (Dye, Moore & Holly 1966, p. 242) The theories of John Maynard Keynes since the depression of the 1930s advocated the economic stimulation through taxation. However, Milton Friedman, in opposition to Keynesians, strongly advocated pure capitalism of laissez faire. Friedman insisted that the Federal Reserve Board's failure to keep the money supply from dwindling by a third caused the Great Depression. (Hodgetts & Smart 1988, p. 29)

> The population of the United Kingdom in 1483 was about five million; and in 1760, nearly three centuries later, it had risen to only around nine million; but by 1830, the population had topped 24 million, almost a threefold increase in seventy years (p. 150).

Europe and the United States had the population explosion in the 19th century. Britain's population exceeded 42 million in 1900.

I mentioned why the Industrial Revolution erupted in England in the earlier paragraphs. However, without the cheap and abundant labour in England the Industrial Revolution would not have eventuated. Why was so much labour available at the time and why did these labourers endure such harsh working conditions for so long? Where did they come from in the first place?

The Agricultural Revolution preceded the Industrial Revolution by 10 years, and they progressed virtually side by side. Redundant labour the former made got the employment in the new factories the latter created. Unfortunately I cannot give the figures confirming the last statement: the figures are simply not available.

Because the division of labour of the Industrial Revolution enabled many of the jobs simple, and a large number of women and children worked in the English factories with less pays than the adult males. The adult males obtained skilled jobs or supervisory positions over women and children. Women and children of poor and working families had little opportunity to obtain jobs outside the factories, and besides these families could not live without the incoming money. One source of employment available was domestic servants with low wages for the middle and upper class families, not engaging in what we call production. Another source was seasonal farm works. Most of them did not have education and they had to have trades to make decent living. The factories gave the opportunity to do apprentice and had to endure the hard working conditions with low wages though education suffered as the result. For instance, in the early stages of the Industrial Revolution two-thirds of the workers for water-powered cotton mills were children. The percentage of children decreased as the revolution progressed; the children grew up working in the factories. The workers who did not want to work or were inefficient or suffered from the debilitating injuries were simply dismissed without compensation. For those who adapted well to the factory work got skilled jobs or supervisory positions and received more benefits than jobs outside the factories. Before the Industrial Revolution women and children worked at home--farms, shops and domestic production--doing various jobs often without pay: however, since they did not work at the factories the problem did not become the social issue.

The capitalists treated the workers harshly to get high return for their capital. This was made possible because in part the workers did not want to lose the paid jobs and in part there was an abundant supply of workers to replace them.

However, the economic situation in Britain was going to change in the middle of the 19th century. The national income of Britain expanded unmistakably after 1850. The proletariat became conscious as a class and they were no longer submissive to the employers, and demanded their rights, among which is the higher wages. All of this brought an end to the Industrial Revolution in Britain. The movement showed up as the concrete laws of the voting rights for most workers in Britain (1867) and British unionism was given the legal foundation (1871 and 1875). Also continental Western Europe and the USA came out as the strong manufacturing nations in the second half of the 19th century. With the flooded commodities the world market changed from the production-orient economy to the consumer-orient economy, which also contributed to the end of the Industrial Revolution in Britain. The Soviet economy after the October Revolution in 1917 clearly showed the production-oriented manufacture and could not deviate from this mode of economy, practically and even theoretically.

Karl Marx focused his attention to the Industrial Revolution of England at its height. Industries at this stage were privately owned and generally small. The owner of a factory was typically a capitalist and at the same time a manager. It is true he could dismiss a worker he did not want; however, he had to be worried about sabotage and wilful damage to the production facilities, as any owners of factories or houses in today's world have to. He would have been more worried in the absence of forensic investigations and insurances of today's standard. When he found out these disruptions he often did not know who did them, and could not take effective actions. He had to hide these serious concerns from the public scrutiny; the disclosure of his emotion on this nature would have been taken as his weakness. Marx did not refer to these matters, because he was either ignorant or chose to ignore them in his eagerness to proceed with his doctrines.

In the first half of the 19th century, the industrial proletariat did not constitute a majority of the working class even in Britain:

The population of Britain in 1784: 9 million; 80% worked in agriculture.
The population of Britain in 1865: 29 million; 60% worked in industry.
(Mercer 1996, p. 846)

Britain at the first half of the 19th century had approximately the following number of workers:

1.8 million agricultural labourers
1 million domestic servants
811 thousand workers in the cotton and woollen industries
(Spielvogel 1991, p. 722)

> The pitiful conditions found in the slums, mines and factories gave rise to ideology called communism. However, since the number of the industrial proletariat was comparatively small, that is, 811 000 workers in the cotton and woollen industries at the time, this ideology remained a fringe movement compared to liberalism and nationalism even in Britain in the first half of the 19th century. (pp. 749-50)

The working class are often contrasted with the possessing and ruling class. In the ancient times, the working class were more often referred to as slaves. In the Middle Ages, they were serfs of the land owning nobility and journeymen in the service of petty-bourgeois craftsmen. In the modern setting, they are agricultural labourers, domestic servants, industrial proletariat and other labourers who use their physical capacity to do the job. In the communist jargon, more often than not the working class are in a narrow sense, meaning the industrial proletariat excluding the other category of workers. (Marx & Engels 1989, p. 87)

The Bronte sisters painted the gloomy pictures of the British society in the middle of the 19th century. *Wuthering Heights* (1847) by Emily and *Jane Eyre* (1847) by Charlotte illustrated the ugly side of capitalism in progress as the young sisters observed; they were left behind the social boon of the Industrial Revolution.

France was beginning to receive the impact of the industrial revolution in the mid-19th century. Though it started in Milan in January 1848, it was in France that ignited the fire of a general European conflagration. The revolution erupted not in the rural areas but in the cities such as Milan, Paris, Frankfurt, Vienna, Budapest and Warsaw. England, the most economically advanced, and Russia, the least economically advanced in Europe, did not experience revolution. Its central demand the intellectuals spearheaded was the constitutional government with a widened franchise. The peasants, the vast majority of people in Europe, kept aloof from the disturbances. The working class who manned the barricades were leaderless. (Davison 1993, p. 237) There were a small number of industrial proletariat in Paris at the time and the small fraction of them had the knowledge of socialism. Outside Paris there were virtually no industrial workers in France. Though *The Communist Manifesto* was published earlier in the year, its impact on the upheaval was assessed to be minimal.

Karl Marx lived in London from 1849 until his death in 1883 and was active in exerting influence on the Labour Movement; however, its effect was marginal. The trade unions were the major power and push for labour representation in parliament at this time. (Rowse 1979, p. 153)

> Various Factory Acts passed through the British Parliament between 1802 and 1867: they were designed to improve the working conditions of the factory workers (Walker 1978, p. 195).

The British Parliament introduced a bill in 1802 banning paupers and their children working more than 12 hours a day. Sir Robert Peel proposed the bill which was unprecedented intervening into the factory life. The parliament passed the First Factory Act of 1819 by the urging of Robert Owen. On June 8, 1847 the Chartists had pushed through a factory law restricting working time for women and juveniles to eleven hours a day, and from May 1, 1848 to ten hours.

Marx agreed that these acts contributed to the welfare of the working people, but considered that the measures were insignificant as a whole.

The various factory acts enacted in Britain during the Industrial Revolution were enforced only in the large factories. The owners of these factories found the way to circumvent the laws and found other methods of exploiting their employees, and the laws were not enforced in the small factories, especially in the home industries. (Marx 1954, pp. 460-1)

> It is not too much to say that until the factory legislation that began in the 1830s the Wesleyan evangelicals were the only people who did much to relieve the suffering and to further the education of the working classes (Randall 1976, p. 407).

The benefits of industrialisation flowed into the working class in Britain after the second half of the 19th century. In fact it was estimated that the real wages of British workers were lowest during the Industrial Revolution. The wages of labourers increased from the middle of the 17th century to the middle of the 18th century. Karl Marx, who was born in 1818 and died in 1883, largely formed his opinions on the experiences of the British Industrial Revolution.

In the United Kingdom average real incomes (per capita incomes adjusted for changes in prices) declined in the early 1800s but the trend reversed by the third decade and generally the trend was upward for the rest of the century. By 1870 average real incomes were double the 1800 level and by 1900 they doubled again. These statistics do not indicate in themselves that the wage-labourers' lot improved as might convey without reservation since the average incomes included the incomes of the rich people as they do today. They show clearly that the total income of the United Kingdom improved dramatically but do not show the spread of the incomes.

The economists agree that after 1850 the national income of Britain expanded so fast that even the poor benefited from the expanding economy and industrialisation. Also the British workers obtained the electoral franchise after the middle of the 19th century. However, as far as the dwellings of the workers were concerned no substantial improvement had taken place, as the Royal Commission 'On the Housing of the Poor, 1885' reported.

> In the mid-19th century Britain dominated the world economy, with over 40 percent of the entire world output of traded manufactured goods produced within the country, and about a quarter of the world's international trade passing through British ports (Mathias 1969, p. 250).

Though the idea of communism dates back to ancient times, the systematic presentation as we know is the product of modern industrialisation and has spread even to the non-industrialised nations. During the Ricardian period of political economy the theory of communism and socialism came into existence and the later economists regarded Ricardo (1772-1823) as the originator of the concept. An English political economist Ricardo is best known for his book *On the Principles of Political Economy and Taxation* (1817) and Labour Theory of Value. Communism was founded on the best produced in Europe of the nineteenth century in the forms of German philosophy, English political economy and French socialism. People said at the end of the 19th century that the Frenchman will begin it and the German will finish it (Lenin 1975, vol. 2, p. 506). Karl Marx also got the direct impetus for the idea from the British Industrial Revolution. Capitalist production rests on the value or the transformation of the labour embodied in the products into social labour as well as the foreign trade and the world market. The working class themselves developed trade unionism; whereas, the propertied class, particularly intellectuals, developed communism. Another leading ideology in the modern times may be religion; however, religion has been so since the dawn of civilisation and still continues to be the leading light in many parts of the world today.

In France the factory workers became a significant and growing element of society between 1880 and 1914. The Syndicalists or the trade unions got underway in the 1890s. Unlike the Parliamentary Socialists, they did not believe in the parliament where the propertied dominated. They tried to get what they wanted by the direct action, especially by general strike. However, they all showed a strong sense of patriotism when the war started in 1914. (Grenville 1994, p. 27)

The large scale production in Germany started from 1840s. By 1870 the worst political obstacles were removed from the manufacturing section; however, it found that in the world market England supplied the articles of mass consumption, and France, the luxury items. Germany could not beat the former on price and the latter in quality. The large scale industry of Germany at around this time was almost exclusively for the home market excepting for the steel industry. The export items were a large number of small articles the rural domestic industries made. (Marx & Engels 1969, pp. 300-1)

In Italy, the Socialists were split into two hostile factions from 1903 onwards. A minority or the Reformists were intent to get reforms within the existing government framework. The majority, the Syndicalists, wanted a class revolution by the general strike. The great strikes of 1904, 1907 and 1908 were all defeated. (Grenville 1994, p. 34)

Attlee labour government (1945-51) reflected well the sentiment of the British people. They were not interested in theories of socialism but the enforcement of social justice. His government nationalised the Bank of England. So were the coal mines, civil aviation, the railways, and gas and electricity by the close of 1947. The compensations were paid to the employers and shareholders. (pp. 345-6)

Major Scientific and Technical Developments after First Industrial Revolution

Though electricity was generated earlier by the chemical reactions and stored in batteries which ran electric motors, Benjamin Franklin, Alessandro Volta and Michael Faraday carried out the pioneering work of mechanical generation of electric current in the early 19th century. Generators and motors underwent substantial development in the middle decades of the 19th century.

New thinking was put into effect in the 1880s in an effort to obtain high rotational speed to generate electricity. The Williams engine and the uniflow engine were based on steam engine and partially successful. However, Sir Charles Parsons achieved a real success by the invention of the steam turbine in 1884. The steam turbines have remained the major design with many improvements for generating electricity. The nuclear energy developed after the middle of the 20th century also runs the steam turbine. The hydroelectric power runs water turbine. The steam turbines have been used for the marine propulsion in competition with the internal combustion engines.

Electricity thus made available found its use. Thomas Edison developed the incandescent light bulb as illuminant in 1879. Towards the end of the 19th century, electric traction came to be used, running tramways and subway systems.

Electricity was not the prime mover, and hence the prime mover to substitute steam engines was sought. The internal combustion engines were put forward as prime movers in the 19th century. Nikolaus Otto came up with the gas engines in 1878, which became a commercial success. The gasoline engines were developed towards the end of the 19th century. Rudolf Diesel patented his diesel engines in 1892. By the end of the 19th century the internal combustion engines were replacing the steam engines in many industrial and transport applications. Though the British developed the steam engines in the earlier century, continental Western Europeans and Americans were largely responsible for the developments of the internal combustion engines. This transition reflected the change of leadership in researches and applications from Britain to continental Western Europe and America.

The widespread use of the steam engines and internal combustions engines led to the research and use of power technology. The coal industry went into rapid development in the early 18th century and went through the continuing expansion and innovation. The petroleum industry experienced the rapid expansion in the United States after the Civil War, and the other nations lagged behind the United States in this field and in fact did not make headway until the 20th century.

Medical technology also made significant progress. Anaesthetics and antiseptics were developed in the 19th century. Technique of blood transfusion, examination by X rays, radio therapy and vaccines came to be used. These advances also made possible complex surgery, apart from prevention, prognosis and treatments. Penicillin, the first of the antibiotics, was discovered in 1928, and its commercial production began in 1941.

The 20th century saw such spectacular development in science and technology that it is said that this century made more progress than the whole of the previous human history. The century is marked by the huge destructive wars of World Wars One and Two and the rivalry of the communist and capitalist nations, all of which contributed to the rapid progress of not only the armaments and industries but the whole range of political and economic activities. It is also characterised by the vitality of the United States which endeavoured to expand by whatever sources of humans and innovations. In this century also the atomic energy came into use for peaceful and destructive purposes, adding another important source of energy for the future of mankind.

Airplanes came into general use in this century, though the experimental works needed were done in the 19th and early 20th centuries. It is well known that the Wright brothers invented and flew the first airplane in 1903, though they built on the works of the predecessors. World Wars I and II greatly accelerated its development.

The electronic industry came into being, electronics being a branch of electricity. Guglielmo Marconi succeeded in transmitting the wireless message on electromagnetic waves across the Atlantic in 1901. The radio broadcast was introduced in Europe and America in 1920s. The electron microscopes, the radar, the electronic computer, the cathode-ray tube for the television were developed. The public in several nations got the television service by the outbreak of WW II.

The Germans pioneered rocket industry in the war effort in the 1930s and developed V-1 and V-2 rockets. The Russians and Americans took over the German rocket research results after the war.

The industrial revolution does not look like to abate in view of people's interest in and desire for consumer goods as well as those of the manufacturers in regard to making money. Though Karl Marx embraced optimism in technology and his pessimism was directed to capital and labour relations, the technological progress has created the serious problems after the 19th century when he lived. Chief among them may be the population explosion, ecological imbalance and harnessing of nuclear energy. (*Encyclopaedia Britannica,* 15th edn, sv, Technology.) The depletion of natural resources per capita is also distinct and serious problem. Huge population increase always accompanied the industrial revolution. The increase of industrial production enables to support more population; however, there is no inevitable relation between the capability and the increased population. Many people in advanced economies today do not make children as many as they can afford. They carry out birth control and it looks that as far as the developed countries are concerned the population is not a serious problem. Marx's attention was not directed to these problems we are currently having.

Formation and Spread of Communist Doctrines

Marxism became a leading ideology of the world prior to the close of the nineteenth century until the late 20th century, that is, roughly for 100 years. The so-called proletarians the world over and a small number of intelligentsia were the major advocates of these politico-economic doctrines. In the opening decades of the twentieth century, there were perhaps a million or so people who believed in communism the world over. (Wells 1925, p. 694)

In October (November by today's calendar) 1917, the successful communist revolution was carried out in Russia. There had been hundreds of revolutions of any note in the history of humankind: however, the Bolshevik Revolution as the above revolution is often called is the first revolution which people designed and engineered according to the set ideology that people had developed and debated for the previous century. This fact reflects the technological age of the 20th century.

> It is possibly true that as far as the challenge to and disruption of the existing society was concerned the French Revolution from 1789 to 1799 was the forerunner and the model of the communist revolution (Carmichael 1968, p. 50).

Lenin also wrote that without the dress rehearsal of 1905, the victory of the October Revolution in 1917 would have been impossible (Lenin 1975, vol. 3, p. 296).

At one time, one-third of the world population and the comparable land mass came under the communist control. As a rule, dedicated revolutionaries perpetrated the communist revolutions under the economically unsustainable predicament of the capitalist countries.

As a student I heard many times, from people who were well acquainted with economics, that capitalism had to give way to communism at some point in the future: capitalism was not sustainable in the long run and the changeover to the communist system was inevitable. Though they did not explain why the process was a certainty, I innocently believed that they knew the reasons which Karl Marx developed but were too complicated for youths. The repetitions and the confident manners by which many authorities presented the proposition to me did not give me any other choice but to believe it. I also heard time and again from the people who visited the communist countries that communism in practice was a poor performer, though it was excellent theoretically. I further remember a university lecturer in economics ridiculing Marxist doctrines which he had studied in some depth, and his text on economics contained a chapter highly critical of communism.

Bertrand Russell wrote that if all the problems of the world had been reduced to material levels, Marxism would have been the solution. He, further, indicated that materialism was only a part of human existence and hence he did not believe that communism was the answer to the woes of the world.

Whether the communist theories as a whole are correct or not, the intelligent and sensible people would think that these doctrines merit some study. To dismiss the communist doctrines out of hand is to make the same mistake of the communists, judging the theories emotionally. In fact we cannot ascertain until we dissect the doctrines if they are correct or not, seeing that there are diverse opinions as to their correctness. Besides, capitalism may learn something useful through the analyses. As a matter of fact, I present a version of communism in Chapter 2 Partial Communism Proposed by which system we can rectify, I believe, the major deficiencies under the current capitalist system.

I have found that it takes a fair amount of intelligence and a great deal of patience, to read and understand Marxist literature. I would imagine many people judged communism emotionally with piecemeal information for good or bad, not dissecting the ideologies as they should have done.

The general public of the world justifiably think that communism and Marxism are one and the same doctrine. People are in a habit of equating the two teachings since Marx dominated the theoretical aspects of communism. It is a taboo for the communists the world over to criticise Marx and his *Capital* (1867; 1885; 1895) in a similar way it is a taboo for the Christians to criticise Christ and the Bible. In case of disagreements among the communists, the protagonists insist that they interpreted the sayings of Marx correctly and the opponents misunderstood them.

Friedrich Engels, a German socialist leader and a successful industrialist, was a friend and collaborator of Marx. It seems that one fundamental source of successful union of the two characters was the fact that Engels acknowledged Marx's superior intellect. Engels not only collaborated with Marx in publishing many noteworthy books but published books of his own initiatives. Vladimir Lenin, father of Russian Communist Revolution, and also Mao Zedong (Tse-Tung), father of Chinese Communist Revolution, were significant contributors to the practical aspects of the communist doctrines. Each of these three individuals left a vast amount of written records to follow up Marx's theories, and even furthered their own views. I often wonder how these people found time to write so many books in spite of their busy public life. They must have been exceptionally energetic with the firm conviction to spur them on.

Dissenting Views among Communist Theoreticians

The communist theoreticians, though all expressed allegiance to the orthodox doctrines of Karl Marx, held different views as to how the theories can be put into practice. Marx's opinions were not necessarily consistent with regard to some applicability and Marx exhibited some uncertainties in applications in spite of his forceful argument in the fundamental theories, which I expound in sections 4 and 5. This uncertainty probably came from his lack of experience in the practical affairs of the society. For instance, Marx wrote that only the industrial proletariat can carry out the revolution he preached, though he expressed different views at times. Also we have to take into account of the view that the practical matters of life do not often conform to the even well-conceived and well-developed theories.

> Marx, Engels and Marxists in general have neglected the peasants in their teachings and relegated them, as petty proprietors, to the bourgeois camp. Lenin, however, came to the conclusion that, if properly led by the proletariat and the party, poor peasants could be a revolutionary force: indeed later he proclaimed even the middle peasants to be of some value to the socialist state. The same *April Theses* that urged the transformation of bourgeois revolution into a socialist one stated that poor peasants were to be part of the new revolutionary wave. (Riasanovsky 1977, p. 518)
>
> Russia, a land of peasants, could not afford to rely for its future on the proletariat alone, and at least the poor peasants, if not the wealthier ones, had to be included to bring theory into some correspondence with the facts. Again, in contrast to, for example, Germany, socialism never acquired in imperial Russia a legal standing or a mass following, remaining essentially a conspiracy of intellectuals. (p. 519)

When Lenin wrote that the toiling mass consisted of nine-tenth of Russian population he meant it the industrial proletariat as well as the peasants in opposition to tsar, nobles and capitalists (Lenin 1975, vol. 1, p. 626).

Marx wrote that in some countries such as France, the revolutionary movement must win over the great mass of people, peasants, for them to be successful. Further, the agricultural population, since they are dispersed over the great area and have a difficulty in an agreement on politics, cannot become an independent movement: They need an initiatory impulse of the proletarians in the towns. (Marx & Engels 1989, pp. 209, 318)

Engels wrote that the farm labourers or the agricultural proletariat can be rescued from their misery only when the landed property was transferred to the common national property. He did not see much difference between the industrial proletariat and agricultural proletariat in their state and solution to their problems. (Marx & Engels 1969, p. 164) He saw parallel in the means of production in the industry and the land in the farming.

Lenin believed that only the urban and industrial workers were able to lead the whole mass of the toilers and the exploited, though he did not discard the participation of the other working people. He did not believe that the Russian peasantry could carry out the communist revolution. In 1914 more than 80% of the Russian population were of peasant families and half of the peasants were illiterate. The Russian peasants lived a hard life indeed, close to subsistence. Both their scattered existence and their illiteracy prevented the peasants, though large in number, from organising their forces. The peasants of the communist usage referred to not only the tenants or labourers but the owners of a small patch of farm. 'But despite tactical manoeuvring he [Lenin] consistently held to the basic strategy of using the revolutionary potential of the peasant land-hunger as an integral part of the socialist takeover.' (Nove 1992, p. 29) He stressed the alliance of the industrial workers and the peasantry, which was essential since the bulk of the Russian population before World War One was of peasant families. In furthering the alliance he made points that the workers and peasants were similar in many ways; they were both toilers; both had common class enemies in capitalists and landowners; both formed the lowest strata in the society; and the industrial workers traditionally came from the peasants ruined on land. However, Mao made a successful revolution in China, a country of predominant agriculture, mobilising mainly peasant army, thus proving that Marx and possibly Lenin were wrong in this respect. Mao came from the prosperous peasant stock with all the hatred to the warlords and bureaucrats who filled the history of China. (*Encyclopaedia Britannica,* 15th edn, sv, Marx and Marxism.) Mao also modified Marxism to suit China and added Chinese characters to the doctrines.

The amounts of the harvest from the lands depend on many factors, the chief of which may be the good soil and the weather. Another characteristic of agriculture is long time required for its productions measured in weeks, months, even generations for timber-growing. Because of this lengthy production time it is set that farming cannot produce great wealth. (Marx 1956, pp. 246, 251) If we look at the extreme end in terms of production time, there are a few peculiar aspects in timber-growing:

- A large tract of land is required for economic gains.
- A small expenditure of human and capital for the production and the maintenance is required.
- A forest will still thrive in soils where the cultivation of grains is no longer profitable.

(p. 247)

There were a few other notable dissents in how to put the theories into practice among the communist theoreticians. They expressed their opinions as to which country would become the first communist state and how it would spread to the other countries. Karl Marx at first predicted that the communist revolution would take place in the industrially most advanced country at the time, that is, Britain. He must have reasoned that the communist revolution in the industrially advanced nations such as England and France would bring about the revolution in the other nations as they mature in the capitalist development. (Marx & Engels 1989, p. 89) Seeing that British workers' lot was improving after the second half of the 19th century, he abandoned this idea. Later in his life he hoped that Russia would be the country which would become the first communist state.

> But, in the 1870s and after, Marx made a number of remarks which suggested it was possible for Russia to jump a stage of economic development and to arrive at socialism without passing through the social dislocation and misery of capitalism (Walker 1978, p. 200).

Friedrich Engels expressed his view in *Principles of Communism* (1914) that the revolution would spread among the most developed countries such as England, America, France and Germany more or less simultaneously (Marx & Engels 1989, p. 96). He predicted in 1895, in the year he died, that a revolution, not necessarily a communist revolution, was imminent in Russia, seeing the intolerable condition of the peasants after the emancipation from the serfdom, and extremely disorderly financial affairs (Marx & Engels 1969, pp. 387, 390, 397). As a matter of fact, it was in Russia that Lenin and a few dedicated revolutionaries formed the first communist government in 1917.

Marx and Engels proposed in *Address of the Central Authority to the League* (1850) that the workers organise a proletarian guard with the commanders elected by themselves (Marx & Engels 1989, p. 189). A proletarian guard, as Marx and Engels meant, was the militia of workers at the time of communist insurrection.

Section 2 Communism in Russia

Preliminary Remarks on Russian Revolution

The Kievan Russia which had started at the end of the 9th century imported Christianity, Greek and Latin cultures from Byzantium, though the Renaissance (from the mid-14th to mid-16th centuries in Western Europe) did not prevail in Russia, and the Russian intellectual life was limited to what was translated for them. The institution of slavery existed in the Kievan Russia which the Mongols conquered in the 13th century; however, the vast majority of the population were free peasants until the serfdom was established. Ivan the Great put an end to the Mongol domination in Russia in the early 16th century. The institution of serfdom had become ingrained in Russia since the sixteenth and seventeenth centuries, when Western Europe was becoming free of serfdom. Though the institution of serfdom could be traced to the Kievan Russia in the 11th century, the vast majority of peasants became bound in full serfdom only in the 17th century. Though serfdom existed in the Russian modern history, Tsar Alexander II (1855-81) abolished it in 1861 in a grand effort of social engineering. The serfs received approximately half of the lands they had cultivated; however, they wanted all and simply there was not enough land for everyone. The reformist tsar created modern military and judiciary, and established the institution of local governments. All these reforms led to the spurts of industrialisation in Russia at the end of the 19th century. The state took the initiatives to create industries, placing an emphasis on heavy industries. It taxed the peasants heavily, and many of them became the proletariat the industries required. The proletarians led appalling lives and became the driving force of the revolutions in 1905 and 1917.

The upheaval of 1905, erupted under the strains of the disastrous war with Japan, did not have any leading ideas or leaders; however, it gave rise to the birth of the soviets which Karl Marx and Lenin did not conceive. The soviets (the workers' councils) played a vital role in the subsequent revolution of 1917, and Leon Trotsky proved his oratorical and administrative skills in the Saint Petersburg Soviet. The soviets were capable of quickly mobilising proletarian forces and of coordinating activities.

The emancipation preserved the peculiar Russian institution called communes. They were the peasants' self-government, having the power of distributing the lands to adjust to the changing needs of the families and available lands. The central government recognised its needs to be responsible for collecting taxes and redemption payments: they thought that the communes promoted stability in the rural area. Before the revolution many economists and politicians recognised that the communes were more hindrance to the economic growth. The communes periodically redistributed land, and hence the farmers did not have incentive to improve their holdings. As a matter of fact the peasants could not leave the lands without the consent of the commune.

The communes in the country were similar to the soviets in the cities. The communes organised the confiscation of the landlords' land and distributed among their members during the revolution. The Bolshevik government was hostile to the communes because they could not control them.

Unlike Western Europe where there was a fierce competition between the church and the temporal powers, no such competition existed in Byzantine history and the emperor was the head of the church as well. The Kievan Russia inherited this caesaropapism. During the Mongol rule the Russian church freed itself from the Byzantine tutelage, and when the Turks conquered Constantinople in 1453 the church became fully independent of Byzantine influence. Peter the Great made the Russian church one government department. The separation of the church and the state did not happen in Russia until 1917.

Russian Revolution

The Marxists in Russia founded the Russian Social Democratic Labour Party in 1898. In 1903 it split to the Mensheviks which aspired to wide membership and democratic decision making process, and the Bolsheviks which aspired for a single centralised party of professional revolutionaries with non-party members of workers and peasants assisting. Lenin led the Bolshevik faction.

Lenin gave concrete expressions to the theories of Karl Marx. Among them, Lenin found answers to his queries concerning the nature of imperialism in the works of JA Hobson, an English radical. However, Lenin's views were often ridiculed and his following, even among Russian socialists right up to the October Revolution of 1917, was a minority. Lenin's origin was not of the people as we might expect. His father, though started from the humble origin, was promoted to the post of provincial directors of schools and addressed as 'Excellency'. (Grenville 1994, pp. 106-7)

During the first few years of World War I, the Russian troops fought in their dogged, tough manners enduring hardships, and with disciplines unknown in the West.

Both the Tsarist Government (autocratic) and the Provisional Government (liberal) simply collapsed, and no revolutionaries or discontented workers brought them down. The former went down because the autocracy as they existed could not carry on the modern war and failed to see the mood of the people. The latter failed because the liberal principles representing the privileged class could not govern the country as it was at the time, not resolving the issues of war, land reforms, and the autonomy of the national minorities. Both imperial and liberal governments had been intent to carry on the war to a victorious conclusion.

The imperial Russia was a multinational empire and the Russians made up only half of the population and the rest was so-called minorities. The Provisional Government clearly could not satisfy the aspirations of the minority races within the borders. Women were second class citizens in the imperial Russia. The Bolsheviks fought for the equality of sexes among the other objectives, hence women played extraordinarily significant role in the revolutionary movement. (Kenez 2006, p. 71)

The minorities in the imperial Russia were not overly conscious of their ethnicity with the exceptions of the Poles and perhaps the Finns before and even during World War One. However, the situations radically altered at the disintegration of the empire and the consequence of the war, and the minorities became a potent force. The Bolsheviks utilised the situation to their advantage and it is thought that one contributing factor in their victory was to have handled the minority question cleverly.

The disastrous war prompted the strikes and demonstrations by the Russian people. The crucial event was the refusals both of the soldiers to obey the superiors and the commanders to carry out the orders. On February 27, 1917 the monarchy was overthrown and the Provisional Government was established. The government took over the administrative apparatus of the tsarist Russia, and all the foreign powers promptly recognised it though it had less power than the Petrograd Soviet. The high command of the army and the masses of workers and soldiers supported the government for now.

During the Provisional Government, the soviets sought supports from the soldiers whom the Mensheviks and the Socialist Revolutionaries mainly controlled, whereas the Provisional Government sought supports among officers of the army. The Social Democrats, divided into the Bolsheviks and the Mensheviks, were fierce rivals to the Social Revolutionaries (SR).

Stalin and Lev Kamenev (Trotsky's brother-in-law) returned from the Siberian exile in the early 1917 and took charge of the party policy. They were moderates and cooperated with the Mensheviks and the Social Revolutionaries. The Germans subsequently allowed Lenin to return to Russia in the hope of contributing to the disintegration of the Provisional Government.

Two million deserters from the army left the front, and the communes seized estate after estate from the great landowners.

The Bolsheviks had no more than 20 000 members as late as February 1917. In any case the Socialist Revolutionaries had the greatest popular support. Formed in 1901, the SR's looked to the peasants rather than the urban workers for support.

The Duma handed over all authority in March 1917 to the Provisional Government which Prince Lvov presided over. Lenin accused the Provisional Government of consisting of landowners and capitalists. The Provisional Government embraced one Socialist Revolutionary, Alexander Kerensky. Lenin returned to Petrograd from the German exile on 16th April 1917. Lenin declared that his aim was not to give a parliamentary republic but a republic of soviets. Within weeks the Social Democratic soviets or councils elected by soldiers and workers sprang up all over Russia. In Petrograd, a council of Soviets of Workers' and Soldiers' Deputies sprang up in defiance to the Provisional Government. The similar soviets had sprung up during the 1905 revolution. Lenin's first aim was to destroy the Provisional Government and put out the slogans: all lands to the peasants and all power to the soviets. Prince Lvov, unable to satisfy the increasingly radical demands of the populace, resigned in July in favour of Kerensky.

By the beginning of 1917 the Russia's repeated defeats in the field interacted with the unrest in the cities and the rumours of the distribution of land, to produce a widespread disintegration in the army. The Liberal Social Revolutionary Government headed by Alexander Kerensky had promised a constituent assembly to give Russia a democratic parliament. However, Kerensky's July 1917 offensive with the army slashed to pieces was the critical blow.

In August, abortive attempt by General Kornilov, commander of the Russian Army, to disperse the Petrograd Soviet with the army forced Prime Minister to relinquish General of the army post. By refusing to resign he effectively mutinied and also mismanaged the mutiny, and was arrested together with the fellow mutineers. This event fatally weakened Kerensky's government. Lenin claimed that Kornilov aimed at the dictatorship of landowners and bourgeoisie, the dispersal of the soviets and the restoration of monarchy (Lenin 1975, vol. 2, p. 228).

At the First All-Russia Congress of Soviets in June 1917, the SR's represented the largest single group. Kerensky was a leading member of SR. The Bolsheviks concentrated their efforts in gaining influence over the soviets, supporting Lenin's cry of 'Peace, land and bread' and 'All power to the Soviets', which were well attuned to the discontents of the people. In point of fact the Bolsheviks were a minority in the important soviets of the country. Leon Trotsky, recognised as vitally important, also returned from exile to Russia in May 1917 and joined the Bolshevik cause. In October 1917, at the Social Democratic Party Congress, the Bolsheviks had the majority delegates. By the time of the October Revolution they had obtained a majority in the local soviets. (Bradley 1988, pp. 188-9)

The Bolsheviks consistently represented the most radical views. The factory committees were formed shortly after the February Revolution by which the Provisional Government replaced the monarchy. They were the most important workers' organisation within the factories, and more powerful than the trade unions. The factory committees were a direct democracy and the Bolsheviks took over the leadership of these organisations.

On October 24 by the old Russian calendar (November 6 by today's calendar) the revolution started with Trotsky as the chief leader. The government lost all power and authority as well as the support of the armed forces. The revolution was completed in a few days, virtually bloodless and the Bolsheviks took control of Russia, thus overthrowing the Provisional (Kerensky) Government.

Leon Trotsky, once Lenin's bitter critic but at the time his closest comrade, supported and initiated the insurrection leading to the October Revolution. Trotsky, not Stalin, was the mastermind and the real driving force behind the coup. As a matter of fact Trotsky had played a leading role in the 1905 revolution too. This revolution lasted for 3 years from late 1904 to mid-1907, exploding just after Bloody Sunday of 22 January 1905. It took the form of strikes throughout the empire in all major industrial centres. These revolutionaries were, as usual, a minority but they had the willpower and a clear objective and a sheer determination to carry through the insurrections.

It is important to note that the Russian nation was disintegrating when the Bolsheviks took charge of the nation (Nove 1992, p. 25). It throws some lights how the Bolsheviks managed to get hold of the power:

- The Bolsheviks were not mature nor strong enough to wrest the political power from the stable government; only thing they had was a strong determination.
- People felt they had to rely on the Bolsheviks so as to prevent the total collapse of the society.
- The Bolsheviks in turn had to rely on the army to maintain the power, and law and order.
- Many of the peasants hated the Reds as much as the Whites, but when faced with choice they preferred the Reds. After all they obtained the gentry land after the October Revolution. However, most intellectuals joined or sympathised with the White Camp. The Reds were the Bolsheviks, and the Whites were a broad term applied to any anti-Bolshevik group being made up of Mensheviks, Socialist Revolutionaries, supporters of Tsar, landlords and capitalists.

The Second All-Russia Congress of Soviets of Workers and Soldiers Deputies was convened in Petrograd on October 25 and 26 (November 7 and 8), 1917. The Bolsheviks formed the majority at the congress. Lenin, as the leader of the Bolsheviks, made reports and decrees and henceforth the congress adopted them as their resolutions. Notable among them were:

- immediate negotiation for peace
- landed proprietorship to be abolished without compensation
- employment of hire labour to be banned
- establishment of the workers' and peasants' government.

(Lenin 1975, vol. 2, pp. 426-27)

In addition to letting peasants seize land--it was more accurate to say that the government did not have the power to effect the orderly transfer of the agricultural lands--the government assigned control over the factories to workers committees and nationalised all banks confiscating private accounts. Foreign trade became a state monopoly, and the government created a special commissariat to handle it.

Lenin believed in a communist party led by a small elite. He thought that he should centralise and unify the party. He also believed that the anarchism and anarcho-syndicalism were bourgeois trends, irreconcilably opposed to socialism and communism. However, he admitted that the anarchists too stand for the abolition of exploitation and class distinction. (Lenin 1975, vol. 3, p. 571)

Lenin permitted immediately after the revolution, the elections for the Constituent Assembly, which Kerensky's Provisional Government arranged. In January 1918, the Bolsheviks did not secure the majority. Out of 520 deputies the Bolsheviks gained only 161, and the Social Revolutionaries held the absolute majority with 267 deputies, supported by the mass of peasants. The assembly was adjourned and prevented from gathering again.

When the Bolsheviks established their government, they included a commissariat of nationalities, and Joseph Stalin became the commissar. He issued Declaration of Rights of the Toiling and Exploited Peoples in January 1918. This document promised self-determination to the minorities, and described the Soviet Russia as a federation of the Soviet Republics. In Central Asia the minority meant ethnicity as well as Islam, and Stalin had to deal with these difficult problems. The document was really the announcement of the intentions and not the policy statement. What really happened later had nothing to do with the above declaration.

> On February 19, 1918, the nationalisation of land was proclaimed: all land became state property to be used only by those who would cultivate it themselves. The peasants, however, had little interest in supplying food to the government because, with state priorities and the breakdown of the economy, they could not receive much in return. The government resorted to the forcible acquisition of crops. (Riasanovsky 1977, p. 530)

Leon Trotsky, at the conference in Brest-Litovsk, tried to prolong the conference as much as possible in the hope that a communist revolution would erupt in Germany. This did not happen and German forces thrusted deep into Russia and Lenin ordered peace at any price before the Germans overthrew his shaky Bolshevik regime. (Mercer 1996, p. 954) Accordingly, the Central Powers and the Soviet Union signed the treaty on 3 March 1918, ending the hostilities.

The American entry into the war in April 1917 more than compensated for the Russian withdrawal from the war.

Seizing power in Russia presented Lenin and Trotsky with entirely different problems from what they had anticipated. The communists at this time controlled only Petrograd and Moscow. Lenin thought that without the world revolution, the communism in Russia would not survive. Many expected that Lenin's regime would collapse. The Whites had many advantages over the Reds. The Whites' leaders were exclusively made up of the army officers of the imperial Russia, and had the backings of the church and the Cossacks, and received allied aid. However, they lacked the determinations and clear goals, in which the Reds excelled. The Reds more clearly saw the needs of the peasants and workers, improvised their strategies, and ultimately the party rather than the individuals prevailed over the enemies. The party had the strength of organisation and mass mobilisation. This fact bore important results in the history of the Soviet Union. It can be evidenced by the facts that in the dual authority between the party and the government the party always took the upper hand, and also Stalin, as General Secretary of the Communist Party in later years, eventually prevailed over the opponents. In any case Lenin won the civil war by 1920 partly by compromise and partly by military conquest. (Grenville 1994, pp. 128-9)

The Soviet Union since its inception brought the mass of people into harmony to the rulers with propaganda, appealing to communist ideals, where this did not suffice, by force and terror. The revolution created an entirely new class of privileged and bound these to the regime. (p. 151)

Similarly the Soviet Union from its inception had to make enforced economic growth from its own resources with the strong emphasis on armaments and producer goods (steel, machinery, coal, electricity and cement) and transport to the detriment of consumer goods and agriculture.

Lenin believed and introduced the idea called democratic centralism, which entailed the election of the higher bodies by the party members. This principle became increasingly meaningless. The Communist Party executives made all the important decisions and enforced all the members to adhere to the party line with the penalty of calling them factionalists or even expelling them from the party. The top echelon of the party, particularly Lenin himself, made all the critical decisions.

Many features within the country were undemocratic. There was only one candidate or candidates of a single party for local and national elections. All the laws the Communist Party proposed passed the legislative procedures without any questions raised. The Communist leaders acted violating the constitutions when it suited them. The Communist Party leaders and members of the bureaucracy enjoyed special privileges despite similar wages to the average citizens. The party also discouraged religious worship and placed various restrictions on the Christians.

As a matter of fact the above features marked the Soviet government through its existence until it collapsed in the early 1990s.

War Communism (July 1918 to 1921)

One obvious result of the revolution was the destruction of the upper class as existed in the imperial Russia. Two million of these people emigrated from Russia. Many people were killed. A few people stayed behind adjusting to the new way of life without wealth and any privileges. Another feature of the revolution was the appalling suffering of the proletariat constituting about three million people before the war. They had existed in the imperial Russia and for their names the revolution was carried out. They were the backbone of support for the revolutionaries, and drafted into the Red Army in a large number and many of them were killed. During the course of the revolution the economy collapsed and the workers could not get a job in the cities. Moscow lost half of its population and Petrograd, two-thirds; many workers simply returned to the villages they originally came from.

> With the summer of 1918, War Communism began to acquire a definite shape. The nationalisation of industry, which began shortly after the revolution, was extended by the law of June 28, 1918. Eventually private industry disappeared almost entirely. Compulsory labour was introduced. Private trade was gradually suppressed to be replaced by rationing and by government distribution of food and other necessities of life. (Riasanovsky 1977, p. 530)

During War Communism, there was little consistency in Lenin's policies: they were mere reactions to the successive emergencies. Lenin made bewildering change of policy with doctrinal justifications but still retained power. After June 1918, industrial enterprises were rapidly nationalised, and workers and managers came under rigid control. Money became virtually worthless. The key problem was how to secure crops from the peasants.

> It is futile to blame social problems on money or to propose to eliminate money without eliminating commodity exchange (as some 'socialist' reformers of Marx's time did) (Brewer 1984, p. 28).

In August 1918, Lenin quoted the following figures concerning Russian farming families:

- There are 15 million of them altogether.
- 10 millions of them are poor peasants.
- 3 million of them are middle peasants.
- 2 millions of them are Kulaks, rich farmers and grain profiteers.

(Lenin 1975, vol. 2, p. 702)

Russia in the turmoil of 1920 recorded the lowest industrial output, equal to mere 13% of the 1913 figure. However, in 1925 Russia recovered to 70% of the industrial output of 1913. (Kennedy 1987, p. 279)

The Bolsheviks, since seizing power, tried to create the effective army but without much success. Immediately after signing the Treaty of Brest-Litovsk, Lenin appointed Trotsky as the Commissariat of War with the task of building a powerful Red Army. Lenin and Trotsky realised that contrary to their utopian notion they had held before they needed the strong army led by competent officers. It was Trotsky's competence and credit that he set up the powerful Red Army using skills and principles of Bolshevik organisation.

> Leon Trotsky, thus, set out to build the army. On 22 April 1918, with the compulsory military service already in force, he launched a massive effort to rebuild a centrally controlled 400 000 strong army. By the end of 1920 there were 5 500 000 men in the Red Army. Backed by this military might, the Bolsheviks were able to impose Soviet rule over all of the old Russian Empire. The election of officers was abolished and discipline, including death penalty, was rigorously enforced. Imperial officers were forcibly enrolled in the Red Army: out of 446 729 serving officers, they amounted to 314 180. They were called military specialists; their families were held as hostages against their desertion, a policy introduced by Trotsky himself. (Bradley 1988, p. 146)

A government decree introduced large scale nationalisations, and the Supreme Economic Council ran 80 per cent of industry by the autumn of 1919. In practice, the workers themselves managed the plants. In 1920 small scale industries were nationalised. In theory, all Russian industrial production was nationalised, and became part of the centrally directed economy. Circumstances also forced the Bolsheviks to abolish free trade and by the end of the civil war, a barter economy was operating. In time barter trading became norm as money lost its values. By 1920 wages and salaries were paid partly in kind. The Red Government made an effort to base its budget on commodities rather than on money.

The Reds put workers and soldiers into the country side to obtain hoarded grain from peasants, either voluntarily or by force.

After the land distribution of 1917-8, there were hardly any landless peasants left; even the poor peasants benefited from the land distribution.

Czechoslovak Legion trapped in Russia, Social Revolutionaries and foreign armies all opposed the Bolsheviks and tried to destroy them, engaging in the civil war operations.

> The greatest conflict between the peasants and the Bolsheviks arose at the end of the civil war when returning Red Army soldiers were encouraged to establish collective farms (kolkhoz). The peasants felt threatened by this form of farming which was more efficient and subsidised by the state. In addition, the Bolsheviks established state farms (sovkhoz) on former crown land which were capitalist enterprises paying their labourers wages for their work. Both forms of agricultural activity preferred by the Bolsheviks gradually alienated the peasantry--but not before the victorious conclusion of the civil war. After the war, the struggle in the country side continued with renewed vigour. (pp. 161-3)
>
> The Bolsheviks (henceforth known as Communists) won the civil war largely because of Lenin's political skills, Trotsky's Red Army and Dzerzhinsky's security police [the Cheka]. By November 1920 the civil war was over but the country was in an appalling state. (p. 166)

Between 1919 and 1922, the Bolshevik Party became a mass movement of 700 000 members.

New Economic Policy or NEP (from 1921 to 1928)

After the October Revolution in 1917, the Russian communist leaders hoped that the world communist revolution would erupt spontaneously. That was what they expected from their cherished theories. They waited until 1919 but with no results. Bolshevik leaders established Comintern in March 1919.

Three factions emerged among the Russian communists during the 1920s:

- Trotsky held left position. It aimed at the worldwide revolution and opposed NEP. He called for the immediate worldwide revolution by the proletariat--the central plank of Trotskyism.
- Stalin led the centre faction. They believed that socialism could be built within one country of Russia.
- Bukharin held right position. They showed compromising attitude and supported NEP.

(Riasanovsky 1977, p. 543)

Just after the Russian Revolution, Trotsky advocated sending the army abroad to cause the worldwide revolution. Stalin strenuously opposed Trotsky on this policy and preached the revolution in one country, Russia. This disagreement was one cause of rift between the two leaders within the Russian government. Lenin had the opinion that socialism can triumph first in one country: The final victory of socialism in one country is impossible. However, the imperial powers would halt their advances temporarily after the communist victory because of the revolutionary movements of the other countries. This is supposed to be one of Lenin's greatest theoretical contributions to Marxist theory. (Dutt 1961, p. 392; Lenin 1975, vol. 1, p. 13) Lenin advocated that the democratic revolution be carried out worldwide (Bradley 1988, p. 21).

Next they postulated if they conquered Poland making it a communist country, the rest of Europe would turn into the communist rule. War was declared in May 1920 between Poland and Russia. Poland was the most critical region: Poland was the gateway to Germany hence the gateway to the world revolution. The Poles, with the French assisting, had opened a new campaign earlier in April in the disputed territories in Ukraine. The Poles, after initial setback, advanced into the Russian territory. The war lasted from the spring of 1920 well into the following year. The treaty with territorial advantage to Poland was signed at Riga, Latvia, in October 1921, and the hostility ceased. The Red Army could not overrun Poland with limited Allied help and had to accept Polish independence. The Bolsheviks in the prosecution of the war discovered to their disappointment that the Poles were nationality conscious and not at all class conscious.

Since then Lenin gave up the idea of revolution in the capitalist countries to spread the communist doctrines among the underdeveloped countries. Marx addressed his doctrines to the workers of industrialised nations; his theories were applicable only to capitalist nations. The communists from this time on saw the opportunity of communist revolution in non-industrialised nations since the workers were exploited even in non-industrial nations.

> And it was against this background of utter destruction and discontent that Lenin, who, besides, had finally to admit that a world communism was not imminent, proceeded in the spring of 1921 to inaugurate his New Economic Policy in place of War Communism (Riasanovsky 1977, p. 541).

NEP is relaxation from War Communism. Many later Russian historians saw this period as the golden age of communism: the communists destroyed both the old order and the chasm between the rich and the poor. Around the introduction of NEP Russia was still in a state of anarchy. The peasants were in a great misery and bitterness against the policies of the new government, and staged uprisings; however, they were not strong enough to topple the Communist government. The workers did not run the economy and the state because the government could not afford to do without the services of the experts. In the summer of 1921, after the new policy was introduced, drought hit the most fertile regions of the country and millions of people died as the result of the food shortage and epidemics; without the American aids many more people would have died.

In the early part of 1921, Lenin wrote that the government had gone too far in regard to nationalisation of industry and trade and clamping down on local exchange of commodities. He further wrote that the government should not prohibit the development of capitalism but rather should channel it into state capitalism. The state capitalism as he meant entailed grain monopoly, state-controlled entrepreneurs and traders, bourgeois co-operators. (Lenin 1975, vol. 3, pp. 511, 527, 539)

Private enterprise, however, was to be allowed in small industries, that is, plants employing fewer than 20 workers each, and in retail trade. Instead of requisitioning the peasants' produce, as had been done during War Communism, the government established a definite tax in kind, particularly in grain, replaced later by a money tax. It was highly characteristic of NEP that 75% of retail trades fell into private hands. (Riasanovsky 1977, p. 542)

A tax in kind replaced expropriations of food; when the currency stabilised the state resumed payments for grain deliveries with money. The government let the peasants sell their surplus grains rather than sell through the black markets. The government also abandoned wholesale nationalisation and revived the private sector. Only heavy industry, foreign trade and banking remained under strict state control. (Bradley 1988, p. 169)

In 1922, the country became known as the Union of the Soviet Socialist Republics (USSR) or the Soviet Union. By the time Lenin died in 1924, the Soviet Union became one party state, banning all non-communist parties.

> The leasing of land and hiring of labour were also legalised, benefiting the more ambitious peasants (kulaks). ... Three-quarters of retail trade was in private hands, and though industry did not react as well as agriculture to the stimuli that Lenin administered to the economy, it began to show signs of recovery. ... N. E. P. seemed to confirm the widely held view in Russia and the Communist Party that only the peasants really prospered in the years immediately after the revolution. (p. 176)

Life was gradually returning to normal. Private enterprise dominated the economy, producing more than 50% of the national income. Agriculture was almost entirely in private hands; even at the end of the period state farms and collective farms occupied only two per cent of the cultivated land. The forcible labour conscription was abolished and the workers could sell their labour either in the private sector or the state sector. The regime abandoned its egalitarian policy on wages and the skilled workers got more wages than the unskilled.

However, the unemployment remained a serious problem, and even in the second half of the 1920s when the economy recovered the unemployment got worse. Once the city life became bearable many people from the country where the overpopulation was the chronic problem flocked to the city looking for jobs. Since the unemployment benefits depended on the length of the working life, the young and seasonal workers, and women particularly suffered.

The Bolsheviks were hostile to the peasant class, 80% of the population. However, tax remained lower than it had been during the imperial Russia because the Soviet power was weak and could not interfere in the villages, and the worker and peasant alliance was the central plank of the government policy. The government especially feared the kulak, five per cent of peasantry though not well defined. They were placed in a dilemma: while they feared the growing wealth and consequent political influence of the kulak class, they had to have the wealthy farmers who supplied food to the cities. The poor peasants made food only for their consumption. The government was too weak to interfere into the lives of the peasantry. Ironically the foregoing circumstances made the peasant class never better in Russia in the second half of the 1920s.

The USSR devoted a large share (12-16%) of government expenditure to defence for much of the 1920s.

The revolution brought tremendous changes in political, social and economic life of the Russian people; however, the cultural revolution was delayed and effected at the end of NEP. The Russian Marxists, more than Marxists elsewhere, believed in their faith on Marxism, and attacked vigorously any dissenting views. They justified the persecution, believing that they were on the right and the opponents, wrong. The government interfered into the life of the activists and publications of undesirable materials. The intelligentsia generally showed hostility towards the Bolshevik government. The government showed more tolerance to scientists than to artists because they needed the former more than the latter.

The Menshevik Party, which was an insignificant shadow of the former self, was destroyed in 1922. The trials of the leading Socialist Revolutionaries followed relentlessly.

Stalin became the General Secretary of the Communist Party in 1922 that directed the organisational matters of the party and made full use of the bureaucracy which had been already in place when he was appointed. He was not a particularly able organiser but a master politician. This post proved to be critical in deciding the party leader after Lenin.

The Russian Orthodox Church always supported the imperial government and also the White movement. However, after the Bolshevik victory, Lenin reasoned that persecuting the church was not a good idea since many peasants in the country clung to the faith in the village priests though many people, particularly the youth, in the cities did not.

At the time of the revolution about 60% of the people were illiterate and the Bolsheviks believed that education was the key to the success of their objectives and set about to raise the standard of education as high as that of Western Europe.

Outer Mongolia was established as a communist country in 1924 by the help of the Comintern because the Mongolians feared the domination of the Chinese more than they did that of the Russians.

By the mid-1920s all major European nations established diplomatic and economic relations with the Soviet Russia, and the Bolsheviks abandoned the hope of immediate world revolution.

<u>Under Stalin (from 1924 to 1953)</u>

Lenin wrote in 1922 that Trotsky was probably the most capable person on the Central Committee; however, Stalin as Secretary-General with unlimited power may not be always able to exercise that authority with sufficient caution (Lenin 1975, vol. 3, p. 680). Lenin died in 1924, and Trotsky was expelled from the party in 1927 and exiled from the Soviet Union in 1929 and eventually assassinated in Mexico. There is ample evidence that Stalin had a hand on all these events, the death of Lenin being included.

Lenin founded one party rule. Stalin even further developed it into the totalitarian state in which he did not permit any dissenting voice or he even denied the dissents to exist.

There was no great appeal in the communist formula to the peasants, who owned the land they cultivated. The city-based workers carried out the revolution, and the peasants always held suspicion and hostility to their ideology.

Stalin maintained his bitter vendetta against the peasants for their strong preference to private plots.

Joseph Stalin issued a five-year economic plan in 1928 to industrialise the USSR, which set the economic pattern of the Soviet Union as long as it existed. At the end of the planning period the Soviet government announced that they achieved the targets though in fact they did not: they announced that the annual industrial growth was 19.2%, which the capitalist economists disputed. The capital required for industrialisation was squeezed out of the peasantry: one of the measures adopted was to raise the prices of the industrial goods which the peasants could not do without. The plan went hand in hand with a revolution in the countryside--the collectivisation of agriculture. In 1928 collectives cultivated hardly more than one per cent of the arable land. It is a general rule that agriculture does not admit division of labour as for industries. This is one reason why the improvement of the productive powers of labour in agriculture lagged so much behind the industries.

Whatever the virtues of collectivisation, the land-owning peasants felt they would become landless proletariat under this system.

In 1928 Stalin declared that expropriating the kulaks would be an act of folly; however, in the following year he ordered their liquidation as a class giving their farms to collective farms when they resisted. Nobody knew how the collectivisation should be carried out nor what consequences it would bring in the society: the collectivisation was a vast improvisation. Early in 1930 there were slightly over 4 million peasants working in collectives; by March there were 14 million collective farmers, some 55 per cent of the peasant class. By 1932, according to official statements, 65 per cent of peasants were collectivised. The collectivisation went hand in hand with dekulakisation, and dekulakisation with half-disguised robbery. According to_Ivnitsky, a total of about 300 000 kulak households were deported; they were roughly 1.5 million people. (Nove 1992, p. 166) By 1934 the entire peasantry was collectivised: typically each village formed a collective farm. The Soviet regime abolished the village communes on the way to collectivisation: the communists could not penetrate and control the system by the natures of the commune setup.

Collectivisation entailed both the state farms and collective farms. The government paid wages not dependent on the amount of the crops production at the state farms. The peasants paid the failure of production in collective farms; the wages depended on labour day for a peasant, and the overall wages came from the performance of the particular farm.

By this time the victory of Stalin was complete; the Soviet political system became the dictatorship of Stalin. He was a Georgian but was a Russian nationalist from his early age, and pushed forward the Russian nationalism, which was quite risky in the multinational empire. He made socialist realism the only tolerated artistic style, abandoning the cultural heterogeneity of NEP. He thought himself a tzar. The constitution adopted in 1936 made little difference to the personality cult of Stalin. Until the mid-1930s the Soviet Union did not have the serious threat of major war and Stalin could concentrate on the domestic affairs until Hitler's army loomed menacing in the latter part of the 1930s. He wanted to keep his country out of war for his tyrannical rule on the Soviet Union.

The Bolshevik Party could not have gained the government unless the instrument of terror was ingrained in its system from the inception, being aware that its government was based on the concept of the dictatorship of the proletariat. Terror was a part of the Leninist system. The Cheka was created in 1917, it became the OGPU in 1922, and it became in turn NKVD in 1934, a part of the commissariat of internal affairs. Stalin used these facilities to liquidate the kulaks and effect the collectivisation of the farms.

At the early stage of collectivisation, the weather was unusually favourable and the adverse effect did not show up immediately; however, the Soviet Union did not recover from the ills of the collectivisation for decades to come. After the good harvest of 1930, two years of disastrous harvests in 1932 and 1933 followed. They were the costliest famine in the Soviet Union and it is estimated that five to seven million people died. It was shocking that the government and the newspaper did not acknowledge the problem, the procurement plans went ahead, and the government removed the grains from the famine struck villages. The city people were spared from the starvation.

> But the government, in its anxiety to appease the workers and in its evident indifference to peasant interests, fixed most prices--food stuff and manufactured goods--in rural areas at 'commercial' levels (p. 206).

The practice of compulsory procurements of the crops at low prices was only one indication of unfavourable treatment of the agricultural sector by the government.

Despite the earlier statement concerning the doubt reaching the production targets, the growth of the Soviet industries was impressive. By 1930 the unemployment was not only eliminated but the industries were to suffer from the shortage of labour. The workers, if capable, moved to administration and technical branch. Millions of people who escaped to the cities from working in the miserable conditions in the collective farms filled the vacancies. The government introduced in 1932 the domestic passport system which had existed in the imperial Russia and had been abolished during the revolution. The new regulation established two classes of citizens: the urban dwellers with the freedom of movement and the collective farm workers who needed the permission to leave the farm from the chairman of the collective farm. The government had to negotiate with the chairmen to release the workers for industrial employment.

In an effort to beat the shortage of labour the industry employed women and even convict labourers. Women made up only a quarter of the labour force in the NEP period but the proportion increased to 40% by the end of the 1930s. The employing industries suffered from the low quality of the workers who were unable to adjust to the industrial life, as well as the high turnover rate. The government allocated the resources to the heavy industries, and the consumer goods made up the loss, though the overall scheme was to sacrifice the peasantry. (Kenez 2006, pp. 94-5) Women also had to bear more children since the government encouraged higher birth rate by the various incentives, though there were no women in the highest leadership of the party at around this time unlike during the revolution and civil war.

The peasants obtained lands through the revolution but the peasants were unwilling to give up their crops with little gains and to proceed with further changes to the Russian society; the peasants shared the disproportionate burden in the Soviet economy. The Soviet Union neglected agriculture in many ways. Even as late as 1940 only 4.2% of kolhozes had any electricity. Any available mineral fertilizer was likely to be allocated to industrial crops. (Nove 1992, p. 246)

In spite of the industrial growth, the economists calculated that the real wages in 1932 was only half of that of 1928 in the Soviet Union.

Artel type of collectives became predominant, where the peasants retained their own livestock and small plots of land to tender on their own time. The machine-tractor station (MTS) provided their machinery and looked after maintenance, though the collective farms were the centres of the Soviet power and became focal points of communist education. Eventually, the artels ran 96% of Soviet agriculture. There was no incentive to work for the collective farms because the benefits were too small. However, the peasants were able to survive by utilising their private plots and animals. The government could not abolish the private plots being such an important part of the national economy.

> On 5 September 1929 the principle of one man management was assented in a decision of the Central Committee. The factory party organisation was told not to interfere with the directors' responsibilities; the trade unions were to be energetic organisers of production activity and of the initiations of the labouring masses, even while upholding the everyday

> cultural amenity and economic needs of the workers. The director was, in principle, in sole charge. (p. 214)
>
> In 1931 Stalin made his famous critique of egalitarianism in wages. Stalin also encouraged a policy of higher pay and privileges for industrial cadres, and abandoned the old rule, established by Lenin, that the party members should not earn more than a skilled worker did. (p. 211)
>
> After the October Revolution, and especially in the 30s, labor unions, to which almost all workers belonged, have served as agencies of the state, to promote its policies and rally the workers behind them, rather than as representative of labor interests and points of view (Riasanovsky 1977, p. 556).

Under Stalin, the trade union became virtually a branch of government.

> During the thirties there was developed the system sometimes known as the command economy, or the Stalin planning model, based on stern centralisation. The system survived for several decades with minor modifications. The overriding criterion at all levels was the plan, embodying the economic will of the party and government, and based not on considerations of profit or loss but on politically determined priorities. Yet, with prices not even in theory capable of fulfilling their role as economic 'signals', there was no other criterion than the plan. A further source of complication was the division of authority between government and party organs, at all levels. (Nove 1992, pp. 267, 269, 365-6)

There were a party structure and a government structure. The leading communists occupied the upper echelons in both party and government, with Lenin and Stalin at the head of both in succession. Production continued to adapt itself not to user demand but to the 'Success Indicators', that is, to plan fulfilment statistics in roubles, tons and square metres.

The command economy entails the following planning by the central planning committee:

- what goods and services to produce,
- how to distribute them,
- what are their prices and people's wages.

(Hodgetts & Smart 1988, p. 35)

The command economy was in fact a production-oriented system; the manufacturing was done from the viewpoint of the producers, that is, to carry on the production on the perceived needs of the consumers.

The depression in the capitalist countries started in 1929. By the summer of 1932, industrial production in many countries was only half that of 1928, and the world trade had shrunk by one-third.

The Soviet Union made the industrial advance at the sacrifice of its own living standard; the workers received low wages. During the depression of 1930s the Soviet economy was free from the mass unemployment of the West but the Soviet citizens lived under misery and hunger.

The number employed in agriculture in Russia dropped from 71% to 51% in the twelve years 1928-40.

> The USSR's manufacturing was expanding during the Great Depression. By the late 1930s, indeed, Russia's industrial output had not only soared well past that of France, Japan and Italy but had probably overtaken Britain's as well. (Kennedy 1987, p. 323)

Only the Soviet Union was immune from the depression of 1930s. This fact gave rise to the popularity of communism during the depression.

However, the agricultural sector remained a problem. Although the farm output slowly rose in the mid-1930s, Russian agriculture was hardly feeding its population and the yields per acre were appallingly low. After 1937, the reorientation of the Soviet economy towards a massive rearmament programme was bound to affect industrial continuity and distort the earlier planning. (p. 323)

The major industrialised nations of the world in the 1930s placed a great emphasis on military applications of science and technology; in fact, this was the key factor of the period. However, Britain after WW I was more concerned with the social questions and in 1933 she spent 10.5% of public expenditure for the armed forces and 46.6% for the social service. (pp. 295, 315)

Stalin imposed the Great Terror from 1936 to 1938 and emerged as an undisputed dictator. He attacked high ranking officers in the party and the army. With a few exceptions the entire leadership of the revolution was exterminated. Stalin purged 90% of all generals and 80% of all colonels.

The Second Five-Year Plan (1933-7) progressed apace. The terror inflicted on the upper echelon of the society spurred the tremendous industrial growth and the profound social transformation. By this time the ex-peasants and women got used to the industrial working conditions. The government set the policies to encourage the increased production such as more pay for the skilled workers and the incentives for high production results. The abolition of rationing in 1935 clearly indicated this trend. The government also put tremendous effort to eliminate illiteracy and train the technical people required for the industries. However, the purges of high ranking people in the community resulted in the slackening of the economic growth at the end of the decade.

Stalin and Hitler were ideological foes. During the Spanish Civil War (1936-9) Spain became an international ideological battleground for socialists and fascists. The war also became the testing ground of the new generation weapons of aircrafts and tanks, and the powers devoted their effort to improve on their mobile armaments. (p. 325)

Adolf Hitler commenced his program of creating a self-sufficient, a thousand year Reich, though Germany had developed the trend for autarky before this program. Hitler, as Napoleon and Germany during WW I did, sought the conquered territories to pay for the war effort. In Germany, by 1938, armaments used 52% of the government expenditure and 17% of gross national product. In fact in 1938, the year of Munich Agreement, Germany spent more upon weapons than Britain, France and the United States combined. (pp. 269, 283, 304)

Hitler was successful without resorting to war in annexing Austria and dismembering Czechoslovakia in 1938.

> On the eve of the Second World War the Russian Communist Party was described as composed of 50 percent of workers, 20 percent of peasants and 30 percent of Soviet intellectuals, with the last group on the increase (Riasanovsky 1977, p. 625).

The Soviet Union wanted to avoid both two front wars with Germany and Japan and the major war at this time. Thus the Molotov-Ribbentrop (non-aggression) Pact was signed on the 23rd August 1939. The German armies invaded Poland on the first of September. The pact contained a secret protocol, which defined the spheres of influence in Europe including Poland between the two parties. Stalin must have reasoned that Britain and France would declare war on Germany at the German invasion into Poland and tie up the German army not giving the opportunity to attack Russia; in fact they did so two days later. Stalin delayed

Polish invasion until the 17th; by this time the Polish army was largely destroyed, and the Russian army took up the positions as the pact specified. To his relief the meeting of the German and Russian armies was peaceful.

The Molotov-Ribbentrop Pact had assigned Finland to the Soviet Union. Stalin undertook the territorial expansions. His army invaded Finland in November 1939 in order to have an easy victory and territorial gains: he wanted to conquer the entire country by the end of the year. The undertaking ended in such huge casualties on the part of the Soviet personnel that the Soviet government did not disclose the figure for many years, and the peace treaty in March 1940 ceded only 10% of Finland to the Soviet Union. The Soviet armies not only suffered a series of humiliating defeats until they secured the victory with the sheer weight of numbers but invited French and English antagonism as well as the Nazi's contempt for the Soviet armies. The League of Nations expelled the Soviet Union on December 14th.

After the fall of Poland Hitler turned west in April 1940 and overran Denmark and Norway, knocked out France by the end of June.

After the fall of France, and the retreat from Dunkirk by the British and other Allied troops in June 1940, Britain was extremely vulnerable. Seeing this Hermann Goering advised Hitler to attack Britain at once. Hitler had always admired Britain and believed that if he offered anti-communist alliance Churchill would accept it. When Churchill refused the offer Hitler could not believe it. Furious, he authorised the attack on Britain in July.

The Battle of Britain was fought from August to October, 1940. The German Luftwaffe bombed extensively south England against the successful resistance by the RAF Fighter Command. The German failure to secure the air superiority in the Battle of Britain put an end to the German invasion of Britain.

All the evidence indicates that Stalin was not sure on which side the Soviet Union would be fighting the war until 22 June 1941 when the German armies invaded his country, though he knew the major war was inevitable. Hitler made clear his intention of attacking Russia in his book *Mein Kampf* (1925), and he did not swerve from this conviction since then. During German-Soviet alliance the Soviet Union supplied Germany with raw material including vitally important oil, Germany with the latest armaments which it mostly did not deliver. At the outbreak of German-Soviet war the Germans owed the Soviet Union 229 million Reichsmarks. Stalin was so unprepared for the German invasion that he retired to his dacha and saw no one for days. After eleven days he collected himself and addressed the Soviet people.

German blitzkrieg marched through along the 2 880 kilometres of the Russian border from the Arctic Circle to the Black Sea together with Finnish, Hungarian and Rumanian allies. The Red Army, clearly unprepared, easily crumbled. The German forces and their allies advanced deep into the Russian territories with the surprising speed of half a year, and got close to Moscow and Stalingrad and even occupied beyond Leningrad, the axis forces encircling this city. General Zhukov stopped German further advance to Moscow during the winter of 1941 to 1942. Also the German and Finnish forces could not force the surrender of Leningrad after the repeated attacks with the siege, that is, 900-Day Siege (Sep 8, 1941 - Jan 27, 1944).

> Sufficient to say that many peasants hoped that the German occupation would lead to the abolition of kolkhozes and the return of private peasant cultivation. They were disappointed. (Nove 1992, p. 283-4)
>
> This and the revulsion of feeling due to the brutalities of the occupying troops, led some peasants who at first met the Germans with indifference, or even welcomed them, to take to the forests and join the partisans (p. 284).

The battle of Stalingrad lasted from August 1942 to January 1943. The Russian army decisively beat the German army, which severely eroded Hitler's military genius.

Hitler deployed the Sixth Army under the command of General Paulus and a part of the Fourth Panzer Army under the command of General Kleist. The Sixth Army was the finest German army and comprised of 330 000 soldiers, and had broken through the Paris defence in 1940 and undefeated. The battle involved 2 million soldiers, equally divided between the two sides.

The German and Axis armies hard pressed the Soviet armies. The Soviet 62nd Army lost half of its troops and it looked like the Germans was going to win the battle. Stalin, alarmed, ordered General Zhukov, possibly the most capable general under Stalin, to head to South Russia. Stalin also appointed General Chuikov to command the 62nd Army; the general was aggressive and determined.

The Russian army under General Chuikov offered incredibly stiff resistance under difficult circumstances and held off. On November 19 General Zhukov launched the counterattack and encircled the German army.

General von Manstein's attempts to relieve the trapped German forces in December failed. The Soviets took more than 110 000 prisoners: and over 800 000 Axis soldiers died; German losses alone accounted for 300 000.

The battle of Stalingrad was in many ways remarkable. The result of the conflict was the first Russian victory since the German invasion into Russia in 1941. The end of the battle marked the turning point of the war: Soviet strength would increase as Germany's would diminish. The Russian victory at Stalingrad remained to be the symbol of Soviet heroism and courage for many years to come. The battle was the bloodiest, largest and longest battle ever fought during the Russo-German war, and possibly for the entire human warfare.

The Soviet Union was taking on two-thirds of the total German military strength during 1942 and 1943. Stalin was begging the opening of the second front.

In response an Anglo-American force landed in Vichy French North Africa in November 1942. The fierce fighting in Tunisia ended in the capitulation of German and Italian troops in May 1943. However, the scale of fighting in North Africa was incomparably small compared with that of the Russian front.

The continuing delays in the opening of a second front in France through 1942, then 1943 must have confirmed Stalin's fears that the reason for delay was mainly political not military.

After the German surrender at Stalingrad in January 1943 the tide of war in Russia reversed and from then on the Russian army took the initiatives. Hitler had always maintained that war with Russia would decide the outcome of World War Two, and had been reluctant to spare his major military resources to the other theatres of war. It seems that Hitler was aware that since the defeat at Stalingrad he did not have any hope of winning the war. After the massive tank battle at Kursk (July 5 - August 23 1943), the Germans called off the Russian offensive. Hitler needed the forces to deal with a new emergency: In July 1943 the British and American armies invaded Sicily.

On 6 June 1944 under General Dwight Eisenhower's supreme command the successful cross-Channel invasion of France by the Allied troops of the Americans, the British and the Canadians began. This was the second front Stalin was desperately asking for, well after the world was certain Russia would defeat Germany. As far as we can postulate the main opposition to the second front was Churchill who opposed vigorously to fascism as well as communism. The Allied leaders were afraid that unless they sent their armies to Western Europe the Russian armies would advance to Western Europe and the entire Europe would become under Russian domination.

It turned out that the command economy with all its faults suited war-time conditions. The industrialisation drive on the emphasis on the heavy industries also turned out to be suitable for the war mobilisation and for the armament production. The Soviet Union mobilised the entire economy for the war purpose far more thoroughly than any other belligerent nations:

15% of the national income was devoted for war production but two years after the start of the war the figure rose to 55%. By 1942-3, Soviet factories produced more planes and tanks than the German counterparts with the matching quality. Agriculture and animal husbandry were left in a dreadful state, and the grain harvests of 1942 and 1943 were only one-third of what it had been before the war. The overall result was that the Soviet system passed the test of war, and Stalin and the Soviet people won the war with deserving credits. It is hard to assess what would have been the outcome of the war without the generous American material aides particularly in trucks and food, though the aides were not available in 1941 when the Soviet Union was under the greatest danger. Stalin had little faith in the Comintern--by now a shell of its former self, and dissolved it in 1943 as a gesture of good will to the West.

Only a small minority of people in the Soviet Union were dedicated communists and fought for the maintenance of the Soviet system. Another minority, perhaps somewhat larger percentage, were hostile to the communist rule and prepared to collaborate with the Nazis. The majority of people were in between and willing to fight the beastly enemy under the communist guidance. The Soviet Union was the multinational empire and many minority peoples were unhappy under the communist rule; however, the racial theory of the Nazis prevented the full utilisation of the minority discontents. The Soviet Government stressed on Russian nationalism and de-emphasised the communist idealism and at the same time slackened the anti-minority and anti-religious policies.

At Yalta Conference in February 1945, Franklin D Roosevelt and Stalin wanted to dominate the discussion but Churchill, though conscious of Britain's comparative weakness, obtained some concessions from the bilateral dominance.

Germany lost battles on all major fronts and the Russian armies entered Berlin in April 1945. On 30th April Hitler committed suicide. On 7th May General Jodl, the Chief-of-Staff of the German Armed Forces High Command, signed unconditional surrender documents for all German forces to the Allies in Rheims, France. In Rheims was located the Supreme Headquarters Allied Expeditionary Force. General Susloparov was present at the conference and signed the documents for the Soviet Government. The above arrangement displeased Stalin. Stalin and even Eisenhower had the opinion that the German High Command should surrender to the Russians, though the Germans wanted to surrender to the Americans. Marshal Zhukov in Berlin insisted that the Rheims ceremony was only preliminary and the Germans should surrender to the Russians who were the main victory contributors and in Berlin which was the centre of Nazi aggression. On 8th May General Wilhelm Keitel signed the similar documents in Berlin explicitly to the Soviet forces in the presence of General Georgy Zhukov.

Just after World War II, the mass starvation and epidemics did not happen through Western Europe as they had happened after World War I. This was in part by the policies of the victorious nations and in part by the effective use of pesticides such as DDT.

When World War II was over, Stalin was well aware of the Western economic and industrial superiority. He maintained a large Red Army to counter this superiority and also the West's hostility against his regime. Stalin placed a facade of representative institutions in Eastern and Central Europe. (Grenville 1994, pp. 338, 344)

Roosevelt, Churchill and Stalin spent a disproportionate amount of time and energy on the question of Eastern and Central Europe especially Poland after the war in the two war-time conferences of Tehran in 1943 and Yalta in 1945. The Western concern over the question came nothing in the face of the reality that the Russian army would occupy and control the regions. The Soviet Government did not have the public opinions they had to consider unlike the Western governments, and instituted the rigid satellite states through Eastern and Central Europe, though these countries were by no means similar in their makeups and responses.

Stalin reasoned that the democracy in these states would go against the Soviet Union, and he did not allow it and had the army strength to enforce his decisions.

In 1950, the USSR kept a huge armed forces of 4.3 million men with the defence expenditure of $15.5 billion, whereas America 1.38 million men with $14.5 billion. We have to take into account the fact that at this time America had the nuclear advantage to balance out the Russian preponderance in conventional forces. The Soviet Union had manufactured its own A-bomb in 1949. In 1953 the Russians also tested an H-Bomb, a mere 9 months after the American test.

> One odd feature of the year 1950 was the decision to increase the nominal gold and foreign exchange value of the already greatly overvalued rouble, from 5.30 to 4.00 roubles to the US dollar. This made all Soviet prices much too high. However, trade with Western countries was conducted in Western currencies, and there was no connection at all between internal prices, foreign trade decisions and the official exchange rate. Or rather the connection was purely one of statistics and accountancy. The rate was used to convert foreign currency into roubles, and thus Soviet exporting corporations, under the Ministry of Foreign Trade, tended to make large losses, which had to be made good out of the budget, while importing corporations, made large profits, which were transferred mostly to the budget. It was, of course, quite impossible to use the exchange rate as a basis for economic calculations. (Nove 1992, p. 323)

The Soviet state survived by:

- military might,
- secret police,
- control of mass media and propaganda.

Although, to be sure, many Soviet communists are people of no special significance, virtually all prominent figures in the country are members of the party. Since the Second World War special efforts have been made to assure that such fields as university teaching and scientific research are largely in the hands of communists. Conversely, it has become much easier for outstanding people to join the party.

After Stalin

Stalin made such an impression on the Soviet history that he and his government created our image of Russian communism. Even after Stalin era the Soviet Union remained a police state, though in somewhat relaxed form.

From the 1950s to the 1980s the Soviet Union maintained the strong army with the nuclear arsenal to achieve the parity with America. However, the economic success did not match this drive for equality with America.

> The extent to which the Soviet Union has been a land of peasants is indicated by the fact that the rural population constituted 82 percent of the total in 1928 and that, after some forty years of industrialization and urbanization, it still constitutes almost 50 percent today (Riasanovsky 1977, p. 628).

As it turned out, however, the peasants have born the brunt of the privations and sacrifices the Soviet 'builders of socialism' imposed. There are two demographic catastrophes in the Soviet history: the First Five-Year Plan especially collectivisation of agriculture and World War II. During the forced collectivisation, 5 million kulaks and members of their family disappeared. Countless peasants, recalcitrant or relatively prosperous or simply unlucky, populated forced labour camps. A large number of peasants got jobs in the factories to become industrial workers. (pp. 628, 629)

> Industrial workers in many ways profited most from the Bolshevik Revolution. The revolution was made in their name, and they gave the new regime its greatest social support. (p. 629)

The reformers in the Soviet Union in the 1960 to 1980 saw the fundamental problem of the centrally directed economy without a market mechanism which could not relate the producers and consumers. This problem was neither tackled nor solved. The relevant ministries decided what to produce, and the consumers represented a mere abstract unit and were not important in any way in the command economy. The ministries could not cope with the complexities of the economy. However, if the consumer demands were important and clarified, for example, for the armed forces and the space enterprise, the Soviet Union made fine products comparable to the best of the West. (Grenville 1994, pp. 804, 806)

Despite all the attention and capital Soviet planners lavished, the agricultural sector of the Soviet Union remained problematic. It grew 4.8% a year in the 1950s but only 3% in the 1960s and 1.8% in the 1970s. By the late 1970s, the Soviet Union was in the embarrassing position of needing to import a large amount of grain and technology. In 1980, the American farm worker produced enough food to feed 65 people, whereas the Russian equivalent only 8. The satellite states of Russia showed similar difficulties as for Russia. (Kennedy 1987, pp. 412, 430-1)

Since Gorbachev became General Secretary of the Soviet Communist Party in 1985, the life in Russia started to change to freer style. Glasnost (openness) and perestroika (restructuring) became the catch phrases of the people. The former referred to freedom of expression in the society, and the latter, to restructuring of the political and economic systems. Legalisation of non-communist parties and the effective parliament were the political reforms among others. The economic reforms were also carried out; private business families and individuals ran were legalised and the central planning system was modified. Since he became president of the Soviet Union in 1990, this trend accelerated. He was a socialist reformer and rejected capitalism.

> In 1988 cooperatives were legalised in the Soviet Union, but private enterprise remained taboo, and private employment was still seen as impermissible exploitation (Nove 1992, p. 407).

A wave of popular revolution swept away communism in Eastern and Central Europe from 1989 to 1991. There were no fears of intervention from the Soviet Army at this time. The Soviet Union dominated these satellite states; however, these nations were heavily reliant on the Soviet economy. When the Soviet economy made a precipitous fall from the 1970s to the end of the 1980s, the satellite states also faced the economic collapse. (Grenville 1994, p. 891)

The hardline Communists vigorously opposed these reforms and staged a coup in August 1991, and removed Gorbachev from power. However the coup soon failed, and Gorbachev returned to power. Shortly after returning to power he resigned as the party head, and retained only the presidency of the national government. By late 1991, most of the republics that made up the Soviet Union declared independence and formed the Commonwealth of Independent States on December the 11th. Subsequently Gorbachev resigned as head of the Soviet government and the Soviet Union formerly ceased to exist.

The Cold War ended in 1991. The Warsaw Pact was dissolved and the United Germany joined NATO. Each republic of the Soviet Union became determined to do what was best for itself. Ethnic strife and economic difficulty undermined the cohesion of the union.

After the collapse of the Soviet economy, it seems that the majority of intellectuals of the world believed that only democracy and market economy can solve the various ills of the society.

Section 3 Communism in China

Adverse Economic Effects of Western Powers on Modern China

I expound the history of China in the modern context in Section 5 China: Ming and Ch'ing Dynasties, Chapter 4, Book One *Idealism and Materialism.*

The unequal treaties in the aftermath of the Opium wars and the subsequent conflicts were the framework of the exploitation. China had to open five ports after the defeat of the First Opium War, and 10 new ports after the defeat of the Second Opium War. China was further forced to open new ports after a series of defeats with the Western powers. The treaty ports were originally confined to the coastal ports but came to include the navigable ports on the rivers. Ports clearly indicated that the Western powers were interested in trade with bulk carrying capacity of ships, and also in the use of warships in case of conflicts with the Chinese. The Westerners enjoyed the protection of extraterritoriality in these ports. Eventually China had about 90 treaty ports. The unequal treaty gave the foreign powers control over China's internal tariffs. China also had to pay a large amount of indemnity as the result of the wars.

In 1870 China's tea export was nearly half of the total value of export; and silk nearly 40%. Forty years later tea made up less than 10% and silk just over 25%. In those years India and Sri Lanka became the dominant tea exporters, mainly because of cheap labour (Roberts 1998, p. 93), and China increased the exports of textile fibres and products.

The first significant growth period for the Chinese modern industry was at the time of the First World War when the Europeans reduced their interests in China.

Traditionally intellectual Chinese identified themselves with the integrity of Confucian culture, and the concept of nationalism as we understand was unknown to them until the end of the nineteenth century when China came widely exposed to the European cultures. Only after the defeat in the Sino-Japanese War (1894-5) the Chinese intellectuals took the challenge of Western cultures seriously.

The Boxer Rebellion (1899-1901) was a warning from the common people in China to the foreigners that they should not encroach into China any further. From about 1895, small groups of people emerged committing themselves to the overthrow of the Manchu (Ch'ing or Qing) Government.

Hsien-feng Emperor reigned 1850-61; Cixi (Tz'u-hsi) was the consort of this emperor and bore his only son. When Emperor T'ung-chih (the dowager's son), a weak and uninterested ruler, died in 1875 at the age of 18, Empress Dowager chose her three-year-old nephew as emperor though it totally went against the dynastic law of succession. She wanted to dominate the government with this arrangement—in fact she did so for half a century from 1861 till her death. In September 1898, Empress Dowager Cixi was officially in retirement and Emperor Guangxu (Kuang-hsu) (her nephew) still lacked experience besides being sickly and depressed. The emperor issued the edict, the Hundred Days Reforms. These reforms were extensive programme of reform and can be looked as a revolution from above. (p. 108)

Although the reformers were executed or dispersed and the emperor was jailed in an island in the Forbidden City gardens and the programme was abandoned because of the opposition by Empress Dowager, the reform period had an enduring significance (p. 111).

Under these circumstances, Empress Dowager called for the suggestions for reform. The reform programme thus adopted covered education, military, administration and constitution. On 2 September 1905, responding to a petition, she issued an edict to immediately abolish the civil service examinations. These reforms were undertaken to preserve the Qing dynasty and not for the national interest. (pp. 117, 121)

Traditionally the educated Chinese wrote in the manner of the classics with the terse abbreviated style, the specialised vocabulary and the allusions, which were incomprehensible to all but the trained scholars. This practice became even more out of touch with the reality after the abolition of the civil service examinations. The novels and short stories used the vernacular of everyday language for centuries: however, the scholars always looked down this practice. The vernacular language movement arose in conjunction with the spread of magazines, text books and ideas such as communism. Mao Zedong (Tse-tung) and Zhou (Chou) En-lai used written vernacular language in spreading the idea of communism. (Milston 1978, pp. 294-5)

Empress Dowager died in 1908. Emperor Kuang-hsu (38 at the time) died the day before without an heir. The empress' final decree passed the throne to the emperor's three-year-old nephew who was to reign as Hsuan-t'ung. This nephew was not next in line to the throne but his father, the brother of the emperor, was, and became the regent to the infant emperor. Judging from these facts we can imagine how powerful Empress Dowager was despite the fact she was not even an empress. Her personality and her machination made it possible on the foundation that she bore the emperor's only son. Hsuan-t'ung was better known as P'u-i, the last emperor of the Ch'ing dynasty.

Yuan Shih-k'ai was implicated for the death of the emperor, and the imperial princes dismissed him. He retired, to come back to politics a few years later. According to another theory the empress had the hand in it. The recent tests show that Emperor Kuang-hsu was arsenic poisoned.

Traditionally in China, the society kept merchants and soldiers in low esteem. However, both classes made ascendancy in the 19th century. Many gentries who passed the civil service examinations were engaged in commercial activities and many wealthy merchants purchased the titles. Alongside the civil service examinations, there were military service examinations and the men who passed the latter acquired the gentry status, though they were not in high esteem.

Double Tenth Uprising at Wuchang by New Army units eventually led to the secession of all the provinces of southern and central provinces from the Ch'ing Empire. They wanted to establish a republic. This is called the 1911 Revolution. This revolution amounted to the shift of power from the traditional emperor-bureaucracy to the provincial merchant-gentry-officer class.

The Nanking Provisional Government announced the beginning of the Chinese Republic on January 1, 1912. Sun Yat-sen became the president on the understanding that he would step down if Yuan could persuade the imperial family to abdicate. Yuan did so, and the edict of abdication was issued on February 12, thus ending a monarchical system of over 2000 year duration. The Manchu Government abdicated on March 1913. Sun Yat-sen stepped down as president, making way to Yuan Shih-k'ai as Provisional President. Thence China had to devise the new form of the central government discarding the outdated institutions and Confucianism. The reform of the intellectual nature interested only a small fraction of the population, and among the fraction only a tiny number of people were really interested in what was best for China and the rest was more concerned with the maintenance of powers and their privileges in their own areas. This unchecked struggle for local power subsequently led to 'the warlord era'.

By the end of the Ch'ing dynasty, the Manchu rank and file were completely sinicised. It was almost impossible to distinguish the two peoples and the Manchus disappeared into the Chinese population.

Yuan in fact wanted to become an emperor. He agreed to most of Japan's Twenty-One Demands made in 1915 counting on the Japanese support. He established an effective dictatorship and began his reign as an emperor on 1 January 1916; however, the fierce opposition made him abandon the idea. He became ill and died in June the same year, thus inaugurating the warlord era, 1916-28.

By mid-1916 China did not have any central governing authority. The general chaos ensued and the warlords seemed to dominate the country with wanton lootings and destructions.

The May Fourth Movement was the intellectual revolution spanning between 1917 and 1921, and aimed at independence and reforms. On *May 4* 1919, the students in Beijing demonstrated against the Versailles Peace Conference, while the conference was in progress. The conference was to permit Japan to keep control of the German holdings in Shandong (Shantung) Province in China. The treaty was signed on June 28th. The above nationalist agitation of 1919 was an important part of this movement and took its name. Among the other aims, its chief objectives were a fierce criticism of Confucianism and a willingness to look to the West for solutions for China's problems. The movement spurred the reorganisation of the Guomindang (Kuomintang), and stimulated the birth of the Chinese Communist Party. Communist writers regarded the May Fourth Movement as the starting point of modern Chinese history.

> Conditions in China's factories in the 1920s were as bad as they had been a century earlier in Britain, with twelve-hour days, seven day weeks, and wide spread child labour, especially in textile mills (Ebrey 1996, p. 274).

19 delegates formed the Chinese Communist Party officially in Shanghai in 1921 combining several Marxist study groups. The Russian communist representatives, the Russian Government being weak and isolated at this time, urged the CCP to join the force with the Kuomintang. The communist delegates in China argued that the KMT's aim was a nationalist revolution, that is, unifying the country and eliminating foreign interference, and the CCP stood for a social revolution. However, they eventually gave in under duress of withdrawing the Russian aides and joined the KMT in September 1922. Anti-imperialism was the main plank of the alliance: the main common objections were the foreign control of tariffs and extraterritoriality in the treaty ports.

The Russian revolution brought new learning to China in the form of Marxism-Leninism. The industrial proletariat led the October Revolution in Russia. In China, the revolutionary core must come from the peasantry by the sheer necessity; there were only a small number of the industrial proletariat at the time. Mao had to rely on the peasants for the recruits and the supplies in return for the promise of the land redistribution.

The consensus of the Russian assessments in the early 1920s as to who would most likely to set up the effective government in China was the warlord Wu P'ei-fu at Peking and Sun Yat-sen in Canton. Wu was ousted from Peking. The Sino-Soviet Treaty was signed in 1924 in Peking between the Soviet representatives and the KMT. Though the USSR insisted the alliance between the CCP and the KMT, the KMT was their main interest as the subsequent treaties with the KMT headed by Sun Yat-sen also showed. Sun Yat-sen had founded the KMT (Kuomintang or Chinese Nationalist Party) in 1911. The Russian aim was clearly strategic rather than ideological on this matter, and some accused them of the Soviet imperialism. At the end of 1924, Sun Yat-sen went to Peking in the hope of some agreement with the warlords. However, he was ill with cancer and died in Peking in March 1925.

Chiang Kai-shek set up his own Nationalist Government at Nanking on 18 April 1927, expelling communists from the KMT. In 1918 he had joined Sun Yat-sen, who appointed him to head the military academy in 1924. The leftist national government at Wuhan looked more legitimate; however, it lost the mass support and succumbed, and agreed to join the Nationalist Government at Nanking in 1928. Chiang Kai-shek had negotiated to limit the treaty rights the foreign governments enjoyed before the establishment of the Nationalist Government. In 1929 the treaties were revised to hand over the control of the tariffs to China. However, England and America did not give in to revoke the extraterritorial privileges in the treaty ports, arguing that the disorder and misuse of justice in China at that time did not guarantee the safety of their nationals. The treaty ports in 1930s included almost all major cities except Peking (not a port city), that is, Shanghai, Tientsin, Canton, Wuhan, Nanking, Chungking, Mukden and Dairen.

The Nationalist Government drew its support from the upper and influential class of China, that is, the business and intellectual communities, the upper echelon of the army and the rural administrative class. The Japanese wanted to turn China into their colony; whereas the Nationalist Government wanted to preserve the privileges of the traditional Chinese elite. Chiang Kai-shek's major attention against the communists rather than against the Japanese aggression did not meet the demands of his supporters. In September 1931, the Japanese army occupied all Manchuria, even ousting the Russians from the Chinese Eastern Railway. He did not reverse his policy of containing the Communists first towards the end of 1936 even when the Japanese were tightening the grip on north China, and all levels of the Chinese society was opposing the Japanese advances. Only after the Japanese attacked Peking and commenced a large scale operation did Chiang order the cessation of the civil war and fight a national enemy. In all these the Nationalist Government lost the support of the people and had to rely on the rural elite, the most conservative class in China. (Milston 1978, pp. 312-14)

When the alliance between the KMT and the CCP officially ended in the mid-1927, the CCP became illegal and its members were liable to imprisonment and execution. The party members were afraid to do any active work, and the membership dropped to about 10 000. The emergency party meeting was held at Wuhan in August 1927, and decided its immediate objective was the agrarian revolution in Hunan and Hupei. Their revolution entailed transferring the land from the landlords to the landless peasants, reducing the rents to 37% of the crops and resulting at the same time in the transfer of political power to the peasant associations. The Red Army had to attend the rural area to encourage the transfer and also to prevent the undoing. They did not participate in the redistributions of the land and the CCP cadres gave advice when necessary. The local people took the initiatives; agreed to reallocations, took the measurements of the lands and allocated the lands. As the time went on, the success of the land reforms brought into existence a self-governing area or a soviet and large Red Army units.

For twenty years the Chinese Communist Party had been distributing land wherever it established bases, but its methods and approaches varied depending on the political exigencies of the moment. Landlords and rich peasants faced not only loss of their land, but also punishment for past offences. How many were executed is uncertain; estimates range from hundreds of thousands to tens of millions. The CCP by killing a large number made sure that the land reform could not be unmade.

After the Long March (1934-5) to Shensi, which was really a desperate retreat driven by the superior Nationalist armies, the CCP decided that the Japanese were the nation's worst problem, hence should be tackled first. They wanted to end the hostility with the KMT, and even to halt the agrarian revolution for a while. Japan proceeded with the major invasions into China in July 1937. Chiang Kai-shek agreed to the joint venture with the CCP in late 1937 only after the nationalists received the credit worth 125 million American dollars from the USSR. However, the war effort by the Nationalist Government against Japan was minimum after 1938. The Nationalist army attack on the CCP army units in 1941 clearly demonstrated the end of the united front. In fact the two parties were incompatible as many of both party members had anticipated from the beginning. From the end of the Long March in

1935 to the end of war with Japan, incredibly the revolutionary movement expanded dramatically in spite of the fact that there were many adverse settings to the revolution.

Mao became an undisputed communist leader in China by 1935. He had to establish the communist bases in the rural regions and spread the revolutions to the populated areas. Therefore the revolution in China took as long as two decades. He was elected Chairman of the Central Committee of the CCP in 1945.

When the war against Japan ended in 1945, it looked that the KMT had more resources, human and material, than the CCP: besides the former had the supports of the USSR and the USA. The CCP had the rural support and the ideological strength and eventually defeated the KMT which showed the organisational weaknesses with manifested corruptions. Chiang Kai-shek, still defiant, moved to Taiwan with his army, air force and navy. Mao declared the People's Republic of China in Peking in 1949.

Breaking with orthodox Marxism-Leninism which regarded that only the industrial proletariat were capable of leading the communist revolution, Mao referred to the poor peasants as the vanguard of revolution. Mao insisted on the sinification of Marxism, adapting Marxism to the Chinese context to be effective.

> The Party [Chinese Communist] grew steadily from 2.7 million members in 1947 to 6.1 million in 1953 and 17 million in 1961. Many of these party members were poor peasants …. (Ebrey 1996, pp. 298, 301)

After World War II the Chinese Communist Party used the revolutionary land reform to obtain peasant support in Manchuria and North China. The peasants obtained the lands belonging to the landlords, the public lands and the collaborators in exchange for taxation, military and labour services, and food.

By the Sino-Soviet alliance treaty of 1949, the Manchurian railways (the China Eastern Railway) were handed back to China.

Mao followed the people's democratic dictatorship. The dictatorship was designed to destroy the enemies of the people. The poor peasants were the vanguard of the revolution. The party policies went on further. The people included not only the poor peasants and the middle peasants and the workers, but also professional people, intellectuals, the propertied merchants and those of limited wealth. However, what really happened later does not necessarily reflect the stated policies.

'The peasants would continue to own their land--even the better off peasants were left in possession--and so were the landlords of the land they themselves farmed.' The Agrarian Reform Law of 1950 confirmed the above setup. (Grenville 1994, p. 423)

At an early stage of the revolution, it was thought that the production of the rich peasants and the industry in private hands were essential for the development of socialism. However, the communist administration exercised increasing control over all production in China. (p. 423)

After the establishment of People's Republic in 1949, Mao ruled China autocratically. In this respect the traditional Chinese rule dominated. Terror was used to mobilise the masses and those who opposed him was ruthlessly eliminated. (p. 633)

The revolutionary land reform was largely completed by 1952. It was estimated that about 43% of China's cultivated land was confiscated and distributed to about 60% of rural population.

Land reform did not produce any substantial increase in output. Official estimates of grain production rose only 12.6% between 1949 and 1952, including the recovery from the ravages of wars. This indicated that China had to adopt collectivisation to increase the output.

(Roberts 1998, p. 223) Thus agricultural collectivisation followed redistribution of land in several stages.

In 1950 Marriage Law was passed, allowing women equal rights with men over property and divorce. It required the free choice of partners and monogamy.

In 1953, the population of China increased by 2.29% and the rate of increase remained at well over 2 per cent per annum. Just after the revolution the Marxists maintained that in a socialist country there cannot be too much population. By 1957 the official line was to encourage birth control. (p. 225)

Just after the Korean War ended with an armistice in 1953, Mao announced that China would head for industrialisation. China initiated its First Five-Year Plan (1953-7) based on the Soviet model. (p. 225)

The plan adopted the centralised planning and one-man management, both of which were practised in Russia. Though the First Five-Year Plan was successful in raising the industrial output, it exposed the weakness in that the agricultural sector lagged behind. China was to discard the Soviet model. (p. 226)

The land reform did not produce the sustained growth in agricultural production to feed the rising population and to provide raw material for industries. The land reform gave only small plots of land to the farmers, which were not large enough to utilise the capital which was lacking in the first place. (p. 229)

Starting in 1954 the small plots of lands were cooperatised. The family retained the private ownership of land and several families got together and mutually aided. In 1955 the decision was taken to amalgamate several cooperatives to collectivise. In the collectives, the private ownership of lands was abolished and the members were paid wages according to labour input. (p. 229) By 1956 the cooperatives (higher stage) held about 90% of the agricultural land.

In the short term collectivisation did not increase agricultural growth.

When the First Five-Year Plan was completed successfully in 1957, Mao wanted to replace the plan with the Great Leap Forward. In 1958 production targets were increased dramatically with the huge increase of the state investment. From 1957 to 1960, the number employed in state enterprises doubled to over 50 million, placing an immense strain to the procurement of food from the countryside.

Mao advocated the Great Leap Forward during 1958-60. Its aim was to hasten the process of industrialisation and increase agricultural production. It entailed organising the population into large rural collectives and adopting labour intensive industrial production. One result was that a large number of professionals and intellectuals were thrown out of their professions and sent to the country side for labour reform. The movement ended in a disaster. From 1960 to 1963 the party returned to more rational planning. The professionals and intellectuals were told they were part of the working people. Private plots and handicraft enterprises were again permitted. (p. 636)

In the country a more dramatic change occurred. The communes as a part of the Great Leap Forward were hailed to solve the various problems of the economy. In 1958, there was a tremendous push to create communes out of the cooperatives. A committee chosen by the people ran the communes. The average commune consisted of about 5000 families. Since a large capital was not available to develop communes, the communes had to mobilise labour in a vast scale. (p. 235)

Peng Dehuai severely criticised the performance of the Great Leap Forward in the letter in 1959. In response Mao stripped him of the portfolio of Minister of Defence and initiated the Second Great Leap Forward in the spring of 1959, stifling the mistakes of the First. The Second Great Leap Forward produced more disastrous consequences than the First. (p. 239)

In 1960 the Western observers reported that China was experiencing an agricultural disaster. The Chinese Government emphatically denied that and the Chinese people kept silent about the matter. According to the data made available in the early 1980s the cumulative deaths from the famine was between 16 and 27 million. (p. 240)

When China launched the Great Leap Forward in 1958, abandoning Soviet economic methods, the Sino-Soviet split was about to come open. The Soviet technical experts withdrew from China in July 1960, thus contributing partially to the failure of the Second Great Leap Forward. (p. 242)

The Great Leap Forward made disastrous decline of the outputs, both agricultural and industrial. In recognising the problems China went through a series of measures to reverse the declining trend. For example, a small proportion of the collectivised land was returned to the peasants as private plots. By 1965 agricultural outputs nearly recovered to the level of the pre-Great Leap Forward. The similar story unfolds in the industrial sector. Centralised planning was resumed and the management practices of the First Five-Year Plan were restored. Also many urban communes were disbanded. From 1963 the sustained growth in the industrial production began. (p. 243)

Jiang Qing began a campaign from 1959 to bring about a revolution in cultural affairs. The Great Proletarian Cultural Revolution lasted from 1966 to 1969 as an active campaign, but was not concluded until Mao's death and the overthrow of the Gang of Four in 1976. It was Mao's and radical group's ambition to rekindle the revolution in the arena of culture.

At another level, the Cultural Revolution was Mao's attempt to regain his political power he lost as the consequence of the failed Great Leap Forwards. His chief opponents were Liu Shaoqi and Deng Xiaoping.

The impact of the Cultural Revolution was minimum and fell far short of Mao Zedong's intentions. Liu Shaoqi was expelled from the party in 1968 and died in prison, Deng Xiaoping was imprisoned, and the opponents of Mao at the various levels of the party were purged. However the political order was intact and the large parts of the rural areas escaped the effects of the Cultural Revolution. The most obvious effects of the Cultural Revolution were the disruption and humiliation brought to many millions of people. It caused about one million deaths. (pp. 255-6)

President Nixon dramatically visited Peking in 1972 and subsequently recognised the People's Republic as the legitimate representative of China rather than the Taipei Government as had been the case hitherto.

Deng Xiaoping was disgraced during the Cultural Revolution but was rehabilitated in 1974.

After the deaths of Mao and Zhou Enlai in 1976, the aspirant successors were Hua Guofeng, the Gang of Four and Deng Xiaoping. However, by 1980 Deng Xiaoping outmanoeuvred the other protagonists and became the effective leader of China until his death in 1997.

For Mao's personal life focusing on his sexual exploits, refer to Section 15, Chapter 1, Book Five *The Sexual Laws*.

Deng Xiaoping's government promoted economic modernisation and an open door policy to the West in 1980s.

The growth in agricultural outputs in China was 3.1 percent per annum between 1966 and 1978. Though the figures were sufficient to meet the needs of a rising population, it was thought to be too low for the high standard of living. The transformation of agriculture began in 1978. The reform was the reversal of collectivisation and communisation which were the earlier trend. The new trend was the effective privatisation of the land and the farmers were allowed to sell any surplus crops, once the quotas were met. (p. 269)

From 1978 an industrial version of the responsibility system was introduced. Managers were now allowed greater freedom of operation. Price controls were removed from many products. Enterprises were now allowed to retain a portion of their profits and distributed it as incentives. (p. 271)

Under Deng's guidance, between 1979 and 1984, the lease system replaced the collectives; the former is hardly distinguishable from private ownership. Deng's initial reforms were centred in agriculture and it seems his agrarian reforms paid off and the production increased remarkably by 1984. The reform of state factories and urban enterprises took off later, in the mid-1980s. In all cases the reforms were set from above. One party control instituted the socialist market economy. (Grenville 1994, pp. 647, 651)

Communist China's effective reforms in summary:

1978 The government introduced to give China's peasants higher reward for more production. A dramatic rise in agricultural products resulted.

1984 Industrial reforms instituted by Deng Xiaoping:

- A million state-owned enterprises became independent.
- The pricing for many products became the market forces of supply and demand.
- The industrial managers got more autonomy.

(Mercer 1996, p. 1096)

The economy in China was highly inefficient when Mao died in 1976. The centralised planning and the large collectives were deemed to be failures. To speed up economic development, Deng also abandoned Mao's insistence on self-sufficiency and began courting foreign investors, even encouraging joint ventures between foreign firms and Chinese government agencies. Foreign manufacturers were attracted to the low labour costs in China, and both set up factories to produce goods for the Chinese markets (such as vehicles) and contracted with Chinese manufacturers to produce consumer goods for Western markets (such as clothing, stuffed toys, matches and bicycles). (Ebrey 1996, p. 324) These reforms resulted in economic growth and improvement in the living standard of the Chinese people.

In the late 1980s, the Chinese university students demanded political reforms such as more freedom and an end to the corruptions in the government. This movement culminated in the demonstrations by hundreds of thousands of students and workers in Beijing's Tiananmen Square in 1989. The government crashed the demonstrators with brute force and subsequently tightened the controls by the government and the secret police.

Deng Xiaoping made his continuing support for market reforms and rapid economic growth as clear as possible in 1992 (p. 330).

Young Chinese responded to Deng's call to make money with the same zeal their parents had shown in response to Mao's call to make revolution. In the early 1990s they were plunging into private enterprise in unprecedented numbers, setting up businesses. (p. 330)

Section 4 Some Fundamental Theories of Communists Presented and Rated

One problem Karl Marx had was a lack of job, especially industrial, experience. His propositions were often too theoretical, not being based on practical problems of industries. Many of these theories were no more than mental exercises and do not have any relevance in solving the practical problems. He devoted himself to many useless and absurd theories since he had ample spare time not having to go to work. Any persons with job experience always asks if any theory is useful for their job or not before they spend some time on it.

Taking into account of the various considerations, I took the format of presenting his theories separately from each other, and briefly explained. This form of presentation in this section should not distort his messages in any way. I selected the theories such that readers would get the good understanding of his doctrines. Compartmentalisation of the communist theories may also be an easy and quick way of understanding them. Further I graded the theory according to my rating. Though I did my utmost for balanced and unbiased presentations, some people may point out that I was subjective in the selections and appraisals of the doctrines. I did my best to assess communist theories fairly and also both not to distort and not to assess them emotionally as some people did. Readers may find the format incredible in that I dare to assess the theories in fractions. I assess them on common sense and fair judgment.

I use only five levels of ratings:

0, a quarter, a half, three quarters, and one
note: A theory rated 0 is totally wrong. A theory rated one is correct without any reservations. The other three represent increasing levels of correctness.

The fraction given to a theory represents correctness of the theory as I judge and hence has nothing to do with its usefulness in practical situation. Marx, being inclined to poetry, expounded his political-economic doctrines disregarding their usefulness; this is especially true with his *Capital*. His writings often reveal that he is conceited and arrogant but I have focused my attention if his theories are correct or not, and not these peculiarities. I would imagine that the usefulness assessment is virtually impossible to make for politico-economic doctrines, since people say a doctrine is good and useful if it matches with their experience or suits them. This fact has a parallel in the subjects taught at school. The students normally do not know how useful the subjects are until they graduate and have some experience in jobs and life; besides, every student after graduation would have different experience and would present different assessments on the usefulness scale. The idea of presenting the theories in this fashion is similar to the assessment techniques widely used in such fields as in the school examinations or the job interviews. The examinees or the interviewees are assessed on the basis how correctly and deeply they understand the questions presented.

One problem in the communist countries in the past was that once the communists assumed the political power, they could not deviate from the original Marxist doctrines, though it was obvious that communism was unworkable in the way Marx presented. If communism had been theoretically correct, there may have been some practical remedies for the past communist nations. This is another reason why we must study communist theories. Until we study the doctrines in some depth, we don't know if they are correct or not.

> They cover up their actual rejection of Marxism by referring to the fact that the Marxist teaching itself presupposes the replacement of out-dated propositions by new ones. But the replacement of obsolete theses by new Marxist proposition has nothing in common with

> rescinding the fundamental principles of Marxism-Leninism that form the very soul of this revolutionary teaching. (Dutt 1961, p. 433)

This section appraises only the fundamental theorems held by the communist theoreticians and does not include the different policies such as described in the foregoing sections. The theories selected are only those peculiar to Marxism, and also do not include what I judge to be ridiculous. In other words, I made it a rule to list only the theories for which the communists were distinguished from other strands of economic thoughts. The propositions which the capitalist economists or the people with common sense readily agree are not included in the list as a rule. For example, the famous catch phrase concluding *Manifesto of the Communist Party* (1848), that is, 'Working men of all countries, Unite!' is truth beyond any question to promote the cause of the proletarians. My analyses do not include this battle cry since uniting the members promotes the causes of any group under any circumstances. It is obvious that the capitalists should be united to further their causes; and the belligerent nations always encourage the united front against the enemy.

A careful survey of the views of capitalist economists reveals that the disagreements among economists are not as great as is popularly supposed. There are many issues of positive economics on which there is a substantial consensus among economists: the effect of rent control, minimum wages and tariffs upon economy as well as the functioning of exchange rate and government spending. There remains two issues of positive economics on which there is major disagreement: role of money and inflation theory. The major disagreements among economists lie in the normative arena. (Samuelson & Nordhause 1985, p. 7)

Among the theses to be brought up subsequently, the two theories may be central to the communist causes. One may be labour theory of value presented as an eternal truth and the other may be the declining rates of profits for the capitalists. The second proposition leads to the worsening working conditions for the proletariat and eventually induces the collapse of capitalism. The theorem implies that the capitalist system is defective and transitory to be replaced by the communist state.

The former theorem justifies the communist revolution even with bloodshed. After the inevitably successful revolution, the working people are to establish the dictatorship since they alone are responsible for the creation of any value according to the proposition. Some communist theoreticians included the farmers, especially the so-called peasants, in the working people. The expropriation of the mass of people from the soil to the factory forms the basis of the capitalist mode of production (Marx 1954, p. 719). Further the communist government thus established has the right to confiscate all the means of production from the capitalists without compensation according to this theorem.

As far as the fundamental theories of the communists to be dealt in this section are concerned, it is immaterial on whose books we base the theories since they are all similar with varying expressions, and Karl Marx formulated them.

> Lenin's work *The Development of Capitalism in Russia* (1899) was about the development of the commercialisation of Russian agriculture and represents a very considerable contribution to the understanding of changes in the Russian agricultural sector. But from then until his death in 1924 Lenin's writings offer no serious advances on Marx's economic ideas. Even after the October Revolution what he has to say about technology and planning amounts to little more than a series of slogans. (Walker 1978, p. 214)

Karl Marx was well versed in the economic theories many eminent economists promoted. He was an avid reader with remarkable memory about what he read. He did not originate many of his theories propounded and, it is widely acknowledged, he borrowed them from the past economic theorists such as Adam Smith and David Ricardo. In particular:

> The germs of many of Marx's ideas are found in his [Thomas Hodgskin] books; and Marx acknowledged, at least partly, his debt to Hodgskin (Roll 1961, p. 246).

One serious problem Marx had is the use of data Engels prepared. Marx based his theories of communism on the prevailing conditions of British industries between the end of the 18th century and the middle of the 19th century, when the lot of the British workers was probably at the worst compared with just before and after. He incorporated a great deal of works done by Engels more than 20 years previously. Even though the British capitalism was forging ahead strongly and the working people's lot was improving considerably when he was writing his *Capital*, that is, in the mid-1860s, Marx relied on the old data to support his argument which reflected the miserable working conditions of more than 20 years earlier. (Carmichael 1968, p. 221)

Marx's ideas expressed in *Capital* are remarkably consistent throughout. 'For example, value is defined in the first chapter of Volume One of *Capital* and plays a fundamental role in the analysis throughout.' (Brewer 1984, p. 15) Marx used logic as his guiding principle and avoided using historical presentation as far as *Capital* was concerned. He formed his views in political economy fairly early in his career. He certainly had his theories firmly set by the time he was 48 years of age when he got published Volume One of *Capital* in 1867, though he had completed the draft of the next two volumes by this time. He spent as long as 30 years writing *Capital,* though he wrote most of it after moving to Britain. Engels got these latter two volumes published posthumously, though Marx had ample time to do so until his death in 1883--in fact 16 years. Engels made an excuse for Marx, saying that Marx was sick during these years.

Progress Publishers, Moscow, published *Theories of Surplus Value* (3 Parts) in 1963. The same publisher also published *Capital,* and *Selected Works* by Marx and Engels. These are the texts I quote in my book. Karl Marx dealt economic history citing many eminent economists in *Theories of Surplus Value* and wanted to publish it as Volume IV of *Capital* complementary to the first three volumes. In Volume IV Marx set forth the whole course of evolution of bourgeois political economy from birth to his time, and completed the draft by 1863. Engels made his intention clear in 1895 that he wanted to publish these books but he died four months later. Kautsky published these books for the first time in 1905-10, and since then his edition appeared in German, Russian and other languages. (Marx 1963, Preface)

There are a few plausible reasons why Marx lost an interest in furthering and completing his communist doctrines, which I disclose in the following hyphenated paragraphs:

- He finished writing *Capital* in the mid-1860s. However, it was increasingly obvious that the British workers' lot was improving beyond any doubt in spite of his confident prediction that the proletariat would be impoverished as the time went on. This prediction was crucial for the arrival of the communist state: If the capitalist economy could improve the life of the working people, there would be no need to create the alternative society of communism.
- Marx obtained a government pension for life one year after Volume One of *Capital* was published hence he did not feel the compulsion to publish the rest for money.
- The sale of Volume One was so disappointingly poor that he did not feel like completing and publishing the volumes Two and Three.
- Not only did he lose an interest in his politico-economic theories, but he could have suspected if many of his doctrines could have been wrong, though none of his works I read indicated that was the case. Logically speaking, he could not possibly admit that after so

many years of fierce debates with the contemporary thinkers.

- His economic theories could not explain and alleviate his personal misfortunes, particularly his poverty before obtaining the pension as well as the deaths of his wife and eldest daughter in his late years.

His doubt on his theories matches with the doubt of some scholars, seeing the absurdities of some theories, if Marx himself really believed in them in the first place. If this implication had been true, many of the communists in the world might have lost interests in Marxism. This is similar in scale in its gigantic consequences to the possibility that Adolf Hitler could have been a quarter Jew, his father being half Jew. Either of the possibilities as facts could have altered the history of the 20th century almost to the degree we cannot even assess with confidence.

Marx was obsessive in defending his theories, though many of his doctrines were not his own making but he borrowed them from his predecessors, as mentioned earlier. He flatly rejected any views which contradicted his and used all his literary skills to denigrate them. As far as I know only Engels and possibly Hegel escaped his bitter criticism. Marx in fact criticised Hegel in *Criticism of the Hegelian Philosophy of Law* (Marx & Engels 1970, p. 79). Marx also wrote: Nothing could be more comical than Hegel's development of private landed property (Marx 1959, p. 615). Marx rejected Hegel's idealistic philosophy and retained only his dialectical method. In spite of all these, I believe he felt admiration for Hegel through his life. And Engels was his co-worker and the division of labour existed between the two. Besides, Engels was his friend and his financial benefactor. Marx was not so out of touch with the reality as to criticise Engels. Let me tell readers that Beethoven used to abuse his pupils in private. He was too steeped in his music to see the absurdity; their parents were the financial contributors to him.

I assess the core theories of communism in this section, and I present the principles of communism in the following section.

I realised in the course of the investigations that I could not give assessment grades to some theories by their nature apart from the reasons for excluding the theories as I mentioned earlier. I am to give examples in the next paragraph. Besides I thought it was a good idea to present the principles--some are assessed and some are not--to give a concise picture of communism.

I cannot give assessment on some theories because of their nature. The following theory is cited as an example since the proposition obviously depends on subjective belief, appealing to individual perception. Many people do not agree with it and even believe that the opposite idea governs the human beings, not being able to give logical explanations for the judgement. However, the theory still forms the core of the communist ideology. These observations are based on my personal judgements.

Theory: Religion is an opium of masses. Though we may have the impression that Karl Marx coined this famous proposition, that is not the case. He got the statement from Hegel who described it in his lecture on *Philosophy of World History* in the context of India.

The following information should assist the understanding of the various communist theories, though they are general knowledge and by no means communistic.

Elements of Production or Elementary Factors of Labour Process
Karl Marx extensively used the concept: e.g., pages 174, 574-5 of *Capital* Volume I; pages 399-400 of *Capital* Volume II.

1. Subjective Factor or Labour Power or Variable Capital or Living Labour

2. Objective Factor or Means of Production or Constant Capital or Congealed Labour or Materialised Labour

   - Subject of Work (or of Labour) or Material of Labour or Circulating Capital
     raw material (undergone human labour)
     soil, fish, timber, water, ores
     auxiliary material

   - Instruments of Labour or Means of Labour or Fixed Capital
     stones, wood, animals, machines, tools, workshops, canal, roads, earth, bones, shells
     note: The instruments of labour include land according to Marx (Marx & Engels 1970, p. 15).

Forms of Business Organisation of Firms
This classification was taken from *Economics* (McTaggart, Findley & Parkin 1992, pp. 87-9). We are familiar with the forms of the firms today; however, it seems that Karl Marx and his contemporary people were not because these forms were not fully developed at the time.

Sole Proprietorship
Unlimited liability
Hire labour
Proprietor = residual claimant
the Profit = the income of the proprietor after subtracting all the expenditures
Small operation in which the proprietor is an expert
Most farms and shops
Capital and labour are combined.

Partnership
Joint unlimited liability
Each partner is legally liable for all the debts of the partnership.
Most law firms and accounting firms

Company
Limited liability
To raise money company issues bonds and shares.

Not-for-Profit Firms
Universities, colleges, churches and mutual insurance organisations

Cooperatives
Members bear the risks of the enterprise and share in its profits.
Credit unions and building societies

Government Business Enterprises
These firms are publicly owned and operated under government supervision.

Resources and Factors of Production
The following classifications were taken from *Economics* (Dye, Moore & Holly 1966, p. 4). However, the classifications can be confusing since some economists may classify them in different ways, such as presented earlier.

Resources
- the materials provided by nature
- the talent and services of human beings
- the man-made tools and techniques used in production

Factors of Production
- land
  note: Land refers to all natural resources--all gifts of nature: arable land, forests, mineral and oil deposits, and water resources.
- labour
- managerial ability
- capital

Fixed Cost and Variable Cost
I also refer occasionally to the following distinctions in this book:

Fixed Cost
It is sometimes called overhead and remains the same regardless of the amount produced unless the amount to be produced far exceeds the capabilities of the factory and a new factory must be set up.
Examples; rent, salaries, insurance

Variable Cost
It changes as the level of production changes.
Examples; cost of raw material, hourly wages of workers, freight charges

Theory: The employers keep the wages of the proletariat to a minimum such that they can buy only the sheer necessities of life for them and their families. In other words, the wages of the proletariat are equal to the basic minimum of living and procreation for them.

Adam Smith developed the above proposition as Subsistence Theory of Wages; the cost of bringing the worker into being as a member and sustaining him in his job. David Ricardo converted it to the Iron Law of Wages; keeping the labouring class to the minimum wages necessary for their survival. (Galbraith 1987, p. 67) Ricardo argued that if the employers paid the workers higher than subsistence wages, they would have more children and live under the subsistence level. The children would grow up and multiply the labourers, thus driving down the wages. So there was no gain in paying higher wages to the workers. (Dye, Moore, and Holly 1966, p. 51)

> Sir William Petty limited the wages of labour to the cost of the food necessary to sustain the worker--which was in fact the prevailing mode of calculating wages in his day--and the remainder of the value of the product he attributed to the land as rent. (Heimann 1964, p. 37)
>
> For Petty, as later for Ricardo and Marx, labour-time thus became the common denominator of all values (p. 38).
>
> But Rodbertus held that the income of the workers is inflexibly tied to the minimum of physical subsistence, and the increment accruing to the national income is reserved to the capitalists exclusively. This doctrine of the falling wage quota was an elaboration of Sismondi's theory and was used by both Rodbertus and Sismondi as an explanation of the deficiency of purchasing power which causes an economic crisis. (p. 137)

Richard Cantillon estimated that the lowest species of common labourers must earn at least double of their maintenance to support their wife and two children (Smith 1991, p. 72).

We may state the proposition in another way. The cost of production of a worker is equal to the means of subsistence he requires for his maintenance and for the propagation of his race.

This proposition fitted so well with the overall scheme of Marxism that it appears in many parts of Marx's literature, though Marx meant it applies not to the individuals but to the species. The production price of the necessary means of subsistence determines the average price of labour. The necessary labour-time required for its reproduction determines the value of labour power. (Marx 1959, pp. 868-70) Marx drew this conclusion focusing his attention on the working and living conditions of the proletariat and their families, a fraction of the total population, during the Industrial Revolution in Britain. He believed it to be the eternal truth under capitalism, ignoring the due considerations. In the first place he did not take into account the time frame in that the lot of the proletariat might improve in the future. He did not even discuss if the wage labourers were single or married with children. The wages of the labourers did not depend on the marital status but depended on their contributions to the employers, on the social customs and the relevant statutes. Further, the financial state of wage workers would have depended also on the spending habits and the health of all members of the families. In addition, the government policies particularly concerning tax and welfare would have had significant impacts on the financial positions of the proletariat.

It is well established that the British workers' living standard improved a great deal after the middle of the 19th century. Adam Smith observed that while he was writing *The Wealth of Nations* (1776), the wages of labourers in Great Britain was evidently more than they needed to bring up their families (Smith 1991, p. 77). The sweeping remark of Marx in the theorem under consideration does not apply to the wage labourers of the industrialised nations of the 21st century. For example, an average working man with a family in Australia today owns a car, a host of household appliances such as a TV set, a refrigerator, a washing machine; and a furnished house possibly with some mortgage.

Wages in Australia today is set out of line with market forces, and protection is used to validate the wages rates. Productivity is central. It determines the capacity for higher living standards. The key reform necessary is an increase in team work and cooperation within each work place and an increase in competitive pressure among the work places. (McTaggart, Findley, and Parkin 1992, p. 254)

In Britain in the latter part of the 19th century, trade unions symbolised the refusal on the part of their members to admit that labour was just another commodity, whose price was responsive to purely natural movements of supply and demand. Producers' agreements were also a refusal to admit the same criteria for 'industrial prices'. (Mathias 1969, p. 387)

I would say that the theorem aptly described the working and living statuses of the slaves in the ancient era the world over or those of the serfs in the medieval era in Europe. It is true that a large number of the British workers during the Industrial Revolution lived under the conditions described but the statement referring to all the working people under capitalist society of all time is contrary to the fact and ludicrous.

my rating = 0

Theory: Communism cannot emerge directly from capitalism but the dictatorship of the proletariat will follow the communist revolution before the government can implement genuine communism. The dictatorship of the proletariat is the transitional political form from capitalism to communism.

Lenin wrote that the soviets are the Russian form of proletarian dictatorship. He further wrote. The Soviet state, after the Paris Commune, is the second step towards the socialist state. Classes will remain everywhere for years after the proletariat's conquest of power. (Lenin 1975, vol. 3, pp. 40, 79, 310) The Paris Commune was a socialist government which ruled Paris from 28 March to 28 May 1871.

We can hardly challenge the theorem since all the countries which went through the communist revolution adopted the so-called dictatorship of the proletariat, though none of them got to introduce genuine communism if survived till the present day. Some of the few surviving communist countries are today desperately introducing capitalist practices into their countries in the fear that the communistic policies may totally obliterate them. However, the above theory itself is true beyond doubt.

The dictatorship of the proletariat is certainly a form of dictator with absolute power, not limited by the laws, and no chance of democratic removal. The phrase is used to indicate the rule by the representatives of the working people only, excluding any other representatives. In this sense the dictator advocated is similar to the Nazi dictatorship, and the violent opposition will meet any attempt to remove the existing government by democratic means. According to Marx the phrase also meant that this form of government was only a transition to more mature government in due course and the eventual abolition of the government in any form.

Lenin wrote that dictatorship of the proletariat is a special form of class alliance. He meant the industrial workers, the vanguard of the toilers, as the proletariat. Non-proletarian strata of toilers, that is, the petty bourgeoisie, the small proprietors, the peasantry, the intelligentsia and so on, join the proletarians. The alliance is against capital. (Dutt 1961, p. 640) Only the military force which will enforce the arming of the masses and insurrection will achieve the dictatorship of the proletariat (Lenin 1975, vol. 1, p. 457). All Marxists and all socialists agreed that a European war would create a revolutionary situation (Lenin 1975, vol. 3, p. 66).

Whatever the theoretical basis of the dictatorship of the proletariat, this form of the government was a sheer necessity for the survival of the communist governments in Russia and Eastern Europe since their establishments, because these communist governments did not have the consent of the majority will of the governed. They had to rely on the military power to maintain the form of the governments, and without the military force to back them up they were simply unable to survive in the face of the oppositions. Therefore, the above concept is in fact an admission on the part of the communist theoreticians that the communists are the minority just after the revolution but still want to govern the nation until they can establish the majority rule.

Hitler's government obtained 44% of the votes when it was most popular in March 1933. The Russian communist government would have got nowhere near that percentage of votes since its establishment till its collapse in the early 1990s. However, this fact does not preclude the possibility of majority communist government in Russia provided the communists alter their strategies radically based on entirely different ideas.

The fact that the minority carried out the Bolshevik Revolution in Russia should not surprise good history students. A small number of people among a large population perpetuated both the Puritan Revolution in Britain and the American Independence War. A small number of casualties in spite of their historical significances reflect this reality. Whereas, the French Revolution and the American Civil War involved the majority of populations in some way or another, thus resulting in a large number of deaths.

my rating = 1

Theory: When the communist revolution is successful, the communist government thus formed should confiscate all lands and all production facilities without compensations.

The communists put into effect this proposal universally after the communist revolutions in the various countries, and we can hardly challenge it as a theory. However, we may criticise it on moral ground. Prior to the successful communist revolution, the land owners and capitalists grew up believing their properties as theirs by unquestionable right. They must have been really shocked to find one day that the working people got hold of their properties and the government decreed to appropriate all their assets to the working people without any compensation. It was a great crime committed on them when looked from their viewpoint.

> The Second Congress of Soviets announced, on November 8, 1917, the abolition of the landlords' ownership of land in all Russia without compensation and declared that all the land in the country was turned into the national property and was being transferred to the use of those who tilled it (Dutt 1961, p. 483).

On the day before, Kerensky and the Provisional Government were ousted in a Bolshevik coup.

After the Bolshevik Revolution in Russia, a law was promulgated in February 1918: Land was nationalised, and the right to use it belonged to the peasants; none should have more than he alone could cultivate since the hiring of labour was to be forbidden. The above land law remained only on paper. Just after the Bolshevik Revolution many peasants in Russia seized land with force and divided up among themselves with impunity from the government. (Nove 1992, p. 41; Wells 1925, p. 695)

For Marx, the capitalists were always bad guys and the proletariat were always good guys. He tried to justify this view using various concepts such as surplus value and the historical inevitability of the proletarian triumph. Even if he could not sustain all these propositions, he would have been still anti-capitalist and pro-proletarian. He sided with the labourers beyond all reasons for rationales unknown to me. I believe that this stance of his was the main reason rather than his theories why the working class the world over hailed him as their hero.

Karl Marx theorised that the working people created all the properties, all of which belong to the working people. The communist leaders, once acquired the political reign after the revolution, placed the theory in focus into practice. The government even used military force at times to confiscate the lands and the means of production, believing in their moral right.

I have some reservation about the moral justification of the theory, whose moral right--the capitalists or the proletarians; however, this section is concerned with political and economic truism and not moral issues. I made a statement that Marxism is in fact based on ethical foundation in a broad measure but I am to judge the individual theory not on morals but on politico-economic principles. As far as the historical events went, the theory stood true, that is, the communists carried out what the theory stated.

my rating = 1

Theory: Value of a commodity is a sum of money to pay for accumulated labour power. The means of production, which comprise of raw material and instrument of labour, are after all commodities made in the past by labour power.

Marx used the term value loosely, which caused some confusion among the economists. I have come to believe that Marx meant cost for value in the above theory; however, the economists normally understand the term meaning price. The value was also used to mean the measure of worth in a general sense, which Marx and the economists used at times.

In the above proposition, labour power means the function of a labourer in the same way the function of a machine is its work. The measure of labour is labour time. The machines create values greater than their own and if a machine gives out only the value expended by labour power in the process of being made no manufactures would buy the machine. (Marx 1954, pp. 224, 504)

Use value is the utility of a thing. Exchange value is the ratio by which one use value is exchanged for another. The commodity is normally sold above its value (cost); this is profit upon alienation. Sometimes people have to sell the commodity below its value (cost) with the resultant loss.

Marx wrote:

> In calculating the exchangeable value of a commodity we must add the quantity of labour last employed the quantity of labour previously worked up in the raw material of the commodity, and the labour bestowed on the implements, tools, machinery and buildings, with which such labour is assisted (Marx & Engels 1969, p. 50).

Karl Marx used the various ways of expressing the above contrast: materialised, antecedent, past labour to living, immediate, present labour. Materialised labour can be in the form of money or commodity. Capital is past labour. Accumulated labour is the definite quantity of materialised labour.

The theorem proposed is termed labour theory of commodity which is produced for commercial selling. If we extend the reference to all physical objects beyond the concept of commodity, it is called labour theory of value: A worker produces a product whether he or she consumes or sells it. The people who supported the above theory went further and asserted that labour is the only measure of the exchangeable value of all commodities. Ricardo wanted to measure the real price by the quantity of labour expended. Adam Smith wanted to measure the real price by the quantity of labour which the commodity would command. They defined the above real price in contrast with the nominal price, the price of a commodity expressed in money.

The purpose of the private firms is to make money for the owners who do not care if the labour theory of value is correct or not. The owners are concerned with how much they pay for the production means and how much they can get out of them and do not care in the slightest if the facilities are worth only the labour input in the process of being made in the past.

The value (exchange value or price) of gold and silver in Europe in the 16th century was reduced to about a third of what it had been before the discovery of the mines in America. Encouraged by the above and other observations, Adam Smith made the following definitive statement:

> Labour alone, therefore, never varying in its own value, is the ultimate and real standard by which the value of all commodities can at all times and places be estimated and compared (Smith 1991, p. 39).

The antecedent of the labour theory of value can be found in the works of Aristotle (Roll 1961, p. 294). The idea is a direct challenge to the physiocrats who maintained that land and its products were the sole source of wealth. The Physiocrats, Parisian economists, regarded agricultural production as the only true form of wealth. Its leader Francois Quesnay expounded this physiocracy in *Tableau economique* (1758). The physiocrats emphasised the importance of land as a factor of production, while the classical economists made a similar assertion about labour. No nation adopted the agricultural (or physiocratic) system, which existed only in the speculation of a few men, notably in France.

Mercantilists advocated that only the trade was the real source of wealth. This creed is merchant capitalism or mercantilism and was predominant for roughly 300 years in Europe, that is, from the middle of the fifteenth century to the middle of the eighteenth century. Spain and Portugal were the notable nations which incorporated this dogma in their national policies. The mercantilists believed that the trade was more important than the production; they thought the latter as important as long as it promoted the former. They thought similarly about the consumers. The productions and consumptions were only the means to achieve the profits through trade. Naturally, the merchants or traders were the primary supporters of mercantilism. The start of the Industrial Revolution in Britain marks the end of its dominance, and the economists often note it by the publication year of *Wealth of Nations* in 1776.

Jevons, [William Stanley] asserted that the origin of value is in utility and scarcity, dismissing labour (Robbins 1998, p. 265).

Karl Marx wrote the statements in his *Capital* which retreats considerably from the above assertion: the soil and labour are the original source of wealth (Marx 1954, p. 475). He wrote an obvious statement that land in its crude state is not a product of labour (Marx & Engels 1969, p. 56). He also referred to labour power and land as the two primary creators of wealth (Marx 1954, p. 566).

Marx further extended the theory to include labourers who were looked as a commodity and stated:

> Value of labour power is determined as in the case of every other commodity, by the labour time necessary for the production, and consequently also the reproduction, of this special article (Barber 1991, pp. 129-30).

Marx and Engels placed a great emphasis in stating that labour power, not labour, is a commodity; the workers sell their labour power, not labour, to capitalists for money.

It follows that the professional people should get more money than the labourers since more money and time are spent to make the former than the latter. However, the above supposition does not explain what is happening under the present capitalist society, when we observe that some professional people make enormous amount of money, some make small money, some even less money than the tradespeople, and some out of work and need the government assistance.

David Ricardo formulated the labour theory of value before Marx:

> In the chapter on wages Ricardo regards labour as a commodity whose value must be determined in the same way as that of any other commodity (Roll 1961, p. 180).

Adam Smith and David Ricardo laid the foundation of labour theory of value. Karl Marx, building up on the works of the predecessors, showed that the quantity of socially necessary labour-time spent on its production determined the value of every commodity. (Lenin 1975, vol. 1, p. 46)

> He [Adam Smith] developed the labour theory of value inherited from Petty and Cantillon; but he also added to it certain elements of the supply and demand analysis of Locke (Roll 1961, p. 156).

In his difficulty of explaining value theory, Adam Smith abandoned the labour theory of value.

> Ricardo's theory is less elaborate than, but essentially identical with, that of Karl Marx (Heimann 1964, p. 99). Ricardo tried to maintain the labour theory without allowing it to lead to a theory of exploitation, as Marx was later to do (Roll 1961, p. 182).

The exchange value of a commodity, reckoned in money, is its price. Wages are a special name for the price of labour power, commonly called the price of labour.

The cost of a commodity includes the depreciation of the machines used and in the same way the wages include the depreciation or reproduction of the workers. The cost of production of simple labour power amounts to the cost of existence and reproduction of the worker. The price of this cost constitutes the wage minimum. The wage minimum does not hold good for the single individual but for the species. The wages of the whole working class level down to this minimum. (Marx & Engels 1989, p. 166)

Capital consists of raw materials, instrument of labour, and means of subsistence of all kinds. All these component parts of capital are creations of labour, products of labour, accumulated labour. Accumulated labour which serves as a means of new production is capital.

In fact you will find both theories in the works of Adam Smith:

- the general cost theory which capitalists advocate,
- the labour-value theory which socialists advocate.

(Heimann 1964, p. 68)

As had the main stream of the classical tradition, Marx approached the problem of value in terms of labour and regarded only physical objects as embodiment of value (Barber 1991, p. 126).

Cost and price in general have the following relationship:
price = cost + profit
where price: the sum of money for which produced commodities are sold
cost: the sum of money paid to produce commodities, including wages and salaries, materials, depreciations of the machines, rent, tax and various expenses
profit: the money sum made after sale subtracting cost
note 1: Profit is the purpose of the whole activity.
note 2: Karl Marx wrote that price, taken by itself, is nothing but the monetary expression of value (measure of worth) (Marx & Engels 1969, p. 53).

A firm's receipts from the sales of goods and services are total revenue. The total payment a firm makes for the services of factors of production is total cost. The difference between a firm's total revenue and total cost is its profits (if revenue exceeds cost) or its loss (if cost exceeds revenue). If the profit is negative, the firm made a loss and there is no point in carrying on the business unless the upturn in the future is foreseen. The capitalists pay for the means of production however the economists ascribe their origins, and it is only an academic interest if the objective factors are actually the accumulated labour power or not.

The labour theory of value reduces to the following argument. The manufacturer has to pay for the means of production, the material of production as well as for the employed for the production to proceed. The means of production, for example a machine, is the commodity made in the past. The manufacturer of this machine pays similarly as above to produce the machine. The repeated processes eventually lead to the suppliers of the raw materials. According to the theory the values of the various materials are in fact the same as the amount of money paid for the labour input, that is, socially necessary labour-time.

Seeing the difficulty in assessing the theory concerned, I am going to substitute cost for value. I present the concrete examples to throw some light on the validity or otherwise of the theory on this substitutioin.

- Some antiques can fetch high prices. However, if the theorem refers to cost and not price, the theory holds true. The antique was made many years ago and the dealer makes a profit by selling the commodity at the price which is far above the cost of production and even the price just after the production taking into account of the inflation.
- A patch of land can be sold at a high price, though the cost incurred in the past may be negligible to make it a commodity. A similar reasoning for antiques can apply: the price accrued to the owner of the land in selling can give the owner a huge profit. Accordingly, the theory holds in this case also.
- Similar argument as above holds for some objects such as gold or works of arts.
- Prospecting for gold is not the kind of situation Marx was thinking when he proposed the labour theory of commodity; however, a gold nugget once found becomes a commodity and the theory holds true in this case also.
- The crops production on the agricultural land heavily depends on two factors of soil and weather. Good soil (fixed for the location) and good weather return a large amount of crops for the same labour. Bad weather reduces the yields. Also the market price determines how much money the farmers get for the crops they want to dispose. All these observations

indicate that the value (cost) of the crops depends on labour. Hence the theorem holds.
- Some girls are born beautiful and very much sought after. In prostitution where the girls are treated as commodities, the good looking prostitutes can command high prices. The costs of bringing up the girls have nothing to do with the prices they may be getting from prostitution. Hence the theory holds true. The same argument hold for people who are born with peculiar voices or bodies sought after for singing and acting.

Labour-value theory cannot explain the well-known consensus that profits should be proportional to the total capital invested rather than to the number of workers employed (Heimann 1964, p. 171). Neither can it explain the fact that the government industries the world over with a huge capital and a large number of the employed, tend to make losses.

F Engels wrote that the proposition by classical economists on the value of a commodity, that is, it is determined by the labour contained in it, is totally inadequate. He further wrote that Marx discovered that not all labour expended on production added a value to a commodity. (Marx & Engels 1989, p. 151)

The theory of labour-value was proven to be false with the far reaching consequences in the modern economic thoughts. Strangely, as might have been expected, Marxism did not collapse. This fact suggests to us that in fact Marxism was not built on the foundation of labour-value. (Heimann 1964, p. 152)

If the value is understood to mean cost there are many instances where the theory hold true as I present in the analyses. However, the overall assessment is that the theory is not valid according to the modern economists. I have no choice but to follow the opinions of the experts.

my rating = a quarter

Theory: As the capitalism progresses the system creates the increasing number of proletarians who are progressively worse off. This proposition is sometimes called laws of increasing number of the proletariat and increasing misery for them.

This seemingly unimpressive proposal is the necessary prerequisite for the establishment of communist state. If capitalism has innate characteristics to improve the lot of the working people, there is no need to have alternative system of economy such as communism. The above theory is posited as the root cause of the breakdown of capitalist society.

Adam Smith and David Ricardo, classical economists, set up three class system in the production environment:

workers providing labour
capitalists providing capital
landowners providing land
note 1: Capital means not only money but the machinery, tools and buildings.
note 2: Land is natural resources of all kinds.

(Lipsey, Langeley & Mahoney 1986, p. 367)

Classical economics is the first modern school of economic thought which Adam Smith and particularly his work *Wealth of Nations* (1776) originated. Classical school economists tried to explain the creation of wealth and advocated free trade, and dominated the European economic thinking until about 1870.

John Stuart Mill (1806-1873), the last major contributor to the classical school, was dismayed by the transition from 3 class system to 2 class system, the aristocrats (landowners), though still powerful at the time, being absorbed into the bourgeoisie.

Smith and Ricardo predicted that only the landowners would improve their lots and the capitalists would be worse off and the labourers would be pushed to the subsistence level. We can see from the above setup that the aristocrats with the huge land ownership were powerful still in the late 18th century in Europe, and even in the early 19th century in the British society. The size of the land the aristocrats owned was the symbol of prestige and identification: they did not want to part with the land, and people in general thought that the landed properties were mostly not marketable commodities as they are today.

Karl Marx set up two class system of the society though he did not invent the idea, becaue money could buy the land, and the land and money were freely interchangeable by the middle of the 19th century. He also predicted that only the capitalists would become better off. Contrary to the above classification, Marx mentioned three class system in conjunction with revenues and their sources (Marx 1959, p. 885).

Karl Marx predicted that a large number of the middle class and a small number of the capitalists would sink to the working class as the capitalism matures, thus swelling the ranks of the proletariat.

It is quite true as Marx detailed in his *Capital* that the British working people went through horrible working and living conditions during the Industrial Revolution approximately from 1760 to 1840. However, we have to take into account the following facts as well. At the commencement of British industrialisation, the British people were not prepared for what they were getting into. They did not have any theory and experience as to what would happen under the widespread machine production. The British economists and hence the decision makers of the firms with scarce capital did not have any role models they could learn from, unlike the other nations which mechanised the industries in the subsequent years.

I would compare the Industrial Revolution to sexual inversion of adolescent boys. Virtually every boy has to go through a difficult period of sexual awakening when he experiences his sexual pleasure with shameful mistakes. As the time goes on the boy, if he is normal, adjusts himself to a sexual reality and learns to live with it. Certainly most males carry the sexual problem in some way or another well into manhood, but not to the extent at the sexual initiation, which has its distinct and acute problems. In a similar manner, newly industrialised nations learn to cope with industrialisation to a great extent after experiencing the initial pleasure of making money with grave consequences.

Ricardo remarked that machinery was in constant competition with labour. Karl Marx theorised that modern industries turned the scale in favour of the capitalists and consequently pushed the wages of labour ever lower. (Marx & Engels 1969, p. 74)

Karl Marx observed closely mostly through the documentations the miseries of the working people during the Industrial Revolution in Britain. The foreman employed and dismissed the workers and even decided the wages and the other conditions of employment. Many factories were small and run by the entrepreneurs eager to make quick profits with the scarce capital. Many of these entrepreneurs did not have formal education and did not hesitate to sacrifice the workers for profits. Marx theorised that as the time went on the fierce competition among the capitalists would force the profit per worker to decrease for the capitalists, and as the consequence the wages of the workers were obliged to come down. This worsening situation would break capitalism into chaos and the communist revolution would inevitably result. Marx justified the terminal nature of capitalism in anticipation of the communist victory.

Marx's prediction simply did not materialise and as a matter of fact the opposite was the definite trend. The real wages of the British workers were lowest during the Industrial Revolution. The wage earners in Britain started getting the benefits of the industrialisation after the second half of the 19th century and ever since they were in ascendancy in gaining political and economic powers with ups and downs of the small cycles as we expect on the matter such as this.

During both World War I and II, the European proletariat rallied behind their own governments, and as a matter of fact the national governments would not have carried on fighting without their cooperation. The wishful thinking of the communists that the workers would fight for communism leaving their respective governments simply did not happen. This was one strong indication that the communist theories were out of touch with the realities and were grossly in error. After the wars, this fact showed itself as the greater importance of the working people and hence resulted from this consideration alone in their more political and economic powers, though there were other contributing factors.

my rating = 0

Theory: The capitalists exploit the working class by skilfully using the ownership of the means of production in the production environment.

Marx defined the capitalist production as the production where capital and labour are clearly separated, that is, labourers do not own the means of production (Marx 1954, p. 668). According to this formula sole proprietorship with unlimited liability, the dominant form of business organisation in the European societies of Marx's life time, where capital and labour are combined as in most farms and shops, are not capitalist productions. He also defined, in another context, capitalist production as commodity production. Commodity can be both the end product and the elements of production for the subsequent manufacturing. The chief characteristic of capitalist production manifests in the fact that labour becomes commodity. If the commodity is consumed individually its value disappears during its consumption; if it is consumed productively, its value is transferred as an additional value to the commodity under production. (Marx 1956, pp. 54, 119)

Sismondi's description of the class division between bourgeoisie and 'proletarians' is almost par with that of Marx, and in his theory of the growing concentration of production and wealth he is the true predecessor of Marx, if not the actual founder of the theory (Heimann 1964, p. 130).

Marx looked at both capitalists and landowners as one class: the former can become the latter and vice versa with the possession of money which can buy the means of production and lands. He insisted on two class system of the society being solely defined on the ownership and non-ownership of capital, that is, capitalists and proletarians. He thought that the other less important classes cluster around the two classes: The other classes do not alter the essence of the two class system.

The two class system has certainly the advantage of being simple. However, it does not totally satisfy the real state of the affairs in the capitalist society in that the society is more varied as the other forms of firms combined carries more economic weight in the society than the companies of the above description. At the same time the capitalists are fighting among themselves for greater shares of the markets and dominance and so are the proletariat from various reasons. Thomas Hobbs may have understood the world deeper than Marx when the former said that the state of the human beings is the war of each against each other.

The first stock exchange in history was set up in Antwerp, Belgium, in 1531. The first stock exchange in England was established in London in 1773. People bought and sold the shares of stock through the brokers before the establishment of the stock exchange. Anybody can buy the shares with their disposal money and the shares become capital. Also the money in the bank account becomes capital. In this sense capital and labour become meaningless. Some people may say capitalists have large capital in their disposal; however, the aggregate of small capital can become huge. Karl Marx formed his economic theories before the stock exchange was fully developed, and consequently his theories were not compatible with what we know about capital and labour in this respect.

The exploiting society--slavery, feudal or capitalist--replaced in the course of history the primitive society or communal tribal system, in which there was no exploitation. With the transition to communism, however, Marx theorised that the exploitation of man by man ceases, and in this respect the communist society resembles the primitive-communal society. (Dutt 1961, p. 104)

Engels wrote that the slave owners and the feudal lords made riches by appropriating themselves the unpaid labour of slaves and serfs in the same way the capitalists do concerning the wage-labourers. There is only money (wages) relation between the capitalists and the wage earners. There was a master and servant relation between the feudal lords and serfs, apart from monetary relation. Before the Reformation the church was in fact the most powerful feudal lords, holding one-third of the land in the Christian Europe. (Marx & Engels 1970, pp. 87, 103) There was only brute force and social sanctions between the slave owners and the slaves.

> Malthus developed an exploitation theory of exchange between capital and labour in crude form, which was fully developed by Marx (Roll 1961, p. 207).

Marx did not deal with racism and sexism. He did not analyse the exploitation within the family except for making the broad statements such as the husbands exploit their spouses and their children. We do not use the term exploitation within the family in spite of the fact the parents spend an enormous amount of money and labour in bringing up their children, because the parents' commitments are emotional and we cannot assess the emotion financially. The parents, if they are happy with their family, do not think their children exploit them under normal course of events.

We normally talk that in private firms the managers exploit the workers. Is this premise really the case, as Marx alleged, for all firms at all times? Today in many small companies, the managers are the owners (capitalists). The large number of shareholders—normally, a small number of people or firms hold a large number of shares and a large number hold a small number of shares--own the large companies and appoint the managers. The majority votes in the share holders' meeting make all the important decisions. A small number of people with a large number of shares--normally 40% or even less number of shares--can control the company. In Marx's contemporary society capitalism was not well developed and people did not make the above distinctions. As a matter of fact many factories at the time were small and did not depend on the large number of contributors in the venture as shareholders. Consequently Marx separated people into capitalists and workers. We know that the workers are victorious now and then in the modern setting. The communists tell us that every struggle between the employers and the employed is a political struggle. We also know that the expanding scope of the communication and transport facilitates the union of the workers of the world.

We start by stating the well-established anomalies of wages:

- The employees bring home more money than the owner in certain circumstances in a small business.

- The staff gets paid more money than their supervisor. This happens especially in the public service sector which acts often inflexibly and illogically. Sometimes the employees have specialised skills and their supervisor has to rely on them, much less to remove them.
- The specialist can earn more money than the head. For example, the music teacher's salary may exceed that of the head master.

Ignoring the contrast between capital and labour, if we focus our attention on the upper and lower strata of a company structure, I can make the following statement with confidence backed by my experience, though the propositions may puzzle the people with no experience in the working of an organisation. Fundamentally, supervisors and subordinates are mutually dependent; in other words, symbiotic. They are also manifestations of division of labour. In some cases the former needs the latter more than the latter needs the former, and in some cases the dependency is the other way around. Normally for supervisors, their subordinates are more important than their own supervisors since the former does their jobs.

In the argument under discussion we have to know that among a large number of nations of the world only a small number of nations operate fully capitalistic economy at the early 21st century. Most of Marx's theories focus on the capitalist economy.

It can be reasonably estimated that roughly one-third of the workers in any capitalist country of today works in the various levels of government. We also know that most of the government departments run on a loss: some by their very nature such as defence, welfare and education; some by inefficiency. Strictly speaking, it is misleading that such departments as defence, welfares and education in the public sectors run on a loss simply because they don't have the clear income and we cannot express meaningfully their contributions to the nation in monetary terms. These departments are making enormous contributions not only in their specified functions but by their expenditures as well as by the incomes of the employees, all of which stimulate the national economy.

Various statutes and conventions protect the workers, manual and particularly professional, in the public sectors. Promotions are largely decided by the qualification and experience, by the willingness to conform to the management or by the personal connections. The employed have little incentive to work hard. If they do, they are valued in their department and they don't get the transfer, and hence the prospect of promotion is often reduced. Apart from the reduced prospect of promotion, the system tends to use the hard workers. I have found these points to be most unfortunate since the managers in the public sectors have the authority to correct; they can transfer and promote good workers as many private firms do. Yet these same managers talk of upgrading the efficiency of their departments in the open. I am sure that the output values of most people in the public service are less than what they are paid. If we use the communist jargon, they are producing negative surplus value and hence are exploiting the government by their inefficiency and laziness. The government are not capitalists in the sense Karl Marx argued about but there are all the ingredients in the public sectors, that is, management, labour, the means of production, exploitation. A man who worked for the government for many years made the above observations.

One-third of the work force today may be self-employed; they don't work for anyone but sometimes they hire labour. The farmers, small shop owners and small business operators are typical examples of this category of employment. They are often referred to as sole proprietorship in the category of business organisation. The proprietors (residual claimants) have unlimited liability and run ordinarily small operations. Here capital and labour are combined; however, they sometimes hire labour, in which case the operations are subject to exploitation. Though many of these self-employed may have the members of their families working within the business, it is generally considered that the family members come under one economic unit. Since the monetary exploitations that may exist within the family are not treated here and were neither by Karl Marx, the exploitation theories by Marx simply does not apply to the family business. Certainly Marx wrote about the exploitations within the families but he was referring to dominance rather than monetary flow.

One-third of today's working people may belong to the so-called companies, which may come, in a broad measure, between the government and the self-employed business in terms of the scales of the operation, that is, the number of the employees and the capital. We find the typical examples of these categories in manufacturing, mining, transport, tenanted farms and service industries. Managers, engineers, accountants, process workers, tradesmen, cleaners, shop assistants and peasants are examples of labour of this category. Here capital and labour fight for dominance and share of the available money. Many employees feel they are being exploited, though it is virtually impossible to gauge the degree of exploitation with some confidence. Karl Marx sometimes fondly assumed the degree of exploitation to be 100%: the surplus value was equal to the wages of the employed. He presented the above formula in a few parts of his literature without proof. It seems that the formula fitted into his various arguments so well that he must have eventually believed the assumption was true beyond any doubt. I have no doubt that surplus value is equal to the wages was out of touch of the reality and was a fairy tale in economics. He made another strange--to me anyway--assumption: the aggregate of surplus value had to pay for the interest of the loan the capitalists obtained for the production and also for the rent of the facilities they used for the production purpose.

There is another serious theoretical problem to arise out of the exploitation theory Marx developed. If the companies collapse with debts, the employees are free to go but the owners are left with the task of sorting out the debts, the nature of the tasks depending on the types of the companies and the prevalent laws. When the companies go bankrupt with so much debt, who exploited whom in these companies whilst in operation? In the co-operative factories, the management arrangement is different and the bankruptcy results in different arrangement. Marx makes brief references to the co-operative factories (Marx 1959, pp. 85, 387).

Capital and labour in the abstract sense and capitalists and labourers in the personified sense are division of labour and they perform the different functions of the companies. They are also symbiotic and one cannot exist without the other in the production environment. Similarly husbands and wives are division of labour and also symbiotic and they cannot exist without the other in the family environment.

There is no question that there is a confrontation between capital and labour in many fields not only of wages and work practices but also increasingly of the company's policies; however, in recent years, some economists have realised that the confrontation between the economic entities and the state is more serious and pronounced (Galbraith 1987, p. 285).

Tax can be seen as a form of exploitation. Throughout the human history, the government placed heavy taxes on the small farmers and small business people. These people were scattered and not united particularly before the introduction of telephones, mass media and public transport, and became easy targets of the government. When the government wanted to raise the revenue for whatever the reasons may be, such as war or building programmes, they picked these insignificant people and got away with it, apart from the fact that the government organisations were inefficient. The government was aware that the taxes from a large number of people, though small individually, made a huge amount of income. Also the various legislations, though possibly they meant well when they were made, were more often than not the restrictions on the people. The people felt that the laws were in fact the exploitations from the government. These exploitations in the form of the legislations were, I am sure, more pronounced in the former communist countries than in the capitalist countries.

Marx chose to ignore these exploitations when he formed the communist doctrines, rather, worse still, he might not even have seen the problems in formulating his theories.

All in all, the theory holds under some conditions.

my rating = a quarter

Theory: Economics is the motor of history, and the economic forces have virtually decided the course of human history. Chance does not form the motives of the masses and classes. They express historical necessity and the law of history. If we focus our attention to a particular era, this doctrine is economic determinism, a doctrine that states that all cultural, social, political and intellectual activities are a product of the economic systems of society, especially of what are produced, how they are produced and the mode of exchange. If we adopt libertarianism the above statement is not valid.

Seemingly in contradiction to the above proposition, Lenin, a prominent communist theoretician and a revolutionary leader, wrote:

> Politics cannot but have dominance over economics. To agree otherwise is to forget the ABC of Marxism. (Nove 1992, p. viii) Politics is a concentrated expression of economics (Lenin 1975, vol. 3, p. 476). Politics means a struggle between classes (p. 432).

The proposition is sometimes termed as materialist conception of history. Marx and Engels thought that the productive forces are the foundation of any society. This foundation builds the general socio-economic system, which in turn generates the ethical and intellectual life of the society. (Carmichael 1968, p. 112) The civil society conditions and regulates the state and not vice versa. The main feature of the influence is the economic relations and their development. The consciousness of men does not determine their social beings but the social beings determine their consciousness. Since the ultimate deciding factor in the society depends on what is produced and how they are produced and exchanged, to support human life, we have to seek the social improvement in the mode of production and exchange rather than cultivating our minds. They further argued that their economic relationships dictate men's collective behaviour. This does not imply that men's motivations are dependent on the desire for material gain but it means that the overall economic pattern of a society ultimately conditions their behaviour.

Marx believed that an economy is a coherent system which objective laws govern. He replaced Hegel's 'spirit' or 'reason' with the process of economic development as a motor of history. Bruno Bauer proved to the satisfaction of Marx and Engels that the authors themselves had fabricated a whole series of evangelic stories of the Bible (Marx & Engels 1970, p. 343).

Engels argued in the following fashion. All history, with the exception of its primitive stage, was the history of class struggles. The classes were products of the mode of production and exchange, that is, the economic structure of the society; the economic forces of the society ultimately decided not only juridical and political institutions but also religious and philosophical ideas. Hegel freed history from metaphysics and established as dialectical process; however, he was wrong in using idealism as his guiding principle. In fact a materialist outlook was definitely the correct principle. (p. 132)

The Marxists-Leninists put forward consistently the primacy of politics over economics and stressed the political form of working class struggles, though the foregoing theory asserts that the material and economic interests decided the course of history. The communists contemptuously looked at the economic struggles by the reformers, and insisted that only the political struggles could alter the true state of the affairs for the good of the working people.

It is interesting to note that Plato believed that the humans are political beings, though his fundamental concern centred in ethics. He formed his philosophical and political views in the Greek world of the 5th-4th centuries BC. The Greeks at the time did not have the sophisticated economic doctrines as Karl Marx and his contemporary Europeans did.

I am not sure if I can pass a judgement on the above assertion. Without any doubt money, the ultimate aim of economics as both a study and myriads of economic activities, has played a vital role in forging human history. However, the accumulation of money is not and should not be the sole aim of the economic activities. Many people are interested in their jobs for their own sake. Many non-economic activities are necessary for defence; the war efforts during war as well as the defence activities during peace. I have learned in my working career that the happiness of the people involved is an important element to measure the worth of an enterprise. There are also other important contributing factors to history such as sex, religion, race, arts and ambitions (personal or group). A historian may tell us what factors played dominant roles in a specific historical event. Another historian may give us quite different assessment to the same event. It is certainly erroneous that economy played a dominant role in every historical happening.

Sigmund Freud asserted that the sex drive is the root of virtually all human activities beyond sheer survival. The Buddhists maintain that human history and even human thinking are illusions and have no values. The Christians seek God's will in human achievements and failings disclosed in history.

I can make the following statements with some confidence. Karl Marx was a Jew and I have come to believe that his proposition that all social ills could reduce to economics gave some deflection from his Jewishness. In Germany where he was brought up, the prejudice against the Jews was quite strong at the time. The proposal is also appealing to people because of its simplicity. It is absolutely true that every human activity has an economic background and every historical event has its economic considerations. Even a hermit in an isolated existence is submerged in the economy the extent of which he is not certain or does not care. However, many historical events whether carried out individually or as a group did not have financial gains as the prime motive. Also it may be wrong to ascribe a single motive to such vastly diverse and complex history as that of humankind except as a means of survival or the biological instinct. Similar inference can be made to our mind activities in our daily life where so many and often contradictory reasoning govern. For example, many people want to stop the habit of smoking, drinking alcohol, gambling and taking narcotics from health and financial reasons but they simply cannot help refraining. In these predicaments the economic reasoning does not apply.

my rating = a half

Theory: A government is only a means of control by one class on other classes. In other words, the state always represents interests of the exploiting (usually a minority) class.

This view is obviously oversimplified, even if we concede that the governments of such disposition have existed in the course of human history. Karl Marx insisted that the above view be the set rule of the governments almost by definition. Marx further argued that the ruling idea of every epoch was in fact the idea of the ruling class which came about by controlling the material force and at the same time by controlling the intellectual force of the society. (Marx & Engels 1989, p. 49)

The laws of all over the world until recently favoured the masters rather than the workers. For example, Adam Smith wrote that the British laws were definitely on the side of the masters. He further pointed out that the British parliament looked favourably the masters' combinations to lower the wages and unfavourably the workers' unions to raise the wages. (Smith 1991, p. 70) The parliament and the government were on the side of the masters, and the workers did not have the right to vote on the elections. Though the franchise extended in the course of the 19th century, the universal suffrage came into force in Britain only in the 20th century. See Section 1 Background of Communism for details.

> The governing class of Great Britain steadily acquired the land and destroyed the liberty of the common people throughout the eighteenth century; and greedily and blindly the new industrial revolution was brought about. The British government, through the decay of the representative methods of the House of Commons, had become both in its upper and lower houses merely the instrument of government through the big landowners. (Wells 1925, p. 548)

Even today in Australia, the coalition of the Liberals and Nationals while in government tends to ignore the welfare of the rural people and the farmers, and their policies tend to benefit the city and business. This is in spite of the fact that the Nationals are to represent the rural people and the farmers. The Nationals are the junior partner of the coalition and they lose against the Liberals in case of the showdown within the coalition. In the first place the number of the farmers is small in Australia and their voting intentions are often not critical to decide who would form the government. In this sense the Australian farmers are a minority of the country at least in the federal level.

History shows that all the interest or pressure groups were ambitious to form the ruling body, and under certain conditions one group was successful and formed a government. Sometimes one group was not powerful enough and had to make an alliance with another group to be effective in governing. The binding force of an interest group can be religious, racial, military, economic, familial, or of class. Marx advocated that one class, the proletariat, should form the government irrespective of the popularity or the number of votes in the elections. There is no doubt that one group (a family, a firm, a political or economic group, a class, a religion, a race, military and so forth) aspires to become dominant as much as each individual as a rule wants to have a greater influence within the group.

Dictatorship of the proletariat, as Karl Marx proposed to come immediately after the collapse of capitalism, is in fact a typical aspiration of one class to form the government. Though the ruling communists the world over insisted that their government represent the majority of people, but in reality it was a minority government, excepting perhaps in Asian communist countries. As a matter of fact, we do not know if the Asian communist parties reflect majority will of the people or not because they have not held free elections.

All the above scenarios do not take into account democracy. The principle of one person-one vote is a rule in modern democratic societies together with secret ballots, abolition of any qualifications such as property, race or sex for the parliamentary candidates. Though we sometimes get the impressions that the government of the day, even democratically elected, protect only the rich and the powerful, in many instances this protection does not come from the laws but rather originates in the frivolities of human beings in bending the social justice. If we study the societies throughout the history, we can certainly find many examples which approximate the setting Marx identified above. However, the proposition is out of reality in the democratic societies of the 21st century against which I am assessing the theory. The proposal that the government favours only one group blatantly as a matter of principle since the supporters of that group elected them can and does happen but should not be the rule in a democratic nation of the 21st century. Karl Marx made the theorem in question when the working people did not have the voting right for the parliamentary elections in Britain.

I am to illustrate the points I made using the Australian example. It is really hard to define the group of people who elect the government. Labour Party is supposed to represent the working people. How can we define the working people? Farmers are working people; however, the National Party who are supposed to represent the farmers are on the other side of the political spectrum of the Labour Party. The members of parliament consist of a variety of people with a variety of ideas. The policy of MPs may not necessarily reflect the wishes of their constituents. When a bill passes the parliament and becomes a law, some laws are obviously advantageous to some people. However, the individuals often have to ponder for a while if it suits them or not: the ramifications of some law may not be obvious for a while in the first place and are hard to assess in the second place because of the complexity of the society.

my rating = a quarter

Theory: In the course of commodity production, the labourers generate surplus value and the capitalists do not create any values in the process.

This proposition is one of the fundamental theories of Karl Marx on which many other communist theories are dependant. The above theorem originates in 'labour theory of value' which Karl Marx quoted in conjunction with communism.

> Adam Smith was the first individual to develop the concept of surplus value and to stress it was bound up with capitalist production. He called it deduction. (Roll 1961, p. 163)
>
> A Smith and D Ricardo regarded surplus accrued to the capitalists as natural, eternal fact of life (Brewer 1984, p. 7).

Surplus value as used today is a communist jargon.

Quesnay, a physiocrat, argued about surplus produced from lands; Marx, from labour. Marx said that surplus value is nothing but unpaid labour. For the physiocrats agricultural labour is the only productive labour, because it is the only labour that produces surplus labour, and rent is the only form of surplus labour. The rent is the return from cultivating the land in excess of production costs and is used here somewhat differently from our everyday use. The physiocrats argued that surplus value is a gift of nature because the labourer produces more than he needs for sustenance (Marx 1963, pp. 46, 51, 83).

Similarly,

ground rent: the rent paid, especially a long period of years, by the owner of the building to the owner of the land on which it is built

economic rent: the extra amount earned by a resource (e.g., land, capital or labourer) in excess of that needed to keep it in its present use

Surplus value is an increment or excess over the original value. This movement makes the original value capital. Capital can take the following forms:

- merchants' capital
- industrial capital
- interest bearing capital

(Marx 1954, p. 153)

Marx said that money, commodities and labour-power are all potentially capital (Marx 1959, p. 355).

Interest bearing capital does not go through purchase and sale for the holders as for merchants' capital, nor production as for industrial capital. Marx's major concern was industrial capital.

> This gain is the differential rent, the word rent denoting a surplus over cost, i.e., revenue that is not required to make production possible (Heimann 1964, p. 96).

Surplus value arises as a result of higher productivity of labour. Marginal (or the least fertile cultivated) land earns no rent. The cultivators consume all the crops and there are no surplus crops left and they cannot pay rent. It is the difference above the marginal land that earns rent and this rent is called differential rent. There are two modes of differential rent. The first category is due to the good fertility, favourable weather and good location of the agricultural land. The second is the additional profit that arises as a result of the successful investment in the land.

The material of variable capital, that is, the mass of the means of subsistence it represents for the labourer, or the so-called labour-fund, was fabled as a separate part of social wealth, fixed by natural laws and unchangeable (Marx 1954, p. 571).

Marx argued that the wages of the labourers cannot go up to eliminate surplus value because the surplus value makes capitalism going. Without it capitalist production does not go on. He was effectively saying the well-established consensus that the purpose of capitalism is profit and unless a company makes a profit there is no reason why the company should go on. Marx asserted that only the workers produce the commodities from the material and add the value to the produced commodities.

We can also define surplus value in the following way. The surplus value is the difference between the value of the product and the value of the elements consumed in the formation of the product. The elements are the means of production and the labour power. (p. 201) The means of production can be further broken down to the instruments of labour and the material in the general usage. The mass of surplus value is the rate of surplus value multiplied by the number of labourers employed (Marx 1959, p. 234). The surplus value can be increased either by the increase of productivity or lengthening of labour time. With a given rate of surplus value, more constant capital and less variable capital necessarily bring in a lower rate of profit. Marx concluded that more surplus value is generated in agriculture where variable capital predominates than in industry where constant capital predominates. (Marx 1968, pp. 55, 93)

> So long as prices are proportional to values, profit is simply another name for surplus value. Further, Marx states that goods are regularly sold at prices that differ from values, so that the profit of any individual capitalist differs from the surplus value produced by his workers. (Brewer 1984, p. 128)
>
> The sum of prices of production is the sum of the cost prices of all products plus total profit, while the sum of value is the sum of the cost prices plus surplus value, so the two must be equal, given Marx's method of derivation (p. 138).

The prices of commodities change under some circumstances but revolve around the fixed value of commodities.

The investors' only concern is the high yield not the number of employees in the companies. Marx claimed that surplus values come solely from the employees and further the surplus values are proportional to the number of the employees. The investors today know well this claim is ludicrous.

> Marx stresses that the capitalist's consumption comes out of surplus value, and hence therefore quite different from the consumption of a petty commodity producer, who consumes the value created by his own labour (p. 91).

Marx stated that surplus value is split up into profit, interest, ground-rent, taxes and likes. Further he stated that rents on land and interest on money are only deductions from industrial profit, coming from the gross profit of the industrial capitalists.

In contrast with the above determination by Marx we find the following rules in the economic history:

Rent enters into the composition of the price of commodities in the different way from wages and profit. Wages and profit are the cause of the price; rent is the effect of it. (Smith 1991, p. 155)

> Even more, it was a strong and historically influential plea for free and unhampered capitalism, and in the history of economic theory it marks the discovery of interest as a cost factor, i.e., a sum the payment of which has an indispensable function in the maintenance of production. Rent, on the other hand, is not an indispensable part of the cost of production; it is a mere surplus and does not therefore have the significance that interest has. (Heimann 1964, p. 60)

According to Marx surplus value (profit) goes into:

- the landlord as rent,
- the moneyed capitalist as interest,
- the employing capitalist as industrial or commercial profit,
- the insurance premiums,
- taxes.

(Marx & Engels 1969, p. 61)

Insurance premiums must be made good out of the surplus value and is a deduction from it (Marx 1956, p. 181).

> Marx counts insurance against disasters as a deduction from surplus value; how disasters and repairs are distinguished is unclear, but it probably makes little difference, since the capitalist pays anyway (Brewer 1984, p. 99).
>
> Once Marx has shown that surplus value originates in production, he relegated exchange to the background (p. 87).

Marx wrote that only the production process creates the values to the commodities; the commercial transactions do not add any values to the commodities. The profits the merchants make is in fact a part of the profit ascribable to the producers.

> There are also costs of circulation; however, he argues that no value or surplus value is created during these stages of the cycle. Profits produced in the sale of the commodities are nothing but the surplus value made during production. (Marx 1959, p. 279)
>
> There are costs involved in trading in commodities. Marx's rule is that labour expended in circulation is not necessary for the production of use-values, and therefore creates no

value. Costs incurred in buying and selling are a deduction from the capital available to produce surplus value. (Brewer 1984, p. 95)

Transportation, unlike simple purchase or sale, creates value because it counts as a transformation of use-values (p. 96).

The useful effect of transport can, however, be thought of a commodity; it can be consumed individually (e.g., a pleasure cruise) or productively (when means of production are transferred). Labour expended in transport creates value. (p. 90)

Only productive capital is divided into fixed and circulating capital, since only productive capital can transfer or process any value at all (p. 98).

The price of certain things, such as land which is not the product of labour, and antiques and works of arts, are determined by many fortuitous combinations (Marx 1959, p. 633).

All surplus value, whatever forms (profit, interest, rent) it may take; it is the materialisation of unpaid labour. One portion of surplus-value is consumed by the capitalist as revenue. The remainder is accumulated. Employing surplus-value as capital for new venture is called accumulation of capital. (Marx 1954, pp. 500, 543, 554)

In *Theories of Surplus Value* which was published posthumously of Marx, he quoted many theories by eminent economists and also put up his own economic truism all in his usual scholarly manner. Though I read the English version translated from the original German edition, it was easy to discern Marx's literary competence.

Upon perusing his voluminous books *Theories of Surplus Value* (1975), incredibly I could not find any proof supporting his thesis concerning who created value in the production process. How many times I went through his papers, I could not find any argument that proved the foregoing premise beyond reasonable doubt. At last I got the impression that being unable to establish the theorem to his satisfaction, Marx resorted to hiding his inability behind a large mass of documents. He could have reasoned that since many readers would not have the patience to read through so many books, they could not disprove his assertion. Or worse still, Marx may not have felt a desire to prove it because his approach was that of a poet and he thought it was OK as long as it sounded true to him.

It is clear that once the search for the origin of the surplus value is abandoned--and this follows from the elimination of the labour theory of value--Condillac's notion of production as a co-operative process in which all factors have equal status, though in varying shares, is the only logical alternative (Roll 1961, p. 321).

It has been a hot economic debate as to what are the rightful shares or functional income distributions to labour, land and capital. It was expressed in the economic history as exploring the determining forces of income distribution; that is, in technical language, the relative values of the contributions of the 'factors of production' (labour, land and capital) to the values of the products. The argument that one's share should be proportional to one's contribution to the production of goods and services has received wide acceptance, satisfying moral and economic standpoints. However, there is a problem of measuring one's contribution.

'Labour is the brain power and muscle power of human beings; land is natural resources of all kinds; capital is all the equipment, buildings, tools and other manufactured goods that are to be used in production.' (McTaggart, Findley & Parkin 1992, p. 14) The economists sometimes add technical know-how to the above factors of production. In the capitalist society of today, the emphasis in the productive environment is on capital since capital enables the employment of labour and land; without capital there will be no production, no labour and no land employed. In the popular parlance, if we have money we can do anything but if we don't have money we cannot do anything.

All the communist theoreticians emphasised the importance of labour for the production to go on. They must have not only labour but money to set up the factory though the government may organise the establishment of the factories. Their theories do not alter the fact that both are needed for production to go on.

The capitalists provide capital and the wage-labourers labour in order for the capitalist production to take place. The part of the capital buys the means of production (constant capital) and the other, labour power (variable capital). This presentation is certainly over-simplified, not mentioning the other important considerations such as the government policies, technology and management. However, the companies sell the commodities thus manufactured at market for the maximum price; the buyers want them at the minimum price and the usual haggling over the price takes place. We all agree up to this point.

Aristotle abhorred taking of interest at loan (Galbraith 1987, p. 12). The Old Testament states that people should not take interest on the loan made to their brothers. The Qur'an (Koran) states that people should not take interest on any loan. The foregoing thinking is idealistic and religious and does not apply to the modern economics.

We derive profit subtracting insurance fees, rents and so forth, from the surplus value. Profit rate thus obtained must be above the interest rate obtainable in the money market; for example, cash deposit rate. This reckoning is the basic premise that the production venture goes ahead in the first place. If the profit rate is smaller than expected and the capitalists do not see any upturn in the future, they will close the factory and invest the capital on some other ventures.

Capital and labour are symbiotic in the production environment. The possession of only one of them can hardly exist on its own. They utilise primary function of each only when they cooperate where both can survive and multiply. Survival and multiplication are the fundamental requisites of all the living things, and under the favourable manufacturing conditions both requisites are satisfied for capital and labour.

Marx asserted that without labour power, the means of production are useless and consequently no products would be made, hence the labourers should get all the credits for the surplus value and the venture itself. Marx recognised that the means of production and management are indispensable for production but argued that they do not add any value to the commodities. He also proceeded with the argument by defining that the rate of surplus value is determined by its relation to its variable capital and not to the sum total of capital (Marx 1954, pp. 187, 220). At close examination, however, these assertions contains many critical flaws.

In the first place, there is definitely some illogicality in Marx's argument. We can say that since capital is also indispensable for commodity production, the capital providers must have some right to the profit, which Marx vehemently denied. In the second place, we must look at the risks involved. If the company makes a loss, the surplus value is effectively minus and the capitalists must make up for the loss, while the labourers do not lose money. When the company goes bankrupt, the labourers can walk free, whereas the capitalists end up losing some or all of the capital which they brought to the venture. At the time of insolvency, the company management sometimes draws up a plan to avoid bankruptcy by calling for the employees' funds. However, we often hear that the employees refuse to hand over their money because both the amount of money and the risks involved are too high. Hence it is fair to say that the capitalists are entitled to some share of profits because of the risks to their capital. The bankruptcies are not the exceptions to the rules as some people might expect: the estimate in Australia in 1990s says that 80% of the firms go bankrupt within 3 years of opening.

We can draw up another reason why the wage labourers are not the only agent which produces surplus value. If a machine or a robot replaces a worker, which is happening more and more, the capitalists will pocket all the profits. Marx may have argued that the labourers make surplus value in the process of manufacturing the machine or the robot. However, there are no logical relationships that the surplus value made in the past is the same at the time of its use. Besides for the capitalists who use the machine or the robot, what happened in the past is not important. All they are concerned is how much money they can make using the new equipment. When we focus our attention to the profit of the present capitalists, a labourer is no different from a machine or a robot: both are money spinning agents. It looks like from this perspective that a worker has no right to profit as much as a machine or a robot has not, beyond what was spent on both agents.

The conclusion was obvious from the start. Both capital and labour contribute to generating the profit. The only question is how much credit each party should take and accordingly how to allocate the profit. Practically this question reduces to the pay issue and the work practices for the workers.

Though the theory is partially correct in saying that labour contributes to the profit, the gist of the statement that capital contributes none at all is definitely false.

my rating = 0

Theory: The communists can change a capitalist society to a communist society not through reforms but only through a violent revolution.

The communists the world over broadly agreed with the above general statement but at times expressed the deviated opinions as to how they could arrive at the communist rule. Contrary to the above assertion, Marx hoped that at least Britain and USA, and possibly Holland might effect peaceful transition to communism through legislative authority (Marx & Engels 1969, p. 293). On the other hand, Lenin went one step further from the above theory and stated that only force can settle major questions in the life of nations. He also reiterated Marx's assertion by stating that the establishment of a democratic republic in Russia is possible only as a result of a victorious popular insurrection. (Lenin 1975, vol. 1, pp. 431, 520)

Lenin was well aware that the proletariat constituted a small minority of the population in Russia just before the revolution, and an agreement between the proletariat holding the state power and the majority of the peasant population must exist (Lenin 1975, vol. 3, pp. 469, 508).

Marx argued that the world economic crisis which was sure to come was the only time to carry out the communist revolution. He effectively disregarded any other time to initiate the revolution except in a few countries above mentioned. (Marx & Engels 1989, p. 198)

In Britain the labour political movement emerged during the last decade of the nineteenth century. Though the clear labour politics did not take place until after the First World War, a broad alliance of socialist parties and trade unions was formed in 1900 and later that year two labour candidates were elected into the House of Commons. The labour movement resolved to work with the existing parties to improve the lot of the working class rather than debating about violence and revolution.

The West European communist parties generally adhered to the policies of the Soviet Communist Party until the 1970s. In this decade there emerged a new variety of communism called Eurocommunism which favoured peaceful transition to communism under the democratic rule. These communists thought that with the alliance with the other parties they had a better chance of achieving their ultimate objective of communism. However, by the 1980s Eurocommunism was largely abandoned and the European communists returned to the orthodox Marxism-Leninism. (*Encyclopaedia Britannica,* 15th edn, sv, Marx and Marxism.)

Many socialists theorised that they can achieve socialism within democracy. The social democrats in Britain and Germany advocated the gradual transformation of capitalism into democratic socialism. Fabian Society was established in Britain in 1884, advocating the gradual introduction of socialism within the democratic process.

People in the democratic system may say that if the communist party wins a majority in the election in a capitalist country, it can form the government which has a mandate to usher in a communist society. They may further argue that winning an election is the only way to make a fundamental change to the social system of a democratic nation and there is no need to rely on the military force to effect the change.

However, Marx insisted that the capitalists block the avenues for the peaceful transition to communism, wishing to preserve their hegemony. He argued that the existing government the capitalists dominate, however democratic it may look, is only a facade to oppress the working class. The army, bureaucracy and financial institutions aid the government in this attempt, and they do all the tricks in the world to oppose any attempt to unseat the bases of their privileged existence. Hence, only a successful military confrontation, Marx lectured, can smash the existing regime and introduce the society of a new social system. While Marx was writing *The Communist Manifesto* which expresses the above view of his, the British workers did not have the right to vote in the parliamentary elections.

In the underdeveloped and developing countries today, as for the advanced countries in the past, the land ownership is more than a symbol of wealth. The number of acres owned by a family is often the best indication of social, political and economic status. It is expected that these rich families would not surrender their lands willingly for the sake of the better economic system.

> Hence, since the material interests of the propertied class were threatened by the inevitability of the new order, it seemed quite obvious to Marx that the only lever for effecting a change in society was force (Carmichael 1968, p. 78).
>
> The ruling bourgeoisie has at its disposal powerful machinery for physical coercion (the army, police, courts, prisons) and ideological influence on the masses (Church, school, press, radio, television, cinemas, etc.). It also has on its side the force of habit, the force of tradition in an exploiting society. (Dutt 1961, p. 440)

Interesting enough, not one so-called communist country has held a free election, obviously because the communist party in power was well aware that they would not command the majority votes in spite of their rhetoric that all the working people were supporting the government regime.

It can be estimated that the proletariat and their families constitute only a third of the voting population in a fully industrialised capitalist nation today. Hence, logically speaking, the communist party does not have much chance to obtain majority votes in a free election in a capitalist country, even if we assume that the majority of the proletarians and their families vote for the communist party and also we make an allowance for radical intellectuals and students who may align themselves with the communists out of the ideological principle. This estimate goes well with the fact that the communist party the world over, except perhaps in the Asian countries where the poverty is the norm and the majority of the populations are just above the subsistence level, had to rely on the military force to acquire the government and to maintain it.

Karl Marx adopted two class system of capitalists and workers. According to this classification the workers mean all working people including professional people. The professional class consists of teachers, accountants, doctors, engineers, managers and so forth, thus making up a sizable population. In reality, however, the communist parties all over the world did not regard this class as a comrade. During the Russian Revolution most of the professional people fought against the Bolsheviks. The core people who perpetuated the Russian Revolution were the industrial proletariat, excluding mostly the other workers. Also Mao's hatred towards the intellectuals was well known. The core people who perpetuated the Chinese Communist Revolution were the peasants. Somebody may propose that if the communists had developed the theories to encompass the other workers especially the intellectuals as their allies, the democratic communist rule must have been possible. In reality the Communist Parties of both nations excluded the workers of not their origin. As a matter of fact, it could not have been anything else by the nature of the revolutions: the communist rule was undemocratic and not guided by the intellectual elements of the societies.

There is ample historical evidence to support that the communists in Europe, though not in Asia, did not have the majority of their population behind their causes both before and after the revolutions. The European communist leaders after the successful revolutions were also aware of this fact and acted accordingly. Some examples are as follows:

- Stalin and the Communist Party had quickly realised after the start of the German invasion into Russia that the Soviet people would not fight for the communist ideology, but would do battle to preserve 'Mother Russia'. Hence, the government propaganda played on patriotic feelings. (Spielvogel 1991, p. 991)
- In the Ukraine and Baltic states, for example, people hailed Germans as liberators from the communist rule, but Hitler's policies of treating Slavic people as subhumans only drove those people to support and join guerrilla forces (p. 986).
- At Potsdam, Truman demanded free elections throughout Eastern Europe. Stalin responded: 'A freely elected government in any of these East European countries would be anti-Soviet, and that we cannot allow!' (p. 998)
- In March, 1933, in spite of the intimidations practised during the election campaign, the Nazis failed to gain a Reichstag majority, though it became a largest party by winning 44% of the votes. The Russian Communist Party would not have obtained the above rate of votes in a free election.
- The Communist Party in Russia has never claimed more than 800 000 adherents, and it has, in truth, probably never exceeded a quarter of a million members (Wells 1925, p. 694).

After World War Two, the Russian government did not, possible could not, disband their huge army and had to keep the armed forces at almost the war-time levels. All the other nations, the victors and especially the losers, broke up the huge army to keep only the minimum necessary at peace time. The broken-up army, not only economically but in terms of personnel, were to be used for peaceful purpose to build up the nation: West Germany and Japan enormously benefited economically by this arrangement. This is one reason why the Soviet Union lagged behind the West in the economic competition, in spite of the stated economic surge of the Soviet Union. The communist leaders were aware that they had to rely on the military to repel the anti-communist forces from both the stated foreign powers and the domestic oppositions. This fact is not surprising for the people familiar with history. The colossal empires such as Roman and British had to keep huge army and navy for their sheer survival, though the governing bodies of both empires appeared to be democratic in spite of the limited electoral franchise for women and some men for some periods. Another example may be the Puritan rule in England perpetuated by Oliver Cromwell. Cromwell reshaped the Civil War's New Model Army into a professional force, and won a series of victories against the Stuart Government forces and took control of the government in 1649. He lacked the civilian support and hence had to rely on the military to govern. After eleven years of rule by the Puritan factions, the vast majority of English people wanted the restoration of monarchy.

The theory Marx put forward is correct though not for the reasons he stated. The history also confirms the assertion.

my rating = 1

Theory: Karl Marx conceived a system of development that combines Feuerbach's materialism and Hegelian dialectic. This combined mode is called dialectical materialism. He did not recognise any other forms of development.

Since I discussed Marx' materialism in the foregoing theorems, I focus attention on dialectic on the following analyses.

According to Marx, dialectic is the most comprehensive and profound doctrine of development. Marx insisted that this mode of development predominate not only the economic field but political, historical, philosophical and even natural spheres of development. In fact he did not recognise any other modes of human evolution. Only two thinkers, Aristotle and Hegel, closely investigated the concept of dialectics. For dialectical philosophy nothing is final, absolute and sacred. Dialectics is the science of the general law of motion, both of the external world and of human thought.

He expounded communism as an ultimate form of human existence: He reasoned that communism once firmly established did not have to change since it had no contradictions. This assertion echoes the fact that the communist ideology has not developed at all since Marx formulated it in the middle of the 19th century, while the capitalist economic thoughts have advanced by heaps and bounds in the same period.

Hegel expounded dialectic logic in his work *Science of Logic* (1812-6). Dialectics is an interpretative method in which a contradiction between a proposition (thesis) and its antithesis resolves at a higher level of truth (synthesis). The synthesis in turn becomes a new thesis and the process starts again until it reaches an absolute, free of self-contradiction. In 1841, Marx read the book *The Essence of Christianity* (1841) by L Feuerbach which criticised Hegel in his idealistic outlook of the world and placed matter or existence above mind or spirit.

Marx used the above doctrines in the following manner to justify the dialectics for his theory of communist revolution. The capitalists challenged and wrested the social dominance from the landed ruling class. The industrial workers in turn will challenge the capitalists to inaugurate the new communist society.

It is well known that Marx obtained the idea of dialectic from Hegel, though he rejected idealism of Hegel. Hegel's theory is termed Hegelian dialectic idealism, in contradistinction with Marx's theory. Though Marx had been impressed with Hegel early in his career, he became dissatisfied with and critical of Hegelian philosophy. He began to search for a more practical mode of expression of social criticism.

There is no question that dialectic process is one form of progress. The problem of Karl Marx on this is that he excluded all other forms of developmental process. He did not provide any proof for his assertion as usual. Can we think of any other forms of development? For example, the evolution seems to be the result of contradictions in the course of interactions among the living things—their own kinds and the other species—and the natural environments. However, if we focus our attention to the growth of the living things, it seems they are quite natural and free from contradictions, thus developing metaphysically. In fact it is hard to prove or disprove the above Marx's theorem. One thing we must be careful about is that the fact nobody came up with the satisfactory alternatives so far does not mean nobody will in the future. For example, most scientists in the past had believed that the sun was the ultimate and only source of life on earth. But recently it was observed that volcanic activities were the source of life in the caves deep under the ocean where no sunlight could get through. Accordingly the original belief was only the assumption and was proven to be wrong. We can see another example in the proposition, as Dalton believed, that nature or humans cannot destroy the atom. If the scientists had held this assertion as the eternal truth, they could not have developed the atomic energy.

> Dialectics, Lenin wrote, is the Marxist theory of cognition (Dutt 1961, p. 110).
> Hegel did not invent the dialectic, which goes back to the Greeks. But before him the conception of dialectic was applied simply to thought or language (Carmichael 1968, p. 33).
> Throughout its history, dialectics has had to fight against metaphysics, a method of thinking and a world outlook that is hostile to it, and that fight continues today (Dutt 1961, p. 69).
> At present, the struggle of dialectics against metaphysics centres chiefly round the question of how to understand development, and not of whether there is development (p. 90).

Metaphysics opposes dialectics. Metaphysics is concerned with the basic nature of reality; existence and essence of things and societies independent of any political ideology or theory of social development. Metaphysics assumes a harmonious unfolding of phenomena and regards the process of development as simple growth.

Do we have to choose one of them at all times. Why cannot we assert that animals, plants and human societies develop metaphysically at some times and dialectically at other times?

Engels argued that nature works dialectically and not metaphysically and works in perpetual evolution. Darwin proved beyond any doubt that all organic beings; plants, animals and humans, are products of a process of evolution going on through millions of years. (Marx & Engels 1970, p. 129)

There is no question that dialectics is the valid theory of not only human and even animal and plant developments but social and ideological developments; however, he is wrong in excluding the other forms of development without proof.

my rating = a half

Theory: As the capitalism progresses the profits the capitalists make ever decreases.

This proposition 'the doctrine of the falling rate of profit', which had occupied a central position in classical thought, supplied the underpinnings to fears about the ultimate emergence of the stationary state (Barber 1991, p. 192).

> The 'law of diminishing return', on which Ricardo based the theory of rent and Malthus the theory of population, is certainly not applicable to conditions of change (Roll 1961, p. 187).
> A Smith made the following statement: Though the profits may fluctuate between these limits, they will tend to fall with the progress of society (p. 165).

Marx further elaborated on the last statement of A Smith:

> Smith had shown that profits on an average tended to fall with economic progress. Increasing accumulation of capital brought with it increasing competition among

capitalists; and this reduced profits. (p. 185)

Marx emphasised that the companies had to adopt larger and larger scale of operation to raise the efficiency, combating the falling rate of profit.

Ricardo drew pessimistic pictures of the future of capitalism. For example, he wrote:
Rent would rise steadily and profits would as steadily decline. The dealings between the landlord and the public are not like dealings in trade, whereby both the sellers and the buyers may equally be said to gain, but the loss is wholly on one side, and the gain on the other. (p. 186)

Many classical economists certainly expressed the opinion conforming to this proposition of Marx's but what happened to the capitalist economies is contrary to the theorem.

my rating = 0

Theory: As capitalism progresses a relative surplus population increases.

As the composition of capital rises, the demand for labour falls relatively, since a larger part of capital goes to buy means of production and less to employ workers. The labouring population therefore produces ... the means by which itself is made relatively superfluous, is turned into a relative surplus population; and it does this to an always increasing extent. (Brewer 1984, p. 75)

This is a crucial theory in Marx's communist views, since it is the presence of the relative surplus population that holds the wages (the price of labour power) down to the value of labour power.

As capitalism progressed the companies had to increasingly mechanise the production spurred by the new knowledge, efficiency drive and competition, thus the company has to spend a large part of capital on the means of production, thus raising the composition of capital. However, the redundant labourers may get another job depending on the status of economy, the nature of their jobs and their age. We all know today that there is no statistical evidence the surplus population ever increased as capitalism progressed. Of course as Marx pointed out in another context that capitalism has the inherent problem of booms and busts whose manifestation is that the unemployment rate is cyclical not progressive. Most likely the statistical presentations of the unemployed as we have today were not available to Marx and his contemporary people. The recession originating in the overproduction of commodities started in the early 19th century in Europe--possibly in 1825, though there were the recessions of different origins earlier. The recession due to the overproduction produced a large number of unemployed and the economists have not been able to overcome this problem even at the early 21st century in the capitalist economy. The recession is cyclic and entirely different in nature from what Marx asserted in the above theory.

The economic history clearly indicates that the theory is false.

my rating = 0

Theory: The working men have no country, and national differences and antagonism between peoples are daily more and more vanishing, owing to the universal development of the fixed relationship between capital and labour.

The above view is sentimentalism and is contrary to what has happened to the working people in the West since the remark was made in the middle of the 19th century.

In all wars fought in the West since the Industrial Revolution of Britain, the proletariat rallied behind their countries. World Wars One and Two did not show any signs that that was not the case. Many people, when they could not find work or were in financial difficulty because of sickness, accident and old age, looked up to their employers and their government for assistance in the absence of insurance covers.

What happened in Germany during World War One underlines the argument of the last paragraph. At the outbreak of the war, the section proposition disappeared promptly. The German socialists voted for the war credits in the Reichstag, and the German soldiers cheerfully marched to the front. As far as I know there have been no instances where the proletariat, as a group in one nation, in dire strait sought help from the proletariat of another country and got it. The last statement refers only to the political or economic sphere and does not refer to the assistance for the natural or human disasters.

my rating = 0

Theory: As the capitalism progresses, the industries tend to be concentrated into a few large companies.

In the manufacturing industries of such as petroleum, automobile, electrical equipment, chemical, aluminium and steel where they require heavy fixed costs to set up and operate, the makers must produce a large quantity of outputs to bring the average cost down. Under these circumstances, there is a strong tendency for the monopoly or oligopoly to dominate the market. These large scale heavy industries under oligopoly are also under competition among them and are capable of investing in research and development, thus producing better and cheaper products as time goes on. It is obvious that the small scale companies in this field simply cannot compete with the large companies and cannot survive unless they, being highly specialised, find a niche in the market.

However, the heavy industries, though large in themselves, do not dominate the manufacturing industries in terms of capital and the number of employees with a huge number of companies existing even in a highly industrialised nation. As a matter of fact retail sales make up 70 per cent of the US economy today.

One way of dividing the national economy for analyses may be to separate it into agriculture, commodity production and services. In the industrialised nations of the early 21st century, it is well established that the number of people employed in services outweigh that in commodity production. Moreover if we divide commodity producing industries into the main components of heavy industries (capital intensive) and light industries (labour intensive), the number of the employed for the latter outweigh that of the former, for example, one to two in Japan today.

Farming and services are huge economic activities with large capital and a large number of people working. The lands used for farming would amount to a vast amount of money if sold at the market prices. Also a huge number of retail shops, a part of service, have large capital and a huge number of people tied in the ventures, though they may be scattered.

Marx did not know that the small firms have many advantages over the large firms for some types of business and the market conditions.

The above theory ignores these due considerations; however, the theory holds true for heavy industries.

my rating = a quarter

Theory: Capitalism has the inherent problem of booms and busts because of its market orientation. The communist society in the past on the other hand with its planned economy did not have the economic fluctuations with the consequent crises.

The capitalist mode of production is the most productive in the social systems that have existed through the history (Marx 1963, p. 199). The capitalist society revolves around capital gearing for production, distribution and service.

Engels wrote. The capitalist production by its nature is ever on the increase, competitive among the manufacturers, having to rely ever more on sophisticated and specialised machines. However, the entirely different laws govern consumption, that is, the markets of these products, and limit the production, however hard the capitalists may try to expand.

This difference of production and consumption showed up as a general economic crisis every ten years or so since 1825 in Europe. This is what we call recession which sometimes degenerates into depression. Marx observed that the modern machine production cannot escape the decennial cycles of booms and busts, whatever the theories for their causes the economists may present (Marx 1954, p. 596). He stated that since the purpose of the capitalist production is to generate profits, the production without the immanent barriers ever tend to exceed the limited consumption. The poverty and restricted consumption of the masses is opposed to the insatiable drive of the capitalists to make money. (Marx 1959, pp. 256, 484)

In the capitalist economy, the individual factory owners, competing one against another, direct the industrial production, hence this leads to economic crises every 7-10 years, resulting from the general gluts and generating an economic and social confusion. In the communist society, the economic plan according to the perceived needs of people regulated the industrial production of the society as a whole. Accordingly, the economic booms and busts were unknown in the former communist countries.

The capitalist economists as well as the communist economists all agree that booms and busts are one of the chief defects of capitalism which no nations have been able to rectify. I have some reservations about the demand satisfactions of the industrial products of the communist nations. For example, the economic planners placed an emphasis on the outputs performance in tons and metres and had the tendency to overlook the demand for varieties in sizes and qualities. The agricultural sector may offer another example where weather played the major role in the outputs after the planners made the production decisions.

However, overall the above claim which the economists make and the people on the street experience is correct.

my rating = 1

Theory: The capitalist system by its very nature must inevitably collapse in the foreseeable future.

The above prediction did not materialised in all these years, and there is no indications at all in the early 21st century that the capitalist system will collapse in the future.

One-third of the least developed capitalist nations came under the dominance of communism by the 1970s when it achieved the widest popularity. It is significant that no economically advanced capitalist nations came under communist rule point-blank contradicting to what Marx had predicted. The so-called communist nations in Eastern Europe and the Soviet Union collapsed economically in the 1990s and are rapidly introducing capitalist elements into their society for sheer survival. The gist of the theory is totally wrong.

my rating = 0

Theory: Once the communists firmly establish the communist state, the state will wither away. The state in this application means the government and not the nation as a whole.

Lenin wrote in the article published in 1921 that the state was necessary without any question (Lenin 1975, vol. 2, p. 107). Lenin left the following notes published in 1929. Historically the state appeared only when there was a division of society into classes, that is, exploiters and exploited. There was no state under primitive communism when slave owners and slaves did not exist. The state is the apparatus for the systematic application of force and the subjugation of people by force. (Lenin 1975, vol. 3, p. 203)

The historical facts go against the proposed theory. The communist states of the past had the most rigid social control and regimentation in the human society ever known. We all heard that how the communist governments imposed the restrictions on the mass media and policed on the personal life of their citizens.

I spoke in 1976 with a few Russians who had migrated to Australia. This was before the collapse of the Soviet Union in the 1990s. They all said that nobody liked communism, and if they opposed the government they could be shot, jailed or sent to Siberia. When I expressed the opinion that how such an unpopular government survived, they said many people tried to wreck but the government survived from unknown reasons to them.

The theory also does not take into account the bad and disadvantaged elements within the nation and also the non-uniform developments of the nations of the world. If any person commits crimes, the police, an arm of the government, must arrest the person and the court, also an arm of the government, imposes a penalty if found guilty; a fine or a jail term. The theory assumes that under the communist rule there won't be any criminal activities, which is absurd. Also the government has the obligation to help temporarily or permanently disabled people, and the unemployed people, and the aged. Further some nations may convert to communist states but some will not change for whatever reasons or whatever length may be. The non-communist nations may make a military attack on the communist nations which cannot defend themselves without the military force, an arm of the government.

The government have many other functions such as education and foreign affairs, which a nation cannot do without.

The theory is absurd.

my rating = 0

Theory: History of human race is but a class struggle, and only revolution is capable of resolving the differences.

Karl Marx and Frederick Engels wrote the following statements in support of the latter half of the above proposition:

- Not criticism but revolution is the driving force of history (Marx & Engels 1989, p. 43).
- The contradiction between the productive forces and the form of intercourse are the bases of social revolution (p. 64).
- Revolutions are locomotives of history (p. 288).
- Revolution and the subsequent commotions make a nation pass in five years over more ground that it would have done in a century under ordinary circumstances (p. 339).

There is no question at all that a class struggle is one underlying conflict of the human race through its history. However, there are other struggles for the humans such as originating in religion, sex, race and nation. It is impossible to place a pro rata rating on the class struggle among the overall struggles of the human race, even for a historical event, much less for a generalised historical doctrine.

The theory is true in that the class struggle has characterised the history of humans; however, at the same time it is wrong in that it disregards the other sources of human conflicts in the history.

my rating = a quarter

Section 5 Principles of Communism

Confucius attributed ills of his contemporary society to the corruption of the ruling class and developed the ethical system which, he hoped, would remove much of the sufferings from the people. Unlike Confucius, Karl Marx attributed ills of the industrialisations to the capitalist system and developed the politico-economic system which, he hoped, would remove all the woes of the industrialisation permanently.

The communist doctrines are not descriptive, but I would say they are normative and more precisely predicative and prophetic. Since Marx elaborated the political and economic system which, according to him, would come into existence in the wake of capitalism, I found it impossible to assess in the last section many of the doctrines except for some theories which I did.

> The task of building communism, a society in which private property, exploitation, the very existence of classes and the state will be abolished once and for all, could be undertaken only by the working class (Dutt 1961, p. 251).

We may be able to say more succinctly that communist revolution is the overthrow of the capitalist government in order to establish the society where private property is abolished. Marx proposed in the communist society he preached that the means of production as well as the means of exchange be appropriated to the society (Marx & Engels 1989, p. 197). The private property in this context did not include the property of the personal consumption, such as houses, household appliances and jewellery. However, Marx possibly meant the personal investment as the means of production or exchange, and hence the state would absorb all the personal investments under the communist rule.

Marx insisted that once the class distinction is abolished, all social and political inequalities would disappear of themselves since the latter depends on the former for their existence (Marx & Engels 1970, p. 24).

In the cooperative farming there will be no exploitation since the workers themselves run the farm, not like the capitalist farming where the capitalist gets hold of the huge profit (p. 474).

Land is the means of production in farming. However, Engels made a categorical statement that after the seizure of the state power by the workers, the state will not expropriate small patches of farming land the peasants own and cultivate. The state will absorb only the large farms with the hired labour. Those small patches of land should be integrated into the cooperatives by the voluntary will of the peasants. He insisted on the advantage of a large scale farming arising from the advantageous use of labour. He again focused his attention on labour. Today we focus our attention to the introduction of machinery, the proper selection of crops by the scientists, the division of labour and the bulk purchase and sale, for the advantage of large scale farming. Engels made a point that the individual farms would be no match against the large scale farming and hence they are doomed. (p. 470)

Karl Marx proposed that the consumer goods would be given to people according to their capacity under socialism, and according to their need under communism. In the 19th century when these doctrines were developed, the depletion of the natural resources and the environmental degradation were not issues at all. The contemporary people of Marx believed in the infinite natural resources and the infinite disposal of consumer goods ignoring both the limited natural resources and the environmental damages, in the same way the ancient people thought that the world was infinite, vast and unlimited, living and making life views accordingly.

Marx further argued that the classes do not have to be abolished by a decree but the abolition of the private ownership necessarily means the abolition of classes and cannot be otherwise (Marx & Engels 1989, p. 98). The private ownership here refers not only to the means of production and exchange but to the dwellings and the other assets. Marx wrote that the social necessity, such as the increase of population and mechanisation, will force the legislation to nationalise the land, overriding the right of ownership by the individuals. (Marx & Engels 1969, p. 288) Likewise he postulated that once his doctrines are firmly in place, the state will wither away without any force or laws.

Lenin wrote in *Pravda* in 1920. It was not difficult to drive out the tsar—that was done in a few days. It was not very difficult to drive out the landowners—that was done in a few months. It was not very difficult to drive out the capitalists either. However, it is incomparably more difficult to abolish classes. (Lenin 1975, vol. 3, p. 417) Plato asserted that the division of labour was the foundation from which the social classes were built (Marx 1954, p. 345).

Lenin wrote that the proletarian state will begin to wither away immediately after its victory because the state is unnecessary and cannot exist in a society in which there are no class antagonisms. He also mocked the idea of anarchists, stating that their idea is muddled and non-revolutionary, quoting Engels as its source. (Lenin 1975, vol. 2, pp. 257, 283)

Engels wrote that under capitalism the state will inevitably feel the necessity of conversion to the state property for the institutions of intercourse and communication; the post offices, the telegraphs and the railways. He further wrote that once the state owns the production and distribution facilities, people don't have any need for the capitalists. (Marx & Engels 1970, pp. 144-5)

The short but famous article *The Communist Manifesto* (1848) well outlines the communist ideals. This pamphlet is the only substantial information I have found which tells us what communism is all about, though Marx's other literatures at times briefly refer to the communist doctrines. Engels published *Principles of Communism* in 1847 and explained communism in the form of questions and answers. However, this pamphlet was used as a draft for *The Communist Manifesto* and does not contain anything radically different from it. Engels also published *Socialism: Utopian and Scientific* (1880), through which we get some insight into the workings of socialism or communism. *Peasants Question in France and Germany* (1894-5) by Engels explains the agrarian policies of communism.

It was quite ambitious of them since they sought to inaugurate a new politico-economic society based on such a small number of words.

> Marx made no systematic analysis of the economic system that would replace capitalism following the collapse he held to be inevitable (Barber 1991, p. 124).
>
> There is no proper price theory in Marx and there is no discussion of the nature or effect of governmental monetary or fiscal policy. Nor, again, does Marx give any real thought to international trade and the effects which two or more economies engage in exchange exert on each other. (Walker 1978, p. 219)

Marx tried to justify the above lapse by saying that 'the organisation of a future society would be determined by its people as they went along and could not be forecast in detail' (Brewer 1984, p. 3).

In the various articles, Marx and Engels advocated that the proletariat wrest the political supremacy from the bourgeoisie and become the ruling class themselves. After the seizure of the political power, the proletariat will gradually reorganise the state organisation which owns all capital, land and labour. The above arrangement will result in abolition of all forms of exploitation as well as bringing about the expansion of production to effect the rising living standard of the population.

Under the socialist economy, labour becomes the only source of income: it is impossible to have a division of society into a working majority, and an idle minority who live by the exploitation of the working people. Under the socialist property the land cannot be sold or bought at all; hence it is no longer a commodity. Nor can labour power a commodity, since the working people, who collectively own all the means of production, obviously cannot sell their labour power to themselves. (Dutt 1961, pp. 711, 716)

> People of the socialist countries are guided by the economic plans which are based solely for the economic welfare of the people, and not by the profit motives (p. 781).

In all the branches of production, such as agriculture, mining and manufacture, national centralisation of the means of production will become the basis of production (Marx & Engels 1969, p. 290).

> Criticism and self-criticism are the main means for bringing to light and resolving the contradictions (Dutt 1961, p. 759). Collective labour based on the socialist property becomes the main driving force of social development (p. 760). In consolidating the socialist property, co-operatives and collective farms are to be advanced to the level of public property (p. 791).

Marx further theorised in *The Communist Manifesto* that in order to achieve the above objectives the following policies must be implemented with some modifications which depend on the national conditions:

a Abolition of property in land and application of all rents of land to public purposes.

b A heavy progressive or graduated income tax.

c Abolition of all right of inheritance. The French Socialist Saint Simon earlier stressed this disinheritance of all property (Carmichael 1968, p. 50).

d Confiscation of the property of all emigrants and rebels.

e Centralisation of credit in the hands of the state, by means of a national bank with state capital and exclusive monopoly.

f Centralisation of the means of communication and transport in the hands of the state.

g Extension of factories and instrument of production the state owns; the cultivation of waste lands, and the improvement of the soil generally in accordance with a common plan.

h Equal liability of all to labour. Establishment of industrial armies, especially for agriculture.

i Combination of agriculture with manufacturing industries; gradual abolition of the distinction between town and country, by a more equitable distribution of the population over the country.

j Free education for all children in public schools. Abolition of children's factory labour in its present form. Combination of education with industrial production.

Many of the above mentioned policies have nothing to do with communism and a capitalist nation can put them into effect. In fact many capitalist countries in the world adopted some of the policies in subsequent centuries, though it is hard to say where these governments got the ideas. Only the policies nos. a, c, e and possibly nos. f, g, h are communistic.

Lenin, before the successful revolution in Russia, proposed among other reforms, an eight-hour working day, workers' inspection of factories, free universal education, election of judges and setting up peasant committees (Lenin 1975, vol. 1, p. 479).

Interestingly enough, *The Communist Manifesto* does not refer to the confiscation of the private properties other than the land and instrument of production. It does not say anything about the dwelling houses, jewellery and other personal belongings at the time of changeover to the communist society. WG Burchett insisted that the personal possessions other than the land and instrument of production be intact and the individuals keep them under the communist rule; however, this was not what really happened in the confusions of the communist revolutions of the various parts of the world.

Communism proposes to abolish the private ownership of all properties. Socialists make distinction between personal properties and collective properties, and propose that only land and means of production, transit and distribution should be collectively owned. (Wells 1925, p. 612) The above line of argument was put forward to clear the writings of Karl Marx.

There is another fundamental confusion among the communists from the inception. The communists have used the term 'workers' in two different ways:

- The workers in the sense of all working people who worked for their living and hence included all levels of working people—industrial workers and staffs, peasants and farmers, soldiers and officers, politicians, managers and professionally qualified people. These workers were in contrast with capitalists and in fact formed and still form the bulk of the population in any community.
- The workers in the sense of property-less, with no higher education and with only manual labouring skills formed the bottom of the social hierarchy and consisted of industrial proletariat, peasants, low-ranking soldiers. These people as a rule can change their jobs only among this group. When workers (hand labourers) are used in this sense, they are contrasted with capitalists as well as professional people (head labourers).

The communist writings sometimes used the workers in the former sense and sometimes in the latter sense to suit their argument under focus. The industrial workers carried out the Russian Communist Revolution and the mainly peasant soldiers, the Chinese Communist Revolution, and hence in either case the workers in the second definition who were often hostile to the professionally qualified people perpetuated the revolution. As a matter of fact, many professional people opposed the communist revolution in Russia and China. Even if the professional people joined the revolutionary movement, they would be a minority expressing the contrary views to the majority. The majority would have ignored or attacked the minority.

Lenin was unambiguous on this point. He stated that the professors, teachers and engineers transformed their knowledge into the instrument of exploiting the working people, serving the bourgeoisie (Lenin 1975, vol. 2, p. 501). He also wrote that the majority of intellectuals gravitate towards the bourgeoisie (Lenin 1975, vol. 3, p. 175). After the proletarian revolution the state will subordinate those bourgeois experts by means of universal accounting and control (Lenin 1975, vol. 2, p. 594). We need the human material created by capitalism as well as the bourgeois intellectuals to build communism (Lenin 1975, vol. 3, p. 367).

Karl Marx's conceptions on capitalism and some theories of communism were way out of the realities when judged in aggregates as I examined in the last section. Some of his theories which I left out of the theory assessment were so ridiculous that many economists doubted if Marx really believed in them. Some doctrines were so much out of touch with realities that when Lenin got hold of the political power in Russia he was unable to put them into practice. However, his main communist idea was not ridiculous as we might expect from the foregoing examinations, and hence it was possible to build a political and economic system based on the notions of communism.

Section 6 Karl Marx Evaluated as Person

Chronology of Karl Marx

His Personal Life	European Events
1818 Marx was born in Trier in the Rhine province of Prussia.	1824 British Parliament passed a law recognising the workers' right to strike.
	1826 Robert Owen admitted his model village, an idealistic socialist Community in Indiana, failed.
	1830 The insurgents forced King Charles X of France to abdicate, and the liberals proclaimed Louis Philippe king of the French.
	1831 GWF Hegel died.
	1832 The law limiting the working hours to 12 hours a day for the teenagers passed the British Parliament.
	1834 Slavery was abolished in British colonies.
1835 October Marx entered Bonn University and studied for a year.	
1836 October Marx entered Berlin University.	1840 PJ Proudhon published a pamphlet *What is Property?* which declared that property is theft.
1841 Marx received his doctorate in philosophy from Jena University.	
1842 October Marx became an editor of the *Rheinische Zeitung* in Cologne.	1842 The Mines Act passed the British Parliament prohibiting women, and children under 10 working underground in coal mines.
1843 March The government closed the *Rheinische Zeitung.*	
1843 June Marx married Jenny von Westphalen after seven years of engagement.	
1843 The Marxes moved to Paris.	
1844 Marx became a communist thinker as we know him.	
1844 The collaboration of Marx and Engels started and lasted for 40 years until Marx died.	
1845 January The Marxes were expelled from France and moved to Brussels, followed by F Engels.	
1847 Marx and Engels founded the Communist League.	
1848 Marx and Engels drew up *The Communist Manifesto*.	1848 Wide spread workers revolts in Europe.
1848 The Marxes returned to Paris briefly.	
1848 June Marx moved to Cologne and founded the *Neue Rheinische Zeitung.*	
1849 May The Prussian Government forced the closure of the above paper which	

vehemently attacked the government.

1849 Marx came to live in England as an exile till he died.

1852 The Communist League was dissolved.

1864 The First International was founded. Although Marx was neither its founder nor its head, he soon became its leading spirit.

1867 First volume of *Capital* was published in German language in London.

1867 Most workers in towns obtained the voting rights for the parliamentary elections in Britain.

1868 Marx obtained pensions for life.

1871 The Paris Commune was declared but was soon crushed by the French military. Before the commune Marx was an unknown political figure but the commune made him an international figure.

1871 The Trade-Union Act of 1871 (and 1875) gave British unionism its legal foundation.

1872 At the congress of the International at Hague, Marx defeated and expelled the the Bakuninists, and the rest of the General Council was moved from London to New York.

1875 Germany's socialists were united and formed the Social Democratic Party.

1876 First International was dissolved.

1881 December Jenny (Marx's wife) died.

1883 January Marx's eldest daughter died.

1883 March Marx died from a lung abscess in London.

1885 F Engels published second volume of *Capital* in German language in London.

1890 Alfred Marshall published the first volume of a massive work *Principles of Economics.*

1894 F Engels published third volume of *Capital* in German language in London.

In this section I am going to assess Marx's works from the perspective of his personal life. It is obvious that one's life story is a good gauge to measure one's works of any sort. If, for example, a priest preaches a good sermon but indulges in debauchery, we can judge that what he preaches is false and has no value, not being a part of his life.

In a novel, the contents do not have to reflect the author's life since this genre, by definition, deals with fiction or product of imagination rather than real life. In philosophy, religion, and political economy such as Marx proposed, what the author teaches must be parts of the authors' life. Marxism is very much philosophical and religious and had to become the object of faith since it lacks scientific foundation. Marx's economic theories are normative and prophetic, containing morals and philosophy and what the society ought to be or do, rather than positive, describing what the society is.

Marx sided with the proletariat beyond any reason like the parents with their own children. This may be the primary reason why the workers supported his theories in spite of their untenable doctrines, not only theoretically but practically, like the children believe in their parents' teachings even when the parents are morally degenerate. The governments of Western Europe sided with the capitalists unashamedly all through Marx's active life since the propertied class elected the governments. The universal suffrage came into force in the 20th century even in Britain.

Karl Marx was the oldest surviving boy of nine children. Both of his parents were Jewish. Marx's father was a Trier's leading lawyer and also an officer of the High Court. It was difficult to be a Jewish lawyer in Prussia at the time, hence his father converted to Protestantism at around the time of Marx's birth. Probably his professional career required it. Karl was baptised when he was six years old. The Jewish background of his family led to prejudices and discrimination of the society.

Karl Marx was nicknamed 'the Moor' early in life because of his swarthy complexion and dark eyes. Rather strangely when he was small, he preferred the companion of adults rather than that of the same age group as is normally the case. His associates as a child were the social elite. He was particularly fond of his father and the Royal Prussian Privy Councillor Ludwig von Westphalen, whose daughter he was later to marry.

As a young man Marx did not show any interest in politics. He was to become a lawyer and attended Bonn and later Berlin University. In Bonn University he attended the subjects of humanities, such as Greek and Roman mythology and the history of art. He participated in the political activities which was rampant at the university at the time. In Berlin University he studied law and philosophy. However, he did not show any interest in law study, either.

> When in Berlin University, Marx devoted his time to understanding Hegelianism, which was quite fashionable at the time. He was thoroughly impressed with Hegelianism by the time he arrived in Berlin from Bonn University, only a few years after Hegel's death. Hegel exercised the most extraordinary influence over the educated classes of his own country and over the whole generations of Europeans--with the exceptions of England and France. (Carmichael 1968, p. 23)

In Berlin University he was also introduced to anti-Christian doctrines which characterised his works.

Marx's paramount ambition in youth was, in fact, to become a poet. After rejection from so many publishers, he was convinced that he did not have talents in making poems, and hence abandoned the idea of becoming a professional poet. After reading a vast amount of his politico-economic treatises, I have not come across his poems, not even a line, which suggests that he was not confident in this field at all and hid his poems from the public scrutiny.

Marx, though he could not establish himself as a poet in the society, could not remove his poetic inclination all his life. This fact had a vital influence on his economic theories. Of all craftsmen, according to Aristotle, the poet in particular is the most in love with his own work (Montaigne 1965, p. 293). Marx did not see his theories contained serious flaws which would make communism unworkable, forcing the annulment of the entire project of communism in the early part of 1990s in the European context. He laid down many of his favourite theories simply because they sounded right to his emotional instincts instead of proving them vigorously as definitely required for the doctrines of politico-economic system. The following is an example; 'the description of evolutionary process as negatives of negatives is mere poetic analogy.' (Engels 1972, p. 61) This poetic aspect of his works appealed to himself and many of the public who became his devoted fans.

Karl Marx is not the only man who indulged in the poetic analogy. Mathematicians and mechanicians called a tool a simple machine and a machine a complex tool (Marx 1954, p. 351). Aristotle wrote that hands were tools of tools. But these are witty comments, and not in the working of political economy. Literature, a form of arts, permits and even encourages the descriptions of this kind.

Karl Marx did not hold a permanent occupation most of his life. In his youth his radical beliefs prevented him from becoming a professor. From 1850 to 1864 the Marxes lived in abject poverty. Except for one occasion Marx could not bring himself to seek paid employment. He once applied for a position of railway clerk without success: probably he was secretly wishing he did not get the job. His main interest was poetry, philosophy and abstract laws.

> Marx at this time was still a radical, an idealist and a dogmatic Hegelian (Carmichael 1968, p. 85).
>
> Up to the mid-1840's, Marx's views were being formed, and were changing very rapidly as he absorbed ideas from a number of sources (Brewer 1984, p. 1).

Marx left Berlin and went to Cologne in 1841, and became a successful editor of the *Rheinische Zeitung* (*The Rhine Gazette*) there in 1842. Marx had been offered the position of the editor-in-chief of this daily newspaper, after contributing only 4 articles to it besides 2 articles to another periodical. (Carmichael 1968, p. 59) From this observation we can gauge the brilliance of his writing skills. Cologne was the centre of the most industrially advanced section of Prussia. For the heresies he advocated, he was sacked and the paper suppressed.

Through the journalistic activities Marx was convinced that he was insufficiently acquainted with political economy and he zealously set out to study it.

In 1843, four months after marriage, Marx and his wife moved to Paris which was the centre of the socialist thought. There Marx first became a revolutionary and a communist and began to associate with the communist societies of France and Germany.

Living in Paris, he realised that French and English cultures were superior to the German. Around this time he changed his attention from the abstraction represented by Hegel to specialised information in the fields of politics and economics.

He learned socialism, economics and history. He also started a lifelong collaboration and friendship with Friedrich Engels around this time. By the end of 1844, he was a socialist through and through as we know him.

> His [Marx's] financial problem was acute. It turned out to be insoluble and remained so for the rest of his life. The year 1844, when Marx turned twenty six, was a turning point--from then on, as long as he lived, he was almost wholly dependent on charity for the support of himself and his family. (p. 88)

While in France, Karl Marx attacked the Prussian Government which retaliated by forcing the French Government to expel the Marxes from France in January 1845. The Marx family moved to Brussels.

Marx and Engels together drew up *The Communist Manifesto* in January 1848 for the Communist League in London, which Marx and Engels founded in 1847. To understand the manifesto well we have to know the following political setup in the middle of the 19th century. The capitalists were wresting the parliamentary dominance from the landowners, and the working class did not have the voting rights. As a matter of fact Marx composed the manifesto and Engels made a few suggestions to improve it. However, Marx was generous enough to put Engels as a co-author.

The first meeting of the Communist League was held in London in November 1847 and dissolved after only 5 years of operation. However, it planted the seed of revolution in the form of *The Communist Manifesto*, whose ideals were to explode in the 20th century.

The Belgian Government arrested Marx without ceremony and deported him in 1848. The French Provisional Government invited Marx to return to Paris, and he did so though briefly.

He moved to Cologne and founded in 1848 the *Neue Rheinische Zeitung,* which the Prussian Government closed in the following year, and was again driven into exile, this time to London.

He spent the rest of his life, that is, from 1849 to 1883, as an exile in England. He never again held a regular job, and had to get by on legacies, gifts, occasional earnings from free-lance journalism and later the pension.

Since Marx came to live in London, he more or less withdrew from the political agitations and devoted his time in studying political economy in the library of the British Museum. He also contributed to *The New York Tribune*. Marx and Engels contributed to the above newspaper, a progressive bourgeois newspaper in publication from 1841 to 1924, from August 1851 to March 1862.

He derived some income from contributing to the newspapers as a freelance journalist. However, his main income after marriage came from his friend Friedrich Engels, a German bourgeois, who helped him financially out of friendship and respect for Marx's scholarship. Engels was a business partner in the Manchester textile firm, the Ermen, and he had a solid business experience. There was a division of labour in many ways between Marx and Engels. Engels' financial assistance to Marx was in a sense a division of labour. Engels was a communism's salesman rather than a theoretician in which Marx excelled. Engels provided data for Marx's writings and Engels also worked as a check to Marx's excessive inclination to abstraction. Engels made an arrangement such that Marx received a yearly pension of 350 pounds for life from the year 1868. The sum was enough for the Marx family to lead a comfortable life.

Judging from these events, the way he made a living was not recommended and, in fact, highly undesirable. This observation matches with my low ratings on his politico-economic theories presented in Section 4 of this chapter.

His financial straits were in contradiction to his claim that the economic factors were the kernel of all human activities. Since he made the above assertion, he should have led his life accordingly. However, he did not organise his daily life for the best economic gains. Instead, he chose not to have a permanent job and as a result he deservedly led a life of poverty until he got the aforementioned pension. He tried to earn his living through freelance journalism after leaving the job of the editor-in-chief, but money from this source was not enough to support his life style. Admittedly Marx' thrust of the argument on economic motivations was on the pattern of the society rather than on the individuals. However, I feel he still has the obligation to conform his personal life to his thrust of the ideas as for some of the other doctrines of his such as exploitation.

Marx married Jenny von Westphalen whose father was earlier mentioned and a baron. She was very beautiful in her youth and in fact known to be the most beautiful girl in Trier. (p. 16) She was said to be intelligent too.

> Jenny was Marx's childhood sweetheart. Her father was both aristocratic in disposition and intellectual. Influenced by her and her father, Marx wanted to become a poet. Her family

> was of Prussian nobility, not of being Jewish and noted for being reactionary: Her eldest brother, Otto, would become a Prussia's Minister of Interior during a most reactionary period of 1850-8. Under these circumstances Jenny's family had vehemently opposed her marrying Marx, though Jenny's father, a follower of the French socialist Saint-Simon, was fond of Karl and did not oppose. (p. 10)
>
> The Marx family had a maid servant, Helen Demuth, living with them through thick and thin. Helen is not a kind of servant girl we today normally expect to be. The peasant girl had been brought up by Jenny, Marx's wife, since childhood and was utterly devoted to her mistress. She was sent to the Marxes by Jenny's mother and was to remain with them until Jenny and then Marx died. (p. 87)

A photograph of Helen Demuth taken at the time shows she was young and pretty. She bore a son, who was named Friedrich. It would not have been difficult for Jenny to guess who the father was. Marx did not show any affection to Friedrich possibly because of Jenny's intense jealousy. In spite of the son's striking resemblance to Marx, the daily life went on the pretence that the boy was a bastard of Friedrich Engels.

Apart from Marx's sexual infidelity with the maid servant, which was not considered to be unusual at the time and even today, their marriage was quite successful. Jenny devoted all her life to Marx, who returned her love with his devotion to her. It seems that Marx believed in love marriage and did not regard any other forms of marriage as proper. That notion naturally must have come from his experience of married life.

Despite his brutish attitude in his public life, Karl was at times a loving husband and a tender father at home though he still showed dominant personality. Probably he was not aware that psychologically his family life was compensating for his hard public life as is often the case for many people even today. In fact the home life for Marx meant more than economics, which is at odd with his philosophy. The fates of his daughters, as I shall describe later, make us suspect that something must have been wrong in his home management, financial or otherwise.

Both Karl and Jenny were terrible in managing their family finances. I would say they did not have any idea how to manage the household budget. Here are two incidences to show the level of their monetary incompetency. When their money problem somewhat eased--temporarily in retrospect--they did not even do what the persons of average intelligence would have done, that is, to save. Instead the family held a rather extravagant ball. Also Jenny bequeathed some money in 1855 and gave the family some breathing spell and the Marxes moved to a house of higher rent. (p. 178) Both decisions reveal not only their poor management skills but also their hidden inclination that they were more concerned with the family comforts rather than the revolutionary ideals. After luxuriating in comfort for brief periods, they got into money problem again and had to ask for financial assistance from Engels on each occasion.

The aforementioned maid servant was the only person who handled money competently in the household. Jenny must have been aware of this fact and hence, I imagine, had to live with her husband's sexual adventures with the maid. Since the family had to keep Helen for sheer practicability, Jenny must have felt that she did not have any other choice but to tolerate her.

> Reading and walking were Marx's favourite past time. He really loved poetry but did not show an interest in other forms of arts such as music and painting. He was a great reader of novels, especially those of Sir Walter Scott, Balzac and Shakespeare. (*Encyclopaedia Britannica,* 15th edn, sv, Marx and Marxism.)
>
> He was particularly fond of Shakespeare: He endlessly recited and discussed and even acted out in the household (Carmichael 1968, p. 184).

It has been well quoted how the Marx family avoided payments for the goods and services rendered by traders. The episodes were often referred to in a humorous fashion: A genius who was the champion of the proletariat the worldwide was contrasted with unimportant dealers who were after petty cash. Personally I don't see anything funny in the setting. It should be pointed out that he exploited and cheated the small people. What he did in his dealings with the maid servant and the traders was worse than what the capitalists did to their employees, though he acted only in a small scale. The capitalists acted within the contemporary laws, which Marx wanted to change. Marx transgressed a moral law vis-a-vis the maid servant, as well as the universal law or cosmic law (both the contemporary law and any law that may be formulated for the sake of communism) vis-a-vis the traders.

Jenny bore seven babies but the four of them did not survive and only three daughters grew to maturity. The three daughters led unhappy lives. When his wife died in 1881, Engels commented that Marx effectively died too. His eldest daughter also called Jenny, Marx's favourite, lived with her husband and children in France but died suddenly two years later from tuberculosis. She was a socialist activist and bore five boys and a daughter. Marx did not recover from these misfortunes and he himself died peacefully in his sleep in 1883 with ever faithful Helen Demuth watching. (p. 246) Laura, Marx's second eldest daughter, was married and active in French working class movement, and all her three children died in childhood. Eleanor, Marx's youngest daughter, also a socialist activist, never legally married and did not bear any child. Both of these remaining daughters committed suicide; Eleanor in 1898, Laura in 1911.

The contemporary newspapers and the general public scarcely noted Marx's death. His fame grew steadily after his death through the spread of his doctrines until he became the champion of the proletariat and the household name. He bitterly criticised Christianity but the Bible says: God will destroy offspring of the unfaithful from the earth and their children from among humankind (Psalms 21:10). The foregoing life records show what really happened whether Marx was right or the Bible was right.

It seems that Marx was not aware that the desire for women was as strong as the desire for wealth for the average men, though certainly the two desires are different in some ways. He focused his attention on the latter, that is, economics in his public life. In his private life he spent enormous amount of money on his wife and household—a far more amount of money, he said, the capitalists exploited off from a proletarian in the production environment, and he did not even see the absurdity of his argument on exploitations.

Some readers may comment that I picked only negative aspects of the great man's life. I did not set out to discredit his life style and did my best to assess him fairly. The assessment of his personal life happens to match with the assessment of his theories: both are poor to the extreme. There is no necessity that the two aspects of the assessment concur: a man can be good at both; a man can be poor at both; a man can be good only at one of them. Still it is significant that he did not lead his life as his theories required. In this regard he breached the conformance of speech and conduct, which I expound in Section 3, Chapter 7, Book One as one manifestation of idealism.

Karl Marx Compared and Contrasted with Adolf Hitler

Though the British Empire was imposing in 1900, there was a clear indication that the vigour of the empire passed the peak. The United States of America based on British democracy in the broad measure came out strongly as an industrial power after World War One. The only material threat outside Europe came from her, and Britain made every effort to resolve the differences with her.

In the troubled post 1919 years, Britain and France were unquestionably status quo powers, though they quarrelled as to the means. After World War I, the British government, labour and conservative, wanted peace to maintain her empire and also believed that the heavy defence expenditure would make her economically weaker, and curtailed the spending on arms.

The power house for the rise of the British Empire was possibly the parliamentary democracy built into the British political system over the centuries. Russia emerged as a world power based on communism before World War Two after the revolution of 1917, though with many unresolved problems. Germany forged ahead mightily as an industrial nation prior to WW II on the concept of fascism. Both of the latter countries became strong industrial powers more or less suddenly during the political life (1900-1955) of Sir Winston Churchill. Both exceeded British outputs of many industrial products on the eve of WW II and posed a serious threat to the very existence of the British Empire. Communism and fascism as ideologies also posed a critical challenge to the British democratic thinking.

Some scholars attributed the comparative decline of Britain in relation to Russia, Germany and the United States to the poor British management skills, though the previous paragraphs may be taken to imply that the problem is in the British democracy. It was well recognised at the turn to the 20th century that British industrial management was not good enough. Some people warned the British by publishing the books such as *Made in Germany* (1896) and *American Invaders* (1902). Britain certainly improved in many ways but the rates of improvements were too low compared with the other leading industrialised nations. The managerial competency is fundamental to the developments of industries, minimising the various problems existing to all the countries at any time. More fundamentally, the British did not see that the world had changed and was still changing and they had to build new relationship with the rest of the world. The various religions teach us that everything reduces to the matter of attitude and way of thinking and they are right in this regard too. In Australia even today, the English are disliked by their arrogant attitude and do not understand that they are living in a different and new world.

Britain had to combat its decline from 1920s to the present day. The government had to struggle against Britain's relative industrial decline, the falling living standard and high unemployment. Actually Britain was remarkably successful in developing the industries of the Second Industrial Revolution; chemical, electrical and motor industries. However, these successes were not enough to change the tide of decline.

The success and failure of the firms depend on the ability of the managers, the market conditions in a broad sense being given. The managers can affect the market in a limited way only, for example, by changing their products to suit the demands or by the advertisements through the mass media or even by influencing the government policies. The majority of the large firms spend a huge amount of money for adverts for their products and their justified existence. And they are very sensitive about the publicities in the media primarily because they affect the consumer perceptions.

I firmly believe that the success or failure, in finance as well as in the happiness of the employees, is mainly dependent on the management not only in the private firms but also in the government sector. The right thinking earlier mentioned decides the management policies. The Small Business Administration in the USA concluded after the survey that 93 per cent of the business failures were attributable to the poor management practices. Another research has shown that even stealing at work is a manifestation of management failures.

The capabilities and willingness of the managers in the main decide the performance of a firm under a given market. If the market is favourable, even the poor management gives out profits. If the market is extremely poor, no management acumen can save the firm. In the absence of a strong market, the good managers will modify their commodities or services to suit and even try to change the market perceptions about their products. In some cases they may withdraw the unpopular products or services, and venture into an entirely new fields. Hence the proposition is valid even under difficult circumstances.

However, the above sweeping statement is not valid for some commodities, especially raw material such as wool and minerals. The prices of these commodities in the market largely decide the fortunes of the organisations, and the management skills have little to do with their success or failure, provided the managers put out the reasonable efforts. Also the weather and the market prices in the main decide the incomes of the agricultural producers, assuming that they are industrious. Irony for the farmers is that bumper harvests often depreciate the prices of the crops and as a result they may get small returns. Further the managers and farmers have little control faced with the foreign competitions: Comparative wages, exchange rates and customs duties largely decide the imports and exports of the commodities. Cheap imports may ruin even the well-managed companies and farms.

All the foregoing observations are not valid in the face of pandemic such as COVID-19.

It is generally believed that the British Empire based its existence on democracy which in turn promoted the empire. This view has a serious flaw in that in spite of the British victories in the two world wars of the 20th century and of the democratic forms it still retains, why the fortunes of the empire went down dramatically in the aftermath of WW II. Possibly trade played more critical role in shaping and undoing the British Empire than democracy: the empire flourished as long as it made money through trade and declined when it no longer commanded the world trade and ceased to make substantial money.

Churchill perceived the dangers from these newly emerged industrial powers on the eve of World War Two. He, who probably lived in the most democratic nation in the modern world, also noted in dealing with the Soviet Union and Germany the strong similarities of the societies which Marx and Hitler dreamed of. However, there were sharp differences between the types of social orders they advocated, though both types may be classed as totalitarian. Churchill remained as much anti-communism as anti-fascism even after the end of World War II.

Marx's view represent extreme left, that is, voicing the opinions of the poor and the lower class. Hitler's views represent extreme right, that is, voicing the opinions of the rich and the upper class.

Democratic capitalism, socialism, fascism and communism. In the ascending order, they move from freedom to control in political, economic and everyday life. Fascism and communism are politically oriented and emphasise the role of the state rather than that of the individuals. (Dye, Moore & Holly 1966, pp. 632, 634) Nazi ideology, fascism Hitler advocated, was not well-developed as Marxism was, as far as the theories were concerned.

Because of the chasm of the two ideological differences, neither side, that is, communism and fascism, did not tolerate the existence of the other ideology and the state thus created, though the democratic nations with their diverse opinions could and in fact lived with the communist and fascist countries. As a matter of fact, the Bolsheviks and Nazis hated each other to the extent they thought that they each other were the real enemies with no hope of reconciliation. (Riasanovsky 1977, p. 572)

Modern fascism is said to have originated in Italy by the person of Benito Mussolini: he instituted the modern fascist movement in Europe.

> Fascism was a movement designed to secure the support of the masses for a leader without the intermediary of a democratically elected parliament. Fascism was a chauvinist male-oriented movement assigning women to the role of child-bearing and raising a family. (Grenville 1994, p. 52)
>
> A meeting in Milan addressed by Mussolini of some 200 followers in March 1919 marks the formal beginning of the fascist movement. In October 1922 Mussolini made himself the head of the government. (pp. 154, 156)

In Italy the National Fascist Party under Mussolini was consolidating its hold after 1922 and internationally the country was relatively quiescent.

The fascist salute borrowed from Mussolini symbolically underscores the point that fascism spread from Italy to Germany. Also the Italian brutality on the defenceless native Abyssinians in 1935-7 was a precursor of Nazi terror in subsequently occupied Europe.

Prior to Hitler's emergence, democracy survived by a narrow margin; however, it died in the depression of the early 1930s, resulting in the race doctrine of Hitler. In the election of July 1932, the Nazis won 37% of the votes, becoming the largest single party. In another election of November 1932, the Nazis lost some ground by winning 33% of the votes but still remained the largest single party. In the election of March 1933, the Nazis secured 43.9% of the votes, failing to secure the absolute majority which Hitler had desperately wanted, after an electoral campaign of unparalleled violence and intimidation.

Hitler came to power during the most serious period of depression and solved the unemployment problem in Germany. Unemployment in Germany:

6 million in 1933
4 million in 1934
2.8 million in 1935

Rearmament and army expansion after 1936 virtually eliminated unemployment in Germany.

We can see the similar concept in the history of humankind. Shi huangdi (Shih huang-ti) of Ch'in put into practice the ideology of totalitarian state, when he unified China for the first time as we know it in 221 BC. We notice the uncanny resemblances of the manifestations between the Ch'in state and the modern totalitarian states, though they are based on the entirely different ideologies. We have an ample evidence that Shi huang-ti as for Hitler genuinely wanted to serve his country well, though their means were often been criticised as being undemocratic and dictatorial. The ideological backdrop of Emperor Shi huang-ti was Legalism Hanfeizi (Han-fei-tzu) (d. 233 BC) formulated. This emperor instituted vigorous thought control. He burned the Confucian books and buried alive hundreds of prominent Confucian scholars who defied his order. He also wanted to regiment the daily lives of the ordinary citizens to the extent that their way of thinking had to conform to a set pattern. He set up the strong army and the bureaucracy to enforce his will.

Karl Marx and Adolf Hitler in their youths wanted to become a professional poet and a professional painter respectively but both were frustrated by the forced realisation that they did not have any talent. Both had a lifelong interest in the art forms they chose and I believe that both showed strong traits of the art in their later professions. I would say they were more artists than a revolutionary economist and a politician respectively: They relied on the impressions and emotions than the vigorous reasoning required in their careers they were eventually known to the general public. On the surface both theoreticians extensively used logic, reasons and facts, all of which were mainly facade to back up their convictions derived from the intuitions.

I do not mean here that the convictions derived from the intuitions are wrong. The intuitions have a proper use under certain circumstances. Immanuel Kant asserted in his book *Critique of Pure Reason* (1781) that intuition comes before reason. Arthur Schopenhauer turned away from spirit and reason to the powers of intuition, creativity and irrational.

Hitler, as for Marx, being a failure as a professional artist, proceeded with his profession without sufficient theoretical trainings, relying too much on impressions and emotions. For instance, I cannot see any concept of time in Hitler's ideologies. When he said in 1933 that his Third Reich would last for 1000 years, he effectively meant it was indestructible and would last forever. Time constrains and governs every ideology. The foregoing observation can be inferred from the fact that there is no time frame in the art of paintings. Artists tend to believe that their works are better than anybody else's, and naturally to denigrate the works of other people. Both Marx and Hitler exhibited this tendency.

Most of Hitler's *Mein Kampf* (1926) was composed in the Landsberg fortress used as a prison at the time, and his cell-mates, Rudolf Hess and Paul Joseph Goebbels, made some contributions in the form of discussions.

Though Hitler did not found the Nazi Party, he became its powerful leader in 1920-1. Hess joined the Nazi Party in 1920 and became Hitler's friend and confidant. Hitler and his party members started the march to Berlin in November 1923 to carry out the revolution in the manner of Bonito Mussolini's march to Rome in the preceding year. The armed police dispersed the 3000 marchers on the way. In 1924 Hitler and Hess were locked up in the above prison as mentioned after being convicted for treason on the Beer Hall Putsch in Munich as the above march is known. Hitler served only 8 months of 5 year sentence. Goebbels made friends with these characters and joined the Nazi Party.

The following chart shows what these two characters were mainly concerned about:

	Karl Marx	Adolf Hitler
frustrated art form	poetry	painting
ideology	communism	fascism
state form	totalitarian	totalitarian
theme of ideology	economy	race, nation
good guys	proletariat	Aryans
bad guys	capitalists	Jews and Communists
major books	*Capital*	*Mein Kampf*
domain of genius	literacy (prose only, not poetry)	oratory

Both picked only one ideology among possibly several of ideologies which are fundamental to the existence of human race, as I outline in 'Introduction to Series', Book One. Necessities of life, sex, religion, idealism, materialism, racism, nationalism, sexism and arts; they are interrelated and dependent concepts, and essential for humans as group existence but some individuals can live without some doctrines on the premise that they have the necessities of life. Many individuals through the human history lived according to one ideology and led happy and successful life. If any one of the ideologies advocating only one of the above concepts dominates the society, many people in the society tend to suffer. If you look at any one concept as primary and the rest as secondary, as Marx and Hitler did, it is conceptually wrong. It may be possible for the society to gain in the short course of time in the chosen field, but that society will eventually stagnate and suffer, since the other ideas are suppressed and don't have proper ways of expressing themselves. Choosing only one survival technique such as economics or race is like studying only the subjects the students like. In the long run they miss out the important and useful supports in life and are not prepared for the varied problems of life.

People may raise the questions. The Christian Church dominated Europe in the Middle Ages, pushing aside the other ideologies. Is that wrong conceptually? Is there good or bad survival technique? It is well quoted that Europe was at the culturally low ebb during the Middle Ages; however, I put up the theory in Book One that without the diffusion of idealism in the society in this era Europe could not have matured in the modern era. Is the survival means of economy, which comes under materialism, or race inferior to that of idealism? I do not see any flaws in idealism of the Bible. Communism and racism advocated by the two characters in focus contained serious defects. I would say that communism and racism, if they are theoretically sound, can dominate the society without causing serious problems. Capitalist economic thinking dominates the economically advanced nations of the world today; however, the intellectuals generally agree that capitalism, though it contains some flaws, is good for the human wellbeing and the development of the societies. Capitalism under democratic rule does not suppress the deviant thoughts if the government judge they do not harm the society.

If the dominant ideology tries to influence the other fundamental ideologies, the latter stall losing the way how to freely express. On the other hand, democracy tries to give harmonious solutions to the political pressure groups arising from the various interests and ideologies, though there are always squabbles among them.

Both of these characters further looked at the ideology in a simplistic manner in good and bad guys as the children would normally do. The simple scripts of this nature appeal to the general public too, as we see from the abundance of the novels and movies depicting the good and bad guy scenarios.

Both Marx and Hitler were dogmatic in their opinions and insisted they were always right, whose attitudes are often observed among the unintelligent people with small knowledge. They and their followers fell into the trap of doctrinaires and did not further develop their doctrines. Generally speaking people who denigrate other people's opinions and are proud in hearts tend to be incompetent, not comprehending even the various issues at hand.

There is no question of Marx's brilliance in writing technique. Not only did he develop his economic theories in a concise and clear manner but he achieved the consistency of his argument throughout his books. Anybody who dares to write a number of books as he did knows that the above two qualities are hard to achieve in practice. However the consistence of the argument contains in itself a germ of manifold errors. For example, Marx defined the value of a commodity as the labour input required to make in Part One of his *Capital* volume I. If this assumption is wrong--in fact the later economists proved wrong--his subsequent argument built on this theory would be all wrong.

Both a superb command of language and a wide range of knowledge mark Marx's writings. They are both out of ordinary and I cannot help admiring. He was a genius in these fields. If he had denigrated other people in their use of language, he would have been right. He showed the above traits in the concrete forms:

- His expressions are appropriate in every occasion.
- He makes proper paragraph developments to suit his purpose.
- He quotes from time to time from the international economic histories superbly matching the occasions, which gives us the impression he picks these quotations from his vast reservoir of knowledge.

Many people acknowledge that Hitler was an expert orator. He thought that the public was so lazy and stupid, that is, from psychological reasons, that he could get through to them better through oratory than through writings. He believed in mass effect and mass influence by the spoken words. His body movement during oration showed an accomplished style reminding of an accomplished circus showmanship, both of which received a ready public acceptance. Mannerism and style are forms of communications.

Betraying our expectation, Hitler was quite sensitive to the German public opinions. He kept secret the terrors carried out within the concentration camps as well as his blonde mistress, Ever Braun. By hiding the existence of his mistress, he wanted to convey to the German public that he was above sexual affairs. The research showed that he was in fact a multi-billionaire at today's standard, also contrary to our expectations. This fact was so cleverly concealed that the researchers got to know only in the year 2002.

These two figures were expert communicators in their chosen methods. Marx was a genius in the literary field, not only in writing expressively which we can perceive through his writing but also in reading capacity with superb absorption of knowledge. Hitler was a genius in oratory. It seems that their sense of superiority came from their superior command of language more than anything else.

There are some problems in respect with the command of language. The Buddha taught his disciples that among body (he meant physical attributes as well as physical achievements or skills), speech (he meant communication by oral or written language as well as by mannerism) and mind, mind is the most important and they should spend major time and effort to improve their thinking faculty. There are good examples in the Bible to illustrate this point. Moses said to the Lord, 'O Lord, I have never been eloquent, neither in the past nor since you have spoken to your servants. I am slow in speech and tongue' (Exodus 4:10), but God chose him to lead the Jews out of Egypt. Also, David did not have an imposing physique as his brothers did, but God anointed him to become the king of the Jews, saying, 'Man looks at the outward appearance, but the Lord looks at the heart' (1 Samuel 16:7). The Bible is teaching by these examples that speech and body are not as important as mind, and God and the Jews approved both of these personalities with sound mind.

Our daily experiences tell us that though body and speech are important in socialising and being popular, the deciding factor as a human being must be the brain which also controls speech and body movements, though not body's attributes. There is a popular maxim that speech never exceeds action. The eloquent people or the people with good bodies did not shape the human history but the people of excellent minds and good workers did: the attributes mentioned earlier were there by chance or contributed in a minor way. Women may have aesthetically better bodies than men and also may be linguistically superior to men, but it has been the rule of the society men dominated over women. However brilliant Marx and Hitler might have been in communicating, ultimately we have to rely on the contents of the messages in assessing their contributions to their chosen fields of economics and politics, though certainly language has its value in the field of communication. Shakespeare' genius lay in the language command, which is an entirely different sphere of human pursuit and in the domain of arts.

We communicate with God through mind, and not by language nor by body. The prophets in the Bible communicated with God by language, but this arose from the sheer necessity of passing the information to the other human beings; the authors did not have any other choice but to use the language. Language cannot express love, often said to be the highest theme of human existence. The Buddha taught that language cannot explain nirvana or Buddhahood, the highest state of mind attainable under Buddhism. Also language cannot adequately explain the cardinal teaching of the Bible 'You shall love the Lord your God with all your heart, and with all your soul, and with all your mind', hence the Bible uses various means to teach people to understand the above concept. Islam changed this concept of love to surrender or submission to God, which is easier to understand.

Marx published the Volume One of *Capital* in 1867. It ended in a bitter disappointment for him since he sold only 200 copies in the first year. He withheld to publish the volumes two and three though he had drafted these manuscripts by this time. Engels wrote that ill-health on the part of Marx prevented him completing the two volumes (Marx 1959, p. 3). Engels completed these unfinished volumes after Marx's death and got them published.

Marx became a firm communist by the end of 1844. He wrote most of *Capital* after moving to London in 1849 to live. From the middle of the 19th century onwards, Britain went through radical changes in many ways. British workers' economic well-being was improving so unmistakably that even Marx acknowledged it. Most workers in British town obtained the voting right for the parliamentary elections (1867), though farm labourers had to wait till 1884 for the same right. Marx's main concern was factory workers. Further trade unionism was legalised (1871 and 1875). Medieval guilds were to serve the common interests of masters and workers, while the modern unions represent only the workers. These social changes were up against the arguments he put up in *Capital*.

In comparison with the dismal performance of the Volume One of *Capital*, Hitler did well in regard to the publication of *Mein Kampf*, in spite of the assessment that this book was difficult to understand even by the admires, though I did not find it particularly hard. The first volume of this book was published in 1925, and 23 000 copies were sold by 1929. The second volume was published in 1926, and 13 000 copies were sold by 1929. By the end of 1933, when Hitler had been in power for almost one year, over a million and a half books had been sold. Total sales were probably of the order of eight to nine million books during Hitler's life time. (Hitler 1992, p. xxvi) After the Second World War the researchers found that many of his personal records in his published books were patently false.

The above sales figures do not indicate the inherent worth of both the published books and the two characters in focus; however, they indicate how popular those books were in their life times and also the amount of money they received as well as the levels of confidence the authors would have derived. After Hitler's death, the general public mostly discredited his racial theory, whereas some sections of the communities of the world over widely recognised the works of Marx to be of prime importance sometime after his death.

Both characters offered simplistic solutions to the complex problems of society, expressing their impressive knowledge with unswerving convictions. However, we sometimes get the impression that they are smart alecks, revealing basic ignorance in their chosen subjects. As is often the case with incompetent megalomania, they had dominant personalities and tried to control the organisations which they belonged to, even by hook or by crook. Both showed a strong sense of love and hate emotions towards some people as is often witnessed among the children and immature persons. Both expressed their mental status in emotionalism rather than rationalism, though they used a veneer of logic in their argument, as is often the case with the crooks who pretend their intentions are good. In forming love and hate relationships, both characters believed that the classes, the peoples or the social creeds had permanent and fixed attributes, like the moral or philosophical creeds. They did not realise that these attributes would change as time went on and the circumstances changed for the former at least though possibly not for the latter.

Section 7 Contributions of Communism

Whether communism is theoretically right or wrong, whether communism can be put into practice or not, we must not forget the fact that it was the leading ideology of the world from the end of the 19th century to the early 1990s. Communism reached its height of popularity and prosperity in the 1970s. Just before the collapse of the East European and Russian communist nations in the early part of 1990s, roughly one third of the world population with as much land mass was under the communist rule. All these countries were still at the stage of the dictatorship of the proletariat and none of them did and in fact could introduce the ultimate aims of genuine communism.

The frivolity of the people may in part explain the above phenomenon of rise and decline of communism. We may partially attribute its demise to the inadequacy of the communist doctrines. The inadequacy of people in general to uphold the new economic system may partially explain. It can be due to the fact that the economic thoughts, whether communistic or capitalistic, stand on the loose ground and come and go as the environments dictate, as happened to many economic thoughts in the capitalist countries. We still have to explain why communism attained such wide acceptance in spite of the poor theoretical backings. Even today there are some rooms for crackpots to make inroads into the economic thoughts of capitalism, and even the well-established economic theories have limited room for applicability because of the difficult environments in the societies with the multitudes of variables and pressure groups.

Communism has contributed to the welfare of human race to the unknown degree. We cannot quantify its input into the human society in any way, and only the following qualitative statements are possible and thus presented. Its negative impacts on the society are a lot harder to assess.

The theories of communism with the proletariat as a ruling class in the hypothetical society gave hope and happiness to a large number of the working people who bore the major burden of industrialisation. Thus in their political and economic campaigns, communism became the common ground and rallying point of the working class. Communism was an international currency of the radical labour movements since the end of the 19th century to the collapse of the Soviet Union in the early 1990s. Communism was also a common language which the left of the political spectrum spoke for mutual support and theoretical backing of their activities. In the above activities, communism became the objects of faith for many communists, who fell in love with the theories of utopian society and did not see its defects in the same way when people fall in love they don't see the ugly sides of their lovers and dream about the utopian married life. When the dreams come true people must face the realities of communism and married life. Religion was, and still is in some parts of the world today, a dogma which has given a strong social cohesion in the history of humankind as communism did for roughly one century.

Communist theoreticians disparaged the capitalist system of production. Hence the capitalist economists had to look at capitalism closely and develop the theories to counteract the criticisms.

The capitalist governments sometimes had to act in favour of the workers for fear of communist revolution. Communism generally acted as the goading whip to the bourgeois governments. From some unknown reasons to me--maybe bloody mindedness or maybe antagonism to the working people--the government of any country has been reluctant to do something good for the people who, though, elected them, unless it was put in a position to be forced to act.

The following paragraphs give examples of the concessions on the part of the capitalist governments to counteract the spread of communism.

The welfare state was born in Germany of Otto von Bismarck (1871-1890) as chancellor of the new German Empire in reaction to the spread of communism. In addition to repressive measures, Bismarck also attempted to woo workers away from socialism by enacting social welfare legislation. Between 1883 and 1889, the Reichstag passed laws that created sickness, accident and disability benefits as well as age pensions paid for by compulsory contributions from workers, employers and the state.

At the Russo-Japanese war of 1904-5, possibly the major cause behind Russian concessions at the negotiating table was that there was a fear of communist revolution in Russia. That fear was in fact well-grounded judging from the ensuing events. The growing opposition to the tsarist regime spurred by the perceived weakness of the government resulting from the defeats of the battles finally exploded into open confrontation on 22nd January 1905. This open revolt was not genuinely Marxist in character, as Lenin claimed it was, though it included the extreme Social Revolutionaries holding Marxist views. Among the participants were also peasants, labourers, dissatisfied ethnic groups and even the middle class. The Peace of Portsmouth to end the war took place in September 1905. The communist revolutionaries finally achieved their objective just over 10 years later in the October Revolution of 1917.

The welfare legislation in Britain 25 years after Bismarck's initiatives was not so much from fear of the revolution but from the good wishes of the well-meaning people. Under the sponsorship of Lloyd George, the National Insurance Bill was passed in 1911 that covered most workers against ill health, but only those in the cyclical building and engineering trades against unemployment.

Between 1871 and 1914, the national state of America began to expand its functions beyond all previous limits. Fearful of the growth of socialism and trade unions, the government attempted to appease the working masses by adopting such social insurance measures as protection against accident, illness and old age. These social welfare measures were narrow in scope and limited in benefit before 1914. Moreover, they failed to halt the growth of socialism. Nevertheless, they signalled a new direction for the state action to benefit the mass of its citizens. The trade unions thus formed learned to demand the big concessions from the financially strong employers: the American industries probably started this facet in the early 1980s.

During the Cold War the United States and its allies had to give military and economic aides to non-communist nations to abort the spread of communism.

Section 8 Overall Appraisal of Communism

As you can see in Section 4 of this chapter, my ratings of Marx on his capitalist and communist theories chosen for evaluation are quite low, in spite of the fact that I left his ridiculous theories out of the assessment. I have no doubt that the communists misunderstood capitalism. It is natural that the communists who dreamed a new society in the wake of collapse of capitalism should denigrate the capitalist system. However, they did so on mostly erroneous notions. If they belittle capitalism at all, they must assess the capitalist theories justly in the first place. In the similar logic, if we denigrate individuals or organisations, we have to base it on the correct observations. I am doing my best to appraise the thoughts of Karl Marx correctly and fairly in this chapter. Karl Marx failed the first test in assessing capitalism. In the second place Marx put too much effort in attacking the other people's economic thoughts and did not build enough of his own communist theories.

The fundamental drive of commerce and industry in capitalism is profit motive which had firmly exhibited as the strong motive power in many human activities through the millenniums, that is, long before capitalism set in. The communists tried to take out this profit motive from the production basis; however, they failed to replace it with something else which was just as strong. They wanted to place instead the concept of state ownership of the means of production and fair distribution of the profit. Even if the concepts might be correct, the communists had to present the concrete evidence that the bulk of the people were financially better off under communism. My research showed what they did was too abstract, too vague, and not convincing.

The communist doctrines must be correct theoretically before the communist government can put them into practice in the same logic that the theoretical aspects of the atom bombs had to be correct before any prototype production can commence. However, I have found I was unable to assess many of them by the natures of the theories, apart from the fact that there is not enough literature concerning communism. Hence I had to rely on the other evidence to try to appraise the communist doctrines, that is, his depths of capitalist understandings and a few theories on building communist society expounded in Section 4, and his personal life in Section 6. On these counts, with all my determinations to be fair and even generous at times, he failed miserably.

One fundamental theory of Marxism is that communist revolution was inevitable in the future; however, any reasonable persons at the early 21st century would disagree strenuously with this assertion. Accordingly we can conclude that Marx's theories and reasoning were fundamentally flawed and in fact in a gross error from this observation alone.

For the proletariat, it is not the correctness of the economic theories, but any theories or any persons that lend support for their cause that is important. *Capital*, Marx's major work, is hard to understand and only a small number of the proletarians would have had the intelligence and patience to read and comprehend its messages. Since life has been hard to all human beings throughout the history, the proletarians who are supposed to have no sizable property, and toil all their life for little gains feel justifiably so under capitalism. For them Marxist teachings that denigrate capitalism and give a hope in the form of communist society in the future must be really a great source of happiness, and the history showed that many of them risked their lives for the sake of communism.

Marx did not practise the conformance of speech and conduct, which manifested as defects of his theories. Though some of his theories may sound marvellous, but nevertheless do not correspond to the realities. Hence they have little value in the practical economic life, though we may agree that some of them may be correct theoretically.

The personal life of Karl Marx did not reflect his teachings. He did not live the life as he preached in his writings. One important teaching that came out from the devotion to idealism in a few parts of the world at the early classical period is that one's speech must conform to one's action or life. Socrates and Confucius were particularly insistent on the correspondence of words and actions. The Buddha and Jesus Christ always led their lives as they taught people to live. Karl Marx said that economic considerations largely decided human history; yet he did not lead his personal life to the best economic advantage. Marx was not capable of running his family economy: He was far below average in his handling of his household economy. Yet he planned to build an economy of the national scale. He said that the capitalist exploitation had to cease; yet he exploited people around him in his daily life. Karl Marx failed the second test of his personal life dismally.

Marx was not an original thinker of his teachings any more than the Buddha, Confucius and Christ were not, though I have some reservations about Socrates. Marx presented the theories in a systematic fashion in the same way the above sages did and hence they give the impression that they were the originators of great thoughts.

Marx came to believe that the economic considerations largely decided the course of the human history after extensively studying the histories of human race and economics, and further only the economics would decide the destiny of the human existence. It is true that the people's desire for wealth is so strong that they are prepared to do almost anything to acquire wealth, which is nothing but the economic activities. However, we cannot ignore the other human concepts such as sex, religion, idealism, race, nation and arts. As I explain in 'Introduction to Series', Book One, pleasure motivates humans overriding the other traits at times. This pleasure principle as for the other traits explains some of the economic activities; however, none of them on its own gives the convincing answer to the totality of the complex human desires and activities.

Though Marx left a vast amount of literature for perusal of later generations, the analyses of capitalism concerned most of it. His famous work *Capital*, as the title suggests, centres on the working of the capitalist society. Contrary to the public perceptions, he left only the elemental concepts of what communism was all about. He did not elaborate the workings of the communist society he preached. In fact what I wrote in Section 5 Principles of Communism of this chapter almost exhausts what he stated about this subject. I noticed further that in his vast written records he wrote a few comments here and there about his communist belief. Lenin supplied a fair amount of information concerning practicability of communism, thus correcting the deficiency of Marx to some extent. For example, John A Hobson developed the theory behind the imperialism as the last stage of capitalism and the imperialist wars, which Lenin took up. Lenin wrote that imperialism is merely monopoly capitalism (Lenin 1975, vol. 2, p. 211), and also imperialism is a superstructure on capitalism (Lenin 1975, vol. 3, p. 115).

However, even Lenin's writings did not elaborate how to run the socialist industries after the successful revolution. Marxism as a whole did not have the blue prints of a socialist future and the communists were not in a position to realistically envisage how to run the government of communist persuasion. (Nove 1992, p. 33)

Marx argued well about deficiencies of capitalism and virtues of communism, but he was not in a position to effect his theories into practice. He had the abstract reasoning required to develop his theories but did not have the practical experience to put the theories into practice. Hence he could not develop his theories to conform to the realities and to be put into the government policies. Plato's *Republic* was meant for argument only and Plato did not have any intention to put its theories into practice. Similarly Marx gives the impression to me that at heart he did not envisage that his doctrines could be put into practice. Lenin also argued well before the successful revolution, but after the revolution what he did was often to present the slogans to the general public. What the two argued was devoid of the substance and far from the reality. We can see the parallel in politics when a large number of the general public attack the government policies in the way they please, which does not mean these people can form and run the government successfully.

There is an episode that throws some light as to how even Lenin was unprepared for the business of communism after the revolution in Russia he led as a leader of the Bolshevik Party. He had the wage structure developed well before the revolution:

> ... technicians, foremen and accountants, as well as all officials, shall receive salaries no higher than workers' wages, ... (p. 35).

In Marx's usage, labourers or workers included all working people regardless of level of skill (Brewer 1984, p. 201) as far as the determination of wages is concerned, though at times he changed the usage. The same pay for all the working people, professional and non-professional, contradicts the Marx's labour theory of commodities. According to him the workers are commodities, and the costs required to produce them set their prices--in this case wages and salaries. The professional people require more labour and money inputs in their training than the non-professional workers, and hence should fetch higher pays.

After the successful revolution Lenin tried to impose the same pay on professional people such as engineers, accountants and lawyers, as on labourers. He was forced to give higher salaries to the professionals when he realised that that was the only way they were prepared to work. He stated after the defeat, sarcastically, that as soon as the workers were competent enough to carry out their tasks these professional people would be forced out of work, obviously smarting from his injured pride and not realising the unreality of his proposition. Marx wrote that the equality of the wages among the labourers is not sustainable, since different costs are involved in educating different classes of labourers. (Marx & Engels 1969, p. 56)

The above incident, taken from his works, shows that Lenin did not understand even the fundamental principles how the wages were decided in a society whether it be capitalistic or communistic. One measure of deciding the wages is supply and demand, another the government legislations, another the cost required to train a competent worker, another the union determination. It also indicates that he did not consider the professionals as his comrades, though these brain workers earned a living by working in the same way as the proletariat of which he claimed he was a champion.

The following episode is exceptional in the history of wages. On the construction work in the Temple of Erechtheus in Athens at the early fifth century BC, an architect and a stone cutter received the same wages. Hiring was quite informal, and the agreements were made only for the performance of a particular piece of work. The state took no interest in regulating the conditions of work or wages. (Roebuck 1966, p. 266)

Marx contrasted capital and labour, and used labour meaning proletarians but varied his usage in some of his writings. Lenin understood the term in the former usage. It was possible to interpret the term labour meaning all the working people including proletarians, professional people, small business people, independent trades people, farmers (landowning and tenanted), and even the managers who work for their salaries. The workers in the latter definition include the bulk of the population and they would have voted for the communists into the government under democratic elections. If the communists understood the workers in the above sense in contrast with aristocrats and capitalists--I believe it can be done with minor modifications, they would have been closer to realities and could have maintained their system of government for many centuries.

> Before the revolution, Lenin called on the soldiers of the imperial army to revolt against officers and advocated the elective command. But once the Bolsheviks grabbed the power, he quickly became the firm supporter of discipline and order, denouncing the foregoing proposals. Also the workers' control was a tactical device and he did not share the political and managerial authority with the workers and kept them under the firm control of the communists. (Nove 1992, p. 50)

Marx delineated the fundamental tenets of the foreign policy in the Inaugural Address of the International Working Men's Association:

> Vindicate the simple laws of morals and justice, which ought to govern the relations of private individuals, as the laws paramount of the intercourse of nations (Marx & Engels 1969, p. 190).

It is interesting to note that he stressed the ethics in the above passage in his rare display. He emphasised the economic aspects of the human dealings, not morals, throughout his vast literature.

The Soviet foreign policies clearly revealed the deficiencies of the communist theories; the dichotomy between revolutionary idealism and conservative nationalism was the prominent feature of the policies (Riasanovsky 1977, p. 565). For example:

> The Bolshevik regime renounced the concessions and special rights obtained by tsarist government in such countries as China and Persia. But it held onto the Chinese Eastern Reailway, weathering the conflict over it with China in 1929. (p. 568)

Lenin stressed in his treaties of pre-revolution era the right of the self-determination of peoples, and in fact just after the revolution the Soviet Government proclaimed it. However, it soon became obvious that the scheme was unworkable and the same government condemned the movement as bourgeois and counter revolutionary. The Soviet Union did not give any political and economic independence to the individual republic, except in the cultural autonomy and the administration. The Soviet Union has been probably the most highly centralised state in the modern era. (pp. 536, 562)

Lenin and Russian Communists hated bureaucracy; however, once they were in power they found that they could not rule without the knowledge, expertise and administration of the bureaucracy (Bradley 1988, p. 172).

> Until Stalin's establishment of the modern Soviet command economy beginning with his forced collectivisation in 1929, the Soviet economy was one in which market relations predominated ... (Walker 1978, pp. 215-7).
>
> Yet according to an official report based on the never published census of 1936, 55 percent of Soviet citizens still identified themselves as religious, while many others presumably concealed their belief. The stubborn fact in conjunction with the general social stabilisation of the thirties made Stalin and the Politburo assume a more tolerant attitude towards religion. (Riasanovsky 1977, p. 645)

At the late 1980s for the East European communists and at the early 1990s for the Russian communists it became apparent that their communist regimes were not economically sustainable. These governments crumbled easily in a short period of time without any external interference which they feared so much since the establishment of communist rule. Thus the experiment of social reform in the name of communism ended in failures or so it seems in the Eastern European and Russian context at least. In spite of the above historical facts to confirm that communism was wrong when assessed in its totality, I believe that it had something to offer to the human race. I have come up with a concept of partial communism, which I am to expound in the next chapter.

It is certainly amazing that the communists with such poor theoretical backings carried out the revolutions risking millions of lives, believing they were on the right. The social experiment of communism seems to have failed in history today. I sometimes wonder how the surviving members of the families would feel if they learned that the member of their families died because of incorrect premises. What happens to the people who died in the process of the revolution? What happens to the people who suffered a great deal in the process of building and dismantling communism? Should we all forget about them? What else can we do?

Karl Marx spoke for only a small section of his contemporary society to which he did not even belong. The industrial proletariat, whom he spoke for, comprise of probably one-third of the population including their families in a fully industrialised nation today. This class was the lowest strata of the working people and was supposed to own no properties. The communists often cited peasants with no lands of their own and low-ranking soldiers as the comrades. If we further added shop assistants, domestic servants and cleaners—they made sizable number of people--but Marx classed them as unproductive workers and did not discuss their plight. The communists in practice did not represent the brain workers such as lawyers, writers, doctors, accountants and engineers, though there were some theoretical deviations. Though Marx insisted that once the communist society was firmly established, no class distinction would exist, not many people (especially the haves in a society) would have believed it. The have-not class Marx advocated was least educated and least successful, and it is not logical that they should be running the government. When the communist society comes about, naturally the most capable persons should come to the top of the various occupations and it is expected that they would form the new elite class, although not a hereditary one. It is beyond dispute that if rank or money does not reward people, they would not work hard and the society would stagnate. Many Russians observed these phenomena even in the height of communist power.

Karl Marx looked at capitalist economy in simplistic, narrow and selective terms, which in fact did not reflect the real state of the society. Consequently most of his capitalist theories were in error in broad terms, though they may be correct partially and look fine theoretically and appeal to some people.

Marx placed too much emphasis on the economic aspects of human existence, and erroneously thought that once a society corrects the economic ills, every other major problem would correct itself. This premise did not produce any difficulties before the revolution. After the successful revolutions, the so-called communist nations did not pay serious attentions to such racial, religious and social problems. The iron fists of the communist rules suppressed these problems. As soon as the communist parties in Eastern Europe and the Soviet Union lost their firm political control and these nations crumbled towards the end of the 20th century, the ethnic and religious conflicts and other social malaise came to the fore. The true state of affairs which the communist leaders had chosen to ignore and hide from the outside world stunned the world. They were not only far behind the Western world in these respects but they did not know how to deal with the problems and were unable to look after themselves in these matters.

There is an ideology in economics which is neither capitalism nor communism. James Burnham (1905-1987) was a communist in Poland. He went to the United States and was so impressed with what he observed there that he proposed a society of new concept in his book *The Managerial Revolution* (1941). According to him, communism does not succeed capitalism but the managerial revolution will take place within the confines of capitalism. In the new society, the managerial class, not the capitalists as they do today, will dominate the society. The managerial class, according to his definition, refers to business executives, technicians, bureaucrats and soldiers. The book published in 1939 by Bruno Rizzi which proceeded on the similar arguments influenced the thinking of Burnham.

My assessment is that communism was the product of the First Industrial Revolution in Britain. Communism was fossilised as Karl Marx formulated in the middle of the 19th century, whereas capitalism went through many evolutions together with the matching theories. The communists relied solely on materialism focusing on the developments of industries and science and engineering, which was in fact grossly an erroneous concept. The communists simply could not cope with the various facets of the human progress, though they were successful in developing science and technology. As I make clear in 'Introduction to Series', the humans have to make use of the various survival techniques; materialism is only one of them if they want to live successfully. Capitalism adopted varied survival strategies; and communism did not, relying on the set doctrines.

In 'Introduction to Series', I made a point that idealism was formulated in a few parts of the world in the early classical era and did not make any further progress. This was because of the nature of idealism. Can we say the same thing about communism? I am certain if capitalism had relied solely on the theories advanced by Adam Smith all these years since the end of the 18th century, the capitalist economy would have collapsed sometime in the past. Communism relied solely on Marxism developed in the middle of the 19th century, and collapsed at the end of the 20th century. I am not sure if communism could have been modified to suit the changing economic needs. Communism did not change and more precisely could not change. The understanding on the economy by the communists was flagrantly erroneous and they also relied mistakenly solely on materialism as a fundamental survival means. Therefore, the communist theoreticians could not develop any further than Marx did. The proposition that communism could not be improved by its nature is in fact one manifestation of communism which are based on many erroneous premises.

Fundamental Flaws of Karl Marx

I present basically uncomplimentary assessments of both Marx's life and his theories on capitalism and communism. In the process of evaluations, I noticed that there were common threads to the defective theories. The flaws may have come from his defective approach which exhibited as the defects in the individual propositions. I have come to believe that these common defects of his originated in his character and thinking, which is in fact generally the case. I can highlight this point by the following illustration. It is well established that many of the nervous disorders don't come from the observable disturbances but rather go deeper and originate in defective characters and thinking and consequent daily life. For more details, see Section 7 Cure of Nervous Problems, Chapter 1, Book Four.

Marx wanted to view the world in a simplistic way and believed that he could extract an essence of political-economy in a concise manner and he formulated his thoughts accordingly. His fundamental arguments reduced to materialism. He looked at capitalism to be replaced with communism, that is, the simple contrast of capitalism and communism. He further reduced the capitalist society to consist of two classes of capitalists and proletariat: only the poverty of proletariat can generate the wealth of capitalists. He sharply defined capital and consumption, not realising that the definition was meaningful so long as it matched with the realities and at the same time served some useful purpose he could nominate. People have no interest in such classification of capital and consumption or the argument that the rent is surplus value but are interested in usefulness in making money which Marx fundamentally agreed. For example, he thought that the attires people wore were nothing but consumption and enjoyment; however, in many professions the clothes were in fact a necessity and hence should have been classed as capital: the appropriate and often expensive clothes were necessary tools of trade to conduct business successfully for many professions such as entertainers, business people and shop keepers. Adam Smith correctly pointed out that clothes and even household furniture in the professional capacity sometimes yielded revenue, and thereby served as a capital (Smith 1991, p. 227). As a further example of the useless classification Marx made, we can cite the following argument he proposed:

- The production workers are productive labour and produce a value, hence are part of capital.
- The unproductive workers, e.g., domestic servants, soldiers, police, mistresses, prostitutes and entertainers, are unproductive labour and produce no value, hence are part of consumption.

(p. 218)

Productive labourers are paid from capital and unproductive labourers are paid from revenue. Capital is expended with a view for profits; and revenue, for immediate support.

In the real world, there are no clear distinctions between the two, besides it is not worth to make a distinction since the same money is spent for them. Karl Marx obtained the above distinction from Adam Smith and used in the sense that productive labour is productive of capital (Robbins 1998, p. 145). However, unproductive labour contributes in some ways to wealth and production; it widens the field of material consumption hence the field of production. Moreover, domestic servants do the chore for the masters, who can spend the saved time for work or leisure. (Marx 1963, pp. 281, 297) Obtaining the necessities of life may be economic activities; however, there are many activities which are uneconomic. For example, men's taking girls out, and entertainments of all sorts are clearly sink of fund for the individuals but for the society as a whole they are healthy economic activities. Exercises (mental and physical) are not productive according to Marx's definition; however, in the long run they contribute to the work, producing more commodities and various ideas and theories. Marx liked walking and reading, both of which contributed to completing his theses.

He believed that the struggles between two classes--the exploiters and the exploited in each stage of the development--made history, ignoring all the other due considerations. For example, he proceeded his argument on the basis that in the capitalist society the capitalists are the exploiters and the proletariat the exploited. I am not sure if I am a capitalist with some capital invested or a proletarian working as a labourer. He was not modest enough to suspect that the theories he did not agree with might have been correct after all, and as a consequence he stifled to develop his thoughts to the fullest possibilities. Also as I noted earlier, the dialectic development was a valid proposition without any doubt but he denied any other forms of development and, hence he failed himself an opportunity for further speculation as to the nature of developments.

Marx wanted to extract the rigid laws governing these simplified pictures of the real world. He ignored the fact that he was dealing with economic laws which alter according to the place and era. He looked into economic activities in search of eternal truth, the kind of which we could find in the field of science and technology or in arts, though the newly developed concepts superseded many fixed laws even in these fields. However, contrary to the above general approach of his, Marx made a statement that the economic laws were historical laws which were valid only for a given historical development, and monopoly and competition were contradictions to be synthesised to be a higher level of order (Marx & Engels 1989, p. 541).

Marx attended the universities to study philosophy, art, mythology and law which mostly dealt with rigid rules and eternal truths. Consequently he deviated considerably from the conventional lines of economic thoughts and carried serious flaws in formulating his economic theories.

He worked as an editor of the newspapers, contributed to newspapers as a freelance writer, founded the Communist League with Engels in 1847, and also was a leading member of the International Working Men's Association (the First International) established in 1864. He virtually had no other work experiences. As a consequence his theories were often way out of realities. He did not sometimes even understand what the people on the street took for granted. For example, the working people were as cunning as any other classes in the society. The common sense of the world told the people that many workers would have exploited the other people or the system if they had had a chance to do. We can say the same thing about the foot soldiers in the army or the so-called minority (racial or sexual) of the community in the past and present. In the real life situation the opportunity of the exploitation by these people was small since they had limited responsibility, hence the general public got the impression that these workers were always pushed around. Another good example may be that the communist society as he dreamed would have or should have a hierarchy of people not of a class but of capability. In his new society some would have been intelligent and diligent and these people should have got professional jobs or have told other people what to do. The society should reward these people for their contribution in monetary terms or otherwise. Without just reward, people eventually would not have felt like working and the society would have stagnated.

He theorised that his propositions concerning the firms and the families were inherent in the system. In actuality there were very few intrinsic qualities in these human organisations and most characteristics were ever changing as a result of the struggles among the contestants, the various social shifts having influences. The corporations of his age were vastly different from those of today, which, I am sure, even the present remaining communists would acknowledge. He could not conceive that in the future the employees of the firms may successfully exploit the employers under certain circumstances. He selected only the parts of the attributes of the events under investigation and thought they represented the whole.

Marx divided the society into two classes of capitalists and proletariat, which was in itself a defective oversimplification. He, further, claimed that the two classes represented incompatible interest, referring to the struggles within the firms. I believe the corporations are similar to the families when we focus our attention to the interests of each member. The members of the family are in competition as well as in cooperation. They compete for money allocation and dominance; however, they are united for the survival of the whole family and in pursuit of happiness. The corporation is no different from the family in this respect. The capitalists and the workers are in for bigger share of the money available and for working hours and the work practices and dominance. However, both parties are united for the survival of the corporation for their own benefits. Prosperity of the firm is good for both. Closure of the firm is bad for both. The families are as complex as the firms if we focus our attention to the difficulties each member must deal; however, the firms are vastly more complex as a whole since the firm involves a larger number of people with different functions. The good employer-employee relationship has a great deal to contribute to the productivity with high incentive and morale, and tend to minimise the strikes and lockouts which stop the production completely. Since the purpose of the production is to make money for both the employers and employees and the good relationship raises the income of the firms, the managers should pay the utmost attention to its fostering. Karl Marx depicted only one aspect of the corporation, that is, competition, dominance and resulting antagonism; and disregarded the other aspect, that is, cooperation, survival and resulting mutual benefits.

In fact, Robert Owen was the first person who experimented successfully in his companies the cooperative potentials between capital and labour (Carmichael 1968, p. 51).

In conjunction with the introduction of communism into a society Marx dreamed up a utopian slogan of 'the commodities will be given to people according to the needs in the communist society'. People with common sense would not believe that it would be realised in the real world and contains the obvious but fundamental problems:

- The depletions of natural resources would force the stoppage of the idea.
- The wanton wastage by some members of the society would also force the stop to the idea.
- The environmental degradation would force the stop to the idea.

If the slogan is possible at all, only the hugely depopulated nations with highly industrial capacities can realise it, such as the Third Prophecy advocates as I expound in Book Four.

My conclusion of the analyses on communism is that it should not have been put into practice with such poor theories. Karl Marx formed his theories based on the Industrial Revolution in Britain, which was radically different from the economic situations of the 21st century capitalist countries. Many of his doctrines were erroneous from the inception and were made even more so as capitalism progressed.

Chapter 2 Partial Communism Proposed

Preface

In studying communism I came up with the idea of Partial Communism. This version of communism does not require deep insight into the economic activities but rather is practical procedures to improve upon capitalism. I don't see any historical inevitability of it but definitely a marked improvement on the current capitalist system. It has obviously something to think about and at least offers the possibility that there is an alternative communism to Marxism.

The Communist Manifesto proposes a number of practical measures to build a communist society, as I explain in Section 5 Principles of Communism, Chapter 1. The Partial Communism adopts only items a and c of the proposed policies within the capitalist frame of the economic system, and discards the rest of the communist doctrines. I am going to restate the two items of concern as follows:

a Abolition of property in land and application of all rents of land to public purposes
c Abolition of all right of inheritance.

If the rents of land are made sufficiently large, the above two measures should give enough revenues for the government such that the government can abolish altogether personal and corporate taxes being charged on the profits at present and being touted as unfair with all the hatred by many sections of the community.

In fact the above two policies are nothing radical and can emerge from the common sense. Hence naturally many people had preached the idea before the modern communism formulated them. In particular, John Stuart Mill (1806-73) proposed the confiscation of accruing land rent and further advocated the abolition of inheritance (Heimann 1964, p. 122). William Godwin (1756-1836) advocated the abolition of private property and the establishment of social ownership of land (Barber 1991, p. 58).

Section 1 Major Economic Defects under Capitalism

This section highlights only the economic, not political nor any other, shortcomings. Some of the ills I bring up are inherent in capitalism, and some are not and exist under any economic systems.

At the early 21st century, it seems that capitalism triumphed over communism. The terminal nature of capitalism was one big thrust of Marx's argument: however, after more than 100 years of his prediction, capitalism is still thriving. However, nobody would doubt that capitalism has its own problems. The Partial Communism is an attempt to address those problems by adopting two communistic policies into the capitalist framework.

Capitalism centres on capital. In capitalist society people with capital take the upper hands in the various dealings. Money in the bank account and the various investments is capital, however small or large it may be. Money saved but hidden in the house is not capital. Also the money spent for the necessities of life and various everyday expenditures is not capital. If a person buys a house whether he borrows money from the bank or not, whether he lives in the house or rents it out, the house is effectively a capital. It is proven beyond doubt that the house prices increase well outstripping the inflation rate whatever the reasons the economists give out, though there are a few exceptions as for any other investments. This fact itself does not tell us if capitalism is good or bad, but tells us that capitalism operates on the mechanism which tries to increase the capital from the various ventures. The human minds have the ingrained desire to increase wealth as well as to have sex. Capitalism operates cleverly in that the ventures are in accordance with the fundamental human desire for wealth. Marx observed that mobility of both capital and labour characterised the capitalist mode of production, resulting in the continual revolutions in the production methods and commercial activities. These changes further created new way of life and thinking of the people. (Marx 1971, p. 444)

The desire for profit makes the producers and traders competitive for the share of the market and survival. The scholars generally agree that the economic competition is good in the overall scheme provided they act within both the laws and the morals. The people strive for efficiency in the various measures: better use of both machinery and labour, minimisation of wastes and so on. One critical problem of the communist countries in the past was that they did not strive for efficiency but chanted the communist slogans instead.

One serious problem of capitalism may be imbalance of production and consumption; the consumption within the nations and the exports are too small to the production capabilities of the capitalist nations. Capitalism has no problem in producing commodities thanks for human greed, the high level of technology, and the competent economists, the well-trained technicians and managers but it has a problem in consuming the commodities thanks for the human propensity to save, which is really another manifestation of human greed. Modern economists established that consumers account for about two-thirds of economic activities of the capitalist nations.

'Laws of Markets' or 'Say's Law' by JB Say (1767-1832), a French economist, was overoptimistic and we know from our observations that it is not true for most of the commodities today. His major publication *A Treatise on Political Economy* (1803) states the above law that the general overproduction cannot happen because supply creates its own demand (Dye, Moore & Holly 1966, p. 52). Up till 1825, when the first economic crisis happened, the rapid consumption compared with the slow production made the development of machinery necessary. The above Say's law was possibly correct until the above economic crisis. Marx referred to the economic crises in Europe between 1800 and 1815 because of the continental blockade (Marx 1968, p. 497). He also referred to the economic crisis resulting from the sudden change in the channels of trade as happened in England after the war of 1815 (Marx 1971, p. 122). However, these economic crises were different in nature from those crises due to the overproduction under advanced capitalist production. He witnessed many economic crises while he was writing *Capital*, and expressed a strong doubt of the correctness of the Say's law (Marx 1968, p. 500). Further, he wrote that the economic crises are inherent in capitalist production and expressed strong objection to the idea that they are only accident or chance (p. 512). He stressed that no overproduction will occur under the socialist production (Marx 1971, p. 118). It seems that Adam Smith (1723-90) was totally unfamiliar with the idea of overproduction and looked at capitalism with unqualified source of both wealth and well-being of the nation (Marx 1968, p. 525).

The imbalance of production and consumption shows up as booms and busts of the economy: especially bad are the prolonged depressions when many factories are closed and many workers are laid off in spite of the fact people are willing to work and the factories have the capacity to take on these people. Marx clearly noted that the life of modern industry becomes a series of periods of moderate activity, prosperity, overproduction, crisis and stagnation (Marx 1954, p. 427).

It is established in the minds of the public today, much more so in the academic circles, that the gluts of commodities from under-consumption, leads to recession and worse to depression. More than 100 years ago, Malthus wrote in *Principles of Political Economy Considered with a View to Their Political Application* (1820): To maximise wealth, a nation has to balance the power to produce and the will to consume.

The aim of the companies is profit maximisation. Profit maximisation is a direct consequence of scarcity. Seeking to make the best possible use of scarce resources is the same thing as trying to make the largest possible profit. (McTaggart, Findley & Parkin 1992, p. 207)

Without sufficient profit for their trouble and with too much risk on the capital, the capitalists are not prepared to put out the venture in the same way the labourers are not prepared to put out their labour without sufficient wages (Marx 1968, p. 544).

Business is not only for living expense and profits but also for distinction and resulting self-esteem. Hence many business people will carry on the operation even if the profit is zero or they make a loss if the upturn of the profits in the near future is anticipated. In fact the many peasants the world over carried on working with near zero profit or even loss at times under subsistence farming for millenniums.

Economic ideas are the product of adversity. People are put under tremendous pressure to face war and economic depression with often good progress in many fields.

Another major problem under capitalist system, sometimes called free enterprise system, as I see, may lie in income taxation and inheritance of properties which I am to explain under the headings of 'Income Taxation' and 'Inheritance of Properties' to follow in some depths. They are the problems not of capitalism but under capitalism, that is to say, they are not inherent in capitalism but have stayed with the various economic systems. Karl Marx, in his analyses of capitalism and communism, left out the proper consideration of tax from unknown reason to me. He makes a rare reference to tax in *Theories of Surplus Value* (Marx 1971, p. 397). Probably tax did not hurt him in his personal life since he had few regular jobs. He discussed the inheritance of property only briefly in conjunction with the establishment of communism.

Another main problem may be monopoly. The power of monopoly can distort the free competitive market, and also the great powers of organised minority groups can hamper the intelligent democratic political actions (Dye, Moore & Holly 1966, p. 633), thus distorting the inherent virtues of capitalism.

I have never heard that the inheritance of properties was the major problem of the society. Many economists and politicians tried to remedy the shortcomings of income taxation and monopoly but failed to give satisfactory solutions. Since all these problems are still in the capitalist nations they may be inseparable from the market economy. This is where communism came into play. Communism tried to solve the various problems with the entirely different political and economic structures, which appealed many sections of the communities. I am proposing the solutions only to the two problems of taxation and inheritance of properties by incorporating a few communist theories into the capitalist system.

Pure competition is often cited as a virtue of capitalism. A good example of pure competition is agriculture, though agriculture existed since Neolithic era to the present with little progress. Agriculture may operate on the principles outside of capitalism. No farmer can dominate the market and control the prices. Hence the farm products were normally not advertised. Recently the vested interest group has come to advertise a particular farm product for increased sale; however, this does not alter the aforementioned fundamental position. The real force of competition is that it pressures enterprises to do things better (McTaggart, Findley & Parkin 1992, p. 253), though again agriculture in many parts of the world have not improved a great deal over these millenniums basically because of the limited land available and the lack of capital. Certainly the farmers introduced a large scale machine production for the maintenance and harvest of land intensive crops in such countries as the USA and Australia. In Australia because of high wages in this country the farmers tend to lose against cheap imports even with tariffs, and also many of them have to deal with frequent droughts and floods more than they can bear, and their numbers are ever decreasing.

We know that the consumer goods made in the former communist countries were no match to those made in the capitalist countries in terms of both quality and price. One obvious reason cited was lack of competition, resulting in lack of market research and production improvements in the former communist countries. The underlying problem may have been that communism was built on many erroneous premises, and the policy makers did not and could not place the remedial policies even if they saw the problems.

Income Taxation

The current income tax system as the Western societies such as Australia exercise is not fair not only in its magnitude but also in the manner it is applied. Most people may agree with the above statement but the fact of the matter is that nobody has come up with better methods of giving the government the adequate revenues to finance its policies. I am to challenge the very existence of the present income taxation in this section. Later in this chapter I detail the better revenue collection methods, though I made a brief reference to them in the preface in this chapter. I am sure that the parliament will legislate the new revenue raising means as long as the system is sound and can raise enough money for the government. I am here decrying only the income tax and not about the other necessary and even beneficial taxes such as tariffs and excise duties.

As a single man, I have always thought the income from any job, professional or unskilled, was more than adequate for my decent living. I have also always felt that the amount of tax I surrendered was too much: about one-third of my gross income had been taken out from my every pay packet without my permission. When we work for a firm, the firm pays the tax for us, and this way of paying tax is called 'Pay as you earn'. The proportion of this tax for the tax department is increasing among the myriads of tax raising methods, the reason being that for the other taxes people can find a way to reduce the tax burden and also people can outright cheat the tax amount in many cases with a slim chance of being detected. Being thrifty by nature, I managed to save nearly half of my net earnings, keeping the unspent money in my bank account. One day I did the reckoning and realised to my horror that the extra tax and the inflation effect combined were as much as or even greater than the bank interest accrued. In effect, I was losing money through keeping the savings in my bank account.

Being thrifty may be recommended for an individual; however, for the society as a whole the consumption is also important. The two extremes of too little and too much saving are detrimental for the society and there must be a point where the consumption and saving are optimum for the economic prosperity of the community. A large consumption as a result of squandering by a large number of people does not leave much money for investment. A small consumption as a result of too much saving does not stimulate the production either. This dilemma is called 'paradox of thrift', and what may be true for an individual is not true for the nation as a whole. Too much spending (consumption) leads to inflation and too little spending (too much saving) leads to deflation, if we focus our attention only to consumption and saving. Obviously, there are other causes for inflation and deflation. The economic downturn is people's reluctance to spend for the commodities and, surprisingly, nothing else. This fact is amazing in view of the various opinions expressed by the eminent economists at the time of recessions and depressions. Many people have noticed this fact. For example, JA Hobson (1858-1940) theorised that excessive savings are the cause of the general gluts in the economy. One thing the government can do during recession is to tell this fact and encourage people to spend more, and producers to curtail production. It is obvious that however enthusiastic people spend the time will come when the production exceeds the consumption unless the production slows down. People can use the disposal income only in two ways; consumption, that is, providing for today, and saving, that is, providing for tomorrow (Dye, Moore & Holly 1966, pp. 57-8, 100, 118).

Next I bought a house getting a loan from a bank and rent it out while I lived in a cheap flat. The monthly loan repayment was not much but heavy on me more psychologically. Tax was minimum since I subtracted the monthly repayments of the loan from the gross income for tax purpose. After 3 years, I fully paid off the loan, and from then I had to surrender as tax approximately one-third of the rent collected: This was where I started. The fact that I had to pay tax from the rent on top of the tax taken out from my salary really hurt me. It is fair to tax the first time income. The way taxation department operates in Australia in this respect is definitely not right. I saved and bought a house whose rent is again taxable. If I had spent all my savings, my tax would have been minimum and knowing this fact many people do just that. The Australian government should be encouraging savings because one problem this country has is lack of capital. The way capitalist countries operate is that the banks channel savings to capital. All the profits made through savings should be tax free, which would encourage savings and as a result business, and reduce enormous amount of various pension payments. This line of thinking is nothing new and David Ricardo insisted that tax falling on profits should be minimised in order to encourage investment and production (Barber 1991, p. 91). The government would have increased tax from increased business activities. Under the current economic system, the chief beneficiary of my venture was, with my ego of owning a home satisfied, was the tax department, though the other participants, the bank and the real estate agent, derived some benefits.

The current income tax in Australia, private and corporate, as in any other Western countries, which is progressive to the profit or net income for people who pay tax as they earn, is not a right measure from another perspective. Why should the successful individuals and firms pay such a high rate of tax provided they earn legitimately? Tax stifles personal savings and entrepreneurial spirit by lessening the net profits which are the main, probably the only, incentive for any investment.

There are other methods of taxing, but they are just unsatisfactory as the taxes on profit or net income. These other taxing methods were applied more often than not in addition to the income tax:

Since the state protects the properties of people, people should pay tax in proportion to the value of property they own (Roll 1961, p. 102). The English economist William Petty (1623-1687) advocated this view. The present land tax may be based on this thinking, though in Australia there is no land tax on the principal residence.

The government taxes on the individual persons whether they have property or not, and irrespective of how much income they have. This tax is often referred to as poll tax. The Ch'in Empire imposed poll tax to raise extra revenue. The Saracen Empire applied on the people who refused to convert to Muslim faith. Margaret Thatcher, as Conservative Prime Minister of Britain, introduced poll tax in 1989 which was widely condemned as extremely unfair. John Major, Labour Prime Minister, replaced the poll tax with the modified property tax in 1993.

Medicare tax as applied in Australia: This tax is primarily designed to help pay the medical expenses.

The Federal Labor Government introduced Capital Gains Tax in Australia. People have to pay tax if a profit is made on the disposal of a capital asset that was acquired after 20 September 1985. Capital assets are defined to be any kind of property or a legal or equitable right that is not property. There are some exemptions in applicability of this tax.

Consumption tax is applied every time the goods or services are consumed. The Federal Coalition Government introduced the Goods and Services Tax (10% of the price) in Australia in the year 2000.

Payroll tax is paid primarily to pay for the unemployment insurance.

Henry George proposed the Single Tax in his book *Progress and Poverty* (1879). According to his proposition, the government should tax away the unearned gains in land values that did not come from the effort or intelligence of the owner but came in effortless fashion from the general advance of population and industry. He reasoned this tax was enough to cover the state expenses making redundant all the other taxes. (Galbraith 1987, p. 167)

Nicholas Kaldor (1908-1986) advocated the expenditure tax which has the effect of exempting savings and investment from levy (p. 189).

Milton Friedman (1912-2006) proposed a radical income tax scheme. According to him the government should introduce a progressive tax, becoming zero at a certain low income and after that progressively returning income, that is, the government pays out money (p. 271).

One pillar of democracy may be the principle of one-person-one-vote. I have come to believe that this principle, though well entrenched in the modern democratic nations, is not really fair when viewed from the monetary contributions of the voters. Some voters pay high tax and some low tax and some no tax and some even receive the government pensions, yet they all have one vote according to the above principle in the process of electing their political representatives. All these people have equal voice in choosing their political representatives as a principle. Many corporations pay a large amount of tax without any voting right.

In the management of the private companies, the process is more democratic. People don't have any say in the management of a company where they don't have any financial contributions. In the companies listed in the stock market which in fact form the bulk of the large firms of private orientation, people have voting power in proportion to the number of shares in that company. They choose their representatives (executives) according to the number of shares in favour.

I believe that the present system of one-person-one-vote in selecting the political representatives irrespective of the amount of tax people pay is not really democratic as many people claim. This fact may partly explain why the political institutions in the civilised world are ineffectual compared with the private companies whose elective procedures the money input decides. This is another reason why we should phase out the current taxes.

Democracy has some deficiencies, which is the reason why democracy often gives way to the other forms of government. It has been proved many times in the course of history that the government by the select few, not passing through the process of election, was better than democracy, because the election process can be flawed in many ways. One of the reasons is that the voters can be quite ignorant about the candidates.

Inheritance of Properties

As far as I am aware, people have never questioned the right of property inheritance by the relations--often the spouse, offspring and sometimes siblings--throughout human history. This system is called hereditary inheritance. Another way of inheritance is by the express will of the property owners who can designate any persons as inheritors of the property. Will normally sits on higher order than hereditary inheritance today and nullifies the social convention of the latter, though I have some suspicion that the order could have been the other way around in a particular era and location in the human history. With the absence of both next of kin and the express will the state confiscates the deceased property.

The empire or kingdom was often passed to an individual who was not related by blood to the deceased monarch--sometimes by the will of the deceased and sometimes by the circumstances going against the will. The inheritance of the empire or kingdom entails not only the wealth in the forms of properties such as estates, lands and investments but also the authority to govern. Before the modern times, the occupation or authority together with the properties were passed in the main hereditarily. In the modern times, the former is separated from the latter and the hereditary inheritance of the occupation or authority is virtually out of existence. Still even today, the hereditary wealth is unchallenged and not many people suspect the prevailing mode of bequest as evil because people are conditioned to think it natural since their childhood, in the same way before the modern times people thought natural to pass their occupation or authority to their relations. It is interesting to note that in the Ch'in Empire the individuals could not inherit the ranks from their forebears and had to earn solely on their own personal merits (Murowchick 1994, p. 96). The modern society uses capability of a person rather than birth in filling a position. They still have not realised the absurdity and illogicality of property inheritance, which I am going to address under the above heading.

Under the existing social custom and law in the civilised countries, when a person dies the assets are passed to the nominated beneficiaries or, in the absence of the will, to the next of kin, or, in the absence of both to the government coffers according to the law of the land. Normally there are a lot of envies and fights among the anticipating beneficiaries such as the families or the favourites of the deceased, the on-lookers observing the events with jealousy.

It is good for anybody to try to become rich by whatever means available to them within the legal limits. Many people strive hard in trying to achieve their goal, which is without any doubt the major driving force of the national development. Some people, apart from making a living, wish to become wealthy by means of hard work, ingenuity, skills, cleverness, chance speculation or even lottery. When they become rich by whatever means, we don't know how much luck can be attributable to successful money making except for lottery. It is the ends that are important and not the means in the race to accumulate wealth, provided people act within the laws.

Moses Hess (1812-75), a Jewish writer from Cologne, challenged the above view. He theorised that as long as the economic inequality and exploitation exist, we cannot achieve justice. Hence he advocated the abolition of private properties for humanistic reasons. (Carmichael 1968, p. 55) The communists advocated the abolition of the private ownership of the means of production for economic and humanitarian reasons. The above Hess's theory influenced Karl Marx.

What I am against as a principle is the inheritance of the property to somebody when the property owners die. The popular maxim states that everyone is born equal. However, some babies are born to the rich families by accident and enjoy good prospect of life. Some are born to the poor families and many of them do not realise the full potential of their capabilities. I am not here to condemn the above scenario. I am saying that the wealth successful persons created should not pass to their beneficiaries or the blood relations when they die, any more than their authorities should not. Under the current system, the property inheritance is unfair in its concept and discriminating on the basis of births.

Section 2 Principles of Partial Communism

Under the proposed form of communism, the private property exists in the same way as under capitalism. All economic activities are capitalistic. The new society retains market economy operating on price mechanism in contrast with command economy the communists in the past advocated. Market economy focuses attention on consumption and command economy on production, each idea emanating from the fundamental concept of each system.

Partial Communism is not a new economic system and facilitates only a few, though fundamental, improvements to capitalism hence does not require vigorous analyses. However, Partial Communism is hardly irreversible by its very nature and people should proceed that this new system stays on the permanent basis. Theoretically at least, it is reversible. If the Partial Communism is unsuccessful and people reject the new system, the society can revert back to the previous capitalism, provided probably at least 75% of the voters consent.

The ultimate aim of the economic activity under this system may be profit seeking and survival of the economic entities, both of which force the entities to be efficient. The competitions among the firms offering similar commodities and services hopefully result in the optimum allocation of resources for the society as a whole. Adam Smith expressed that the invisible hand of God guided the economic activities based on laissez faire. The various markets coordinate individual decisions through price adjustments (McTaggart, Findley & Parkin 1992, p. 15). The resources here refer to labour and capital needed for the running of the corporations. The government may address some of the deficiencies that may arise under this social system as for the present system.

Karl Marx declared that only the violent revolution would enable the society to change from capitalism to communism. However, the Partial Communism has to take place under parliamental democracy by its very nature. The ideas proposed here may be discussed in parliament over many years, not to mention by the media and the debates among economists and politicians and general public. What I am giving out in this chapter is only the idea and the outline, and I expect many people, the scholars and the general public, will put their inputs into the scheme, and the programme will be much more complicated and detailed. When there is a general consensus about the proposal, the government has to initiate a referendum to get the consent of the people on the principles. Only after the solid yes vote, of probably 75% or more of the total cast votes, can the government proceed to change the constitution which integrates the Partial Communism. If the public reject the proposal, the Partial Communism dies unless some people try to get it up again. The constitution thus altered must get another approval of the people before it can be proclaimed as binding to all the people within the nation from the date specified.

The Partial Communism imposes the following policies on the capitalist nation:

A Abolition of private property in land and application of all rents of land to public purpose. Thus the government, actually all the people, owns all the land within the national boundary as well as offshore land and minerals. The government referred here is the national government and not the state or local governments. Possibly from practicability, the government may end up owning many of the buildings--residential, commercial and industrial.

B Abolition of all right of inheritance. When a person dies, the government confiscates all the properties of that person except for the properties the laws specify to cater for the spouse, the under-aged children, and the incapacitated or aged dependants.

C The revenues from the above two items together with the government businesses should be large enough to abolish all personal and corporate taxes which are currently based on profits or net income. In other words, the government sets zero tax on all profits, personal and corporate, as well as the net income within the national boundary. Abolition of corporate tax will encourage the influx of foreign capitals and also the abolition of personal income tax will motivate many wealthy foreigners to come and live within the country. The foreign capital and people are subject to the law of the country when these people die as when being alive for any other matters such as sickness benefits, and the national government will absorb the deceased properties. The inflow of wealth is good for the country. However, the government has to decide who should be allowed to settle and also how to prevent the outflow of wealth just before the settled foreigners die.

D Some taxes must remain imposed for social order and stability. For examples, import duties must remain, and excise taxes for anti-social and anti-healthy items such as tobacco, alcohol and some drugs must be put in place. However, the other taxes such as capital gains tax, consumption tax and stamp duty should be phased out of existence, since these taxes do not have any social benefits apart from contributing to the government coffers.

E The government may carry out any business in competition with the private sectors as long as they can make sufficient profits to make it worthwhile. The government may set up a business to challenge the monopoly of the dominant business or it may become a leading organisation to promote research and development if the industry is underdeveloped in comparison with foreign companies: The government is prepared to lose money in these capacities.

Section 3 Principles Expounded

I am to expound in this section the principles given in the last section under the same item numbers.

A Nationalisation of All Land within National Boundary

The idea is to nationalise all the lands within the national borders for the better running of the nation. The constitution is to establish such that the private citizens cannot own the land and any users have to pay the rent for the use of the land for any purposes--residential, commercial, industrial, farming and so on. This idea is nothing new and many people who were not associated with communism have put up. For example, Franz Oppenheimer (1864-1943), a German-Jewish sociologist and political economist, proposed abolition of landed-property. He argued that if the government owned all lands, they could put unemployed people locked into a land to become farmers. The reasoning argument is quite weak at today's prevailing marketing of farm products and personal freedom.

John Stuart Mill, in *Principles of Political Economy* (1848), made a proposition that the nationalisation of all lands should be effected to confiscate (ground) rent. Henry George, in *Progress and Poverty* (1879), proposed that the land rent should be taxed away: he set the exorbitant rate of more than 50% (Jackson & McConnel 1985, p. 539; Lipsey, Langeley & Mahoney 1986, pp. 393-4). Gossen and Walras demanded the nationalisation of all lands for the best possible use (Heimann 1964, p. 205).

The government owns all the land within the national boundary. There are to be no purchase or sale of land. The government may opt to rent out annually a block of land or longer depending on the use and the prevailing market conditions. For example, for farming and industry the lease has got to be longer than one year and perhaps we are looking at something like 10 years. The leaseholders can be private citizens or corporate bodies who are proven to be responsible. The land charge thus imposed is similar conceptually to the present council rate but is larger than that to cover the large part of the government expenditures. It is certainly not proportional to the profits accrued to the leaseholders.

Obviously the fixing of the charges needs a great deal of tact. If the charges are too high, there won't be much incentive to rent the land for residential or business purposes. The government may lower the charges to stimulate the national economy when the recession is on. In fact this arrangement gives the government the tremendous power to control the national economy: They can encourage or discourage the development of some sectors as they judge for the national benefits. The government may initiate a large scale building programmes for factories, houses, units and shops. Also the government may have to engage a fixed term lease agreement spanning for many years to encourage the investors to build houses, shops, factories or whatever. At the end of the lease, the investor may renew the lease or the government may have to purchase the buildings from the investor for a price an independent commission deems fair or another investor may buy the property as an investment with assured lease agreement of the land. The holders of the lands with good buildings can lease with high rents. The land fees for the different purposes must be on the different scales: the fees for residential, commercial, industrial and farming must be all different. The land in a good location should command higher fees than the land on a poor location of the same category. The government may have to resort to an auction if they are uncertain as to what charge is appropriate for the block of land.

Apart from the fee considerations, the government may have to make a rule such that the current occupier of a parcel of land should have priority over other interested parties who may be prepared to pay the same or even higher charges: This arrangement should give both the stability of tenancy and a peace of mind to the current tenant. Only the public sector can own the land; however, the public sector, the corporate bodies or the private citizens with appropriate arrangements can build and own the buildings of the various purposes. Non-government sectors have to obtain the lease agreement of the land with the government when they plan the building of any purpose.

Further Rationales behind Government Ownership of Land

- The system increases the land efficiency in that people try to occupy as small an area as possible in an effort to reduce the government charge. In the past and at present, the investors have tried to buy more land than necessary as the available money permits, in an anticipation of higher land price in the future.
- The system gives the government a strong voice, actually the final say, in deciding the developments of land use. Hopefully the government does it taking into considerations of the environmental issues with a coordinated planning under democratic guidance.
- The system increases the diligence of people in an effort to make money out of the rented land since they don't have to pay any tax on profits.
- The public ownership of all land eliminates the problem of division of farmland among the large number of children and also the land right for some countries such as Australia.

How to Transfer Privately Owned Land to Public Trust

First the government decrees based on the new constitution that there shall not be any purchase, sale or gift of the land after a fixed date. Then there are a few possible ways of transfer and they can exist side by side, rather than the government has to make a one-off decision on the alternatives.

- The government wait until the registered owner dies, when its land goes into the public control without compensation. For the land belonging to a company listed in the stock market, the government confiscates the shares when a shareholder dies and the government gradually increases the land ownership as the more shareholders pass away. The drawback of this approach may be a long time involved--up to half a century--for the major process to complete.
- The government purchase the land from the individuals or the firms as money becomes available. The government may have to issue bonds to obtain money for the purpose. Once they purchase the lands money from the rents aids the process. Both parties have to reach a mutually agreed price, which we expect to be a long and painful process. However, the private owners, knowing that when they die the land would be seized with no right of passing to their beneficiaries may opt for a quick resolution. Some owners may prefer to receive the compensation in the form of annuity for life rather than the lump sum.

Communism circumvented the above problems by forceful confiscation of the lands by the government and the citizens in the heat of communist revolutions.

Effect of Public Ownership of Land on House Price

Virtually everyone sleeps with the walls around and under a roof. Under the proposed system, the registered owners of the residential buildings of various types have to pay the government fees on both the buildings the government own and the land where they are placed. The government fees include what we call council rate today. The registered owners also have to pay the utility charges such as for water, electricity and gas. People who choose to rent, stay at a hotel or live in a boarding house don't make any direct payment to the government;

however, obviously the registered owners charge these people extra money to cover the government fees.

The registration and renting of the factories, shops, offices, farms and so on operate in a similar fashion. The registered owners of these premises have the separate accounts with the government in addition to the residential if they register any residential in their name.

Since the construction cost of the house is not expected to change whether the government own the land or not, the house price, not taking into account of the land, is the payment to the builders initially, and later varies according to the appreciation and depreciation of the house and the inflation of money: We expect the effects of the other market conditions to be minimal. Also we do not expect that the house price goes beyond the price before the changeover with the land attached. An average house in Sydney, for example, may go down as much as one-third to two-thirds when the government confiscates the land under the house. Up to 70% of house prices in Sydney and Melbourne are made up of the value of the residential land.

People will be much less attached to the house ownership. One reason may be the houses are cheaper. Another may be the government owns the land and can give notice to quit, at the end of the lease or under the valid lease for a set amount of compensation if the owner misbehaves or the government approve a development plan. Psychologically people will also be less attached to their houses since they are all temporal occupants. The government will find that their various development projects being in less opposition than at present since the decrees can remove the residents easily.

Effects of High Land Fees

If the government charges on land become too high there will be all sorts of problems emerging as a result:

- People are not interested in investing in houses, shops, offices, farms, factories and so forth.
- The children, even after becoming financially independent, may opt to live with their parents, thus avoiding to pay the government fees.
- The registered owners of the residential houses may let their friends or relatives or even strangers live with them for small rents. As a result people may crowd the houses creating unhappy and unhygienic living conditions.
- The non-fee-paying crowds may live on the streets, in the cars or in the parks, filling the streets and parks.

The above options people take will reduce the government revenues. Also as a psychological consequence, the government will become bureaucratic and inefficient, losing interest in initiatives and welfare of people, solely relying on high land-charges for its running.

The government must avoid the high land-fees, and setting the optimum level of fees is absolutely necessary if the scheme is going to survive.

B Disinheritance of Property in Practice

Registrations of Valuable Assets

When the disinheritance constitution passes the parliament of the nation, each individual starts the race to acquire wealth theoretically at least in equal terms, that is, without any assets to its name.

In a civilised society of the 21st century, some assets such as buildings, shares, bonds, bank accounts and cars have clearly registered owners. Some assets such as jewels, furniture and the various household appliances are not registered. Though these latter items indisputably belong to the family, they, more often than not, don't have distinct owners within the family. I call these items unregistered properties. For the sake of effective disinheritance I am proposing, the owners may have to register some unregistered but important or expensive assets to avoid confiscation when a death occurs within a family.

The joint ownership of the assets as practised today does not cause any problems in the proposed disinheritance, provided there is a law stating that the joint ownership of the assets by the children (by blood or by adoption), even they are over 18, is not permissible. The government simply takes over a portion of the asset when a person dies. For example, if a man and a woman hold a bank account in both names, the government takes over the half of the money when one of them dies. So goes with every other asset. If the asset the joint owners of a number of people hold is a solid object such as a house or jewellery, the government is entitled to the portion of the asset of the passed away and negotiate with the remaining people what to do with the asset. Keep it as it is or sell it to apportion the money among them or they pay the government the fees for the full ownership. The laws are to deal with the compensations for the spouse, the under-aged children, the incapacitated or aged dependants. The stipulations for these categories would be all different. Most likely last three groups of people will become the state awards if the spouse does not want to or cannot support them. The people can keep only their belongings and do not have the right to have registered properties if they are under the state care.

It is up to the owners to decide if they register an unregistered asset or not. In the first place, the value of the item must be considerably higher than the registration fee to be worth registering. The government set the registration fee which is once only to minimise the fuss for the government and the registerers considerably high so as to pay for all the recording, monitoring, transferring, auditing and deregistering jobs of the bureaucracy, though as an alternative it may be possible to introduce the annual payment of registration. These fees are uniform and not proportional to the values of the assets, and the parliament set them. Some people may not be bothered from the various reasons, apart from the fee consideration, to make an application for registration of their valuable properties. Registration is an insurance against confiscation when a member of the family dies. Some properties are so small in market value that even burglars are not bothered to steal. In practice most of the household appliances and furniture are not worth registering. Though we pay substantial money at purchase, we get disappointedly small cash at disposal of these items. The main items to be registered, which are not registered today, may be jewellery, antiques and works of arts. One rule which the government must insist may be that every item must be registered separately and the group registration of a large number of items of small values should not be permitted.

I believe that the existing technology is capable of marking and recording all the above mentioned articles.

One benefit of keeping the records of the properties with the government may be less incentive for the burglars to steal as long as these records are frequently audited. It is an insurance against theft for the items not registered at present, such as jewellery, antiques and works of arts. Naturally registering and auditing a huge number of the properties require a large bureaucracy which is comparable to that of the present taxation department. I would expect that the disinheritance in practice would be as complicated as the present tax collections in practice and the offices handling the registrations would have about the same number of people working as in the present tax offices.

When a person dies, the government officers move into the house and confiscate all the registered assets belonging to the dead person as well as all the unregistered assets. The chief asset of the average family may be a house or a unit, followed by the investments. The officers look for the valuables in the house which are not registered: it is expected that the remaining family would nominate only the articles they don't want and hide the unregistered small and valuable items somewhere--in the residence or outside. The government officers cannot reach these valuable items because the family breaks the law: the court of law, possibly not the criminal law court but the court especially set up to hear the case of this kind, can punish them severely if it proves the breach of the law in due course. This is parallel today not to declare the taxable incomes. They may have to prove where they got the valuables at the time of registration if they want to register at all. The authority knows that most unregistered properties don't have any commercial values and hence don't even pay for the handling cost. They don't touch unvaluable items used by the remaining members of the family. Most likely they arrange that the charity organisation come and take unwanted items away. Still the fact that the government confiscates all the unregistered properties is important as a principle such that people make sure that the valuable items are registered to the member of the family: only if they are registered to the surviving member of the family, the family can keep them legally.

After bequeathing the various assets by virtue of the death of the asset owner, the government decides what to do with them. It may transfer the investments to the government coffer, or it may opt to rent the house, to keep the jewels or the shares depending on economic, legal or ethical considerations.

One Serious Problem on Disinheritance of Properties

There is a critical problem which may threaten the very introduction of the scheme: How to prevent people giving away assets just before they die? It is well established in our world that people are possessive of their properties even in their death bed and many people will hang onto what they have until they breathe their last. However, knowing the non-transfer legislation of their properties at death, many of them may try to transfer their assets to a beneficiary before their departure from this world. The government has to legislate that the transfer of a property can be validated only after the specified period--similar to the current conveyance of a house--focusing the attention to the above problem; the transfer is complete only after that period. We cannot differentiate the various circumstances such as of genuine sale or of legitimate transfer or of false sale with a pittance price.

My conclusion is that there is no way the government effectively prohibit people transferring their property to another body if the owners wished so in anticipation of their death. Let's hope, for this scheme to be successful, that people are greedy and keep their assets to their name till they die. Since the government discard the will of the diseased in regard to the property transfer, the sudden deaths of the wealthy as the results of wars, diseases, accidents and so on--in fact many deaths are without warnings--will become boon for the government and will raise the revenue for the delight of the budget allocators. I would estimate that as a rule of thumb, the government coffers will get at least one-third if the validation period is set as six weeks. The government will have virtually all if it is set as one year. The long validation period for comparatively small value assets has the practical problem, say for a cheap car or a low priced house. The government may have to devise the graded validation periods depending on the asset values. Naturally we expect a fair degree of tug of war between the surviving family and the authority in this regard in a similar fashion as we have today regarding the income taxes.

C Abolition of Personal and Corporate Income Taxes

By abolishing the right of inheritance, the government of the day can collect a huge amount of money annually. The government also can collect a large sum of money through rents, tariffs and excise duties. In addition it can raise a large sum of revenues through the running of the profitable businesses as I will expound later in this section. All these revenues should be enough to cover the government expenditures and the government can abolish all personal and corporate income taxes. However, I cannot quantify the above sums of money. In the first place, I have not made an attempt to set any of the rents except for making a statement that if the rents are too high it would make the national economy stagnate. In the second place, I have no access to the statistical way of computing the government revenues with some accuracy. However, I am certain that all the rents combined with the assets of the deceased would give more than enough revenue for any national government of the world: Unless we establish statistically this proposition beyond any doubt, Partial Communism cannot go ahead. Theoretically the rents are set to balance the budgets but they should not burdensomely high to damage the economy.

The current tax system as practised in Australia favours the people with capital, though the income tax is imposed progressively with higher income. By borrowing money from the bank for any business ventures the rich, or who can afford to buy their investments by taking out the loans, can write off the income against the monthly repayments, thus reducing the tax payment. After the introduction of Partial Communism, this scheme will become out of existence completely since there will be no income tax to start with.

D Custom and Excise Duties

The custom and excise duties must be in place in the proposed society in order to effect proper control of the society as it is done today. A tariff or customs duty is a tax applied on imports to protect the local industries, which has the effect of raising the price of the imported commodity. However, the academic circles have severely criticised the tariff protection in recent years despite its popularity among Australian community, because people have to pay higher price on imported goods and are subsidising the local inefficient industry. The scholars argue that without this subsidy many industries will make more profit and hire more people. The tariff in effect helps the inefficient industries by sacrificing many other industries. However, excise taxes must be applied not only to alcohol, tobacco and some drugs to suppress manufacturing these not so recommended commodities but also possibly to petroleum and coal. These forms of taxes make considerable contributions to the government income.

E Other Government Revenues

The public sectors can start various businesses if they can make money out of the ventures. I may suggest the following spheres of the economic activities as having potentials to raise the revenues:

> telecommunication, postal service, transport, gambling, distillation, productions of narcotics for medicinal use, prostitution, garbage disposal, house building, tourism and farming.

If they cannot make the individual industry in the black, they should let the private sectors take care of the industry within the relevant laws. If the government business cannot make money on the principle of 'user pay', then the business should fold with the resulting job losses for the employees who are partially responsible for the collapse. This position is the same with the private industries at all times. The government should carry on the enterprise with a loss only when the specific reason not to close is established.

Some government services such as defence, police, foreign affairs, education and research do not produce recognisable immediate financial gains. Still these activities have to be carried on in adequate manners even though they require huge monetary outlets with no discernible monetary returns. Also the government have to carry on with welfares with enormous expenditures with no other functions than helping the disadvantaged temporarily or permanently depending on the natures of the disadvantages.

Section 4 Some Theoretical Considerations of Partial Communism

Disinheritance of the properties in itself undoubtedly makes people less inclined to acquire wealth. Many people would say what is the point of becoming rich if they cannot pass the wealth to their children. However, we also have to take into account of the measure that there are no income taxes, personal and corporate, in the proposed society. Though naturally it is hard to predict quantitatively the propensity for wealth under Partial Communism, we would not be far out of the mark, if we estimate that the above two tendencies going to the opposite directions may roughly cancel each other out and people will be just as eager to make money as today. If this premise is correct, we will have as much enterprise and bustle as today and thus Partial Communism will assure the economic prosperity. There are so many variables for the economic activities that even if the above assessment is incorrect, that should not make a great deal of difference to the daily economic life of people.

We must base democracy on fairness and justice. Both land charge and disinheritance are fair and just since they apply to all the people and the firms. The exception may be on people who opt not to live under roof for the former and people who do not have any sizable assets for the latter. In any case we do not expect these people to pay tax under any tax system. Both are also broadly based and hence should raise large revenues for the government.

Democracy has many merits but tends to make the practising government of the creed weak by its very nature. History has shown repeatedly that democratic rule if not based on the strong tradition degenerates into dictatorship whose perceived advantage over democracy may be strong and unambiguous ruling body. It is estimated that the famous Athenian democracy in the ancient Greece lasted--to our surprise--less than 140 years (Freeman 1996, p. 217). The abolition of income taxes (corporates and individuals), the public ownership of all lands, and the disinheritance of the assets all make the government strong and yet democratic. In the first place the new government has ample revenues at its disposal and in the second place all three of the above fundamental policies were born out of the desire for fair and egalitarian society. The government ownership of all lands will give the elected body a powerful bargaining position, not restricted to the development projects. Thus democracy and strength set the new government on healthy financial basis, and they will dare to override the individual rights when the nation's welfare and benefits are at risk.

Partial Communism seems to be a hybrid of capitalism and communism at first sight; however, it is in fact capitalism whose serious defects are taken out and replaced by a few communistic theories supplemented with a few common ideas. As a matter of fact, the economic activities under Partial Communism are mostly capitalistic and we don't find much communistic concepts. It forces efficiency in the economic entities from the competition for survival and profits. Also price mechanism and profit motives force the efficient resource allocations. There are good reasons why this economic concept carries the name tag of Partial Communism instead of a version of capitalism.

The least reason for that may be that Partial Communism originated in the two of the slogans the communists advocated.

The two communistic policies of Partial Communism, that is, abolition of private possessions of land and disinheritance of personal properties, can be problematic in the light of natural rights of human existence. I am sure that some people insist the basic human rights come before the constitution of a nation. As discussed earlier, the parliament will amend the constitution to include the above two principles, after the successful referendum on the introduction of Partial Communism by the democratic process. According to the natural rights as our common sense dictates, once an individual owns a property (land or non-land), nobody can take it away from the individual unless:

- the individual pays tax according to the law of the land,
- the individual agrees for whatever the reasons; sale, charity, gift and so forth,
- the court of law orders to dispose it by virtue of the debt or the criminal activity of the property owner.

Accordingly if a person owns a block of land, the government has no right to appropriate the block to the public use, unless the above mentioned events take place. Similarly when an individual dies, the government has no right to confiscate any property of that individual except they satisfy the aforementioned conditions. This consideration makes the said provisions of Partial Communism mockery. So as to circumvent this difficulty we may have to develop the following lines of thoughts.

As was discussed before, the constitution of the nation which embraces Partial Communism contains the clauses stipulating the necessary requirements. Thus the argument advocating the natural rights of the individuals concerning their properties becomes purely academic. The High Court challenge refusing the handover of the personal property, even well intentioned, becomes a void.

Another way of obviating the problem may be the total denial of private property conceptually, as the extreme communists advocated. Thus the national government owns all the properties (land and non-land). The government decrees by virtue of the constitution that the citizens cannot sell or buy land since they have no right to own any piece of land. The government also owns conceptually all the other properties including investments, buildings, cars, jewels, household appliances, furniture and all the hosts of belongings. Theoretically the individuals temporarily keep all these assets for the services to the state. A person is born naked and goes to the nether world naked, with nothing to its name, everything belonging to the state. Under this system, people can sell or buy the non-land properties as they do under the capitalist society; however, people have to recognise that the national government which represents all the people within the national boundary owns all the assets. When a person dies, the government has all the right to confiscate what are naturally its assets from the beginning. In fact this is the main reason why I adopted the term Partial Communism for the proposed politico-economic system.

Reference List with Text Citations Marked

Barber, WJ 1991, *A History of Economic Thought,* Penguin Books Ltd, London.
60 61 80 87 117 121

Bradley, John 1988, *The Russian Revolution,* Bison Books, London.
23 27 (27) (27) 28 29 (29) 110

Brewer, A 1984, *A Guide to Marx's Capital,* Cambridge University Press, Cambridge.
26 51 71 72 (72) (73) 73 (73) 74 (74) (74) (74) 81 87 94 109

Carmichael, J 1968, *Karl Marx: The Passionate Logician,* Rapp & Whiting, London.
17 51 68 77 80 88 93 94 94 (94) (95) (96) (96) (96) 96 (97) 115 124

Davison, Michael Worth (ed.) 1993, *When, Where, Why and How It Happened,* Reader's Digest, London.
3 13

Dutt, Clemens (trans. and ed.) 1961, *Fundamentals of Marxism-Leninism,* Foreign Languages Publication House, Moscow.
28 50 56 57 65 77 80 80 (80) 86 88 (88) 88 (88) (88)

Dye, Howard S; Moore, John R & Holly, J Fred 1966, *Economics: Principles, Problems and Perspectives,* Allyn and Bacon Inc, Boston.
10 10 (10) 11 11 54 55 99 118 119 121

Ebrey, Patricia Buckley 1996, *The Cambridge Illustrated History of China,* Calmann & King Ltd, London.
43 45 48 (48) (48)

Engels, Frederick 1972, *The Origin of the Family, Private Property and the State,* Lawrence & Wishart, London.
94

Freeman, Charles 1996, *Egypt, Greece and Rome: Civilizations of the Ancient Mediterranean,* Oxford University Press, New York.
134

Galbraith, John Kenneth 1987, *A History of Economics: The Past as the Present,* Hamish Hamilton, London.
55 67 75 122 (122) (122)

Grenville, JAS 1994, *The Collins History of the World in the Twentieth Century,* HarperCollins, London.
15 15 (15) 22 25 (25) 37 39 39 45 (45) (45) 48 99 (99)

Heimann, Eduard 1964, *History of Economic Doctrines,* Oxford University Press, New York.
55 (55) (55) 60 60 62 62 64 72 73 117 127

Hitler, A 1992, *Mein Kampf,* trans. Ralph Manheim, Pimlico, London.
104

Hodgetts, Richard M & Smart, Terry L 1988, *Economics,* Addison-Wesley, California.
10 11 11 (11) 33

Jackson, J & McConnel, CR 1985, *Economics,* 2nd edn, McGraw-Hill Book Co, Sydney.
127

Kenez, Peter 2006, *A History of the Soviet Union from the Beginning to the End,* 2nd edn, Cambridge University Press, New York.
22 32

Kennedy, Paul 1987, *The Rise and Fall of the Great Powers,* Random House, New York.
9 (9) 11 (11) (11) (11) (11) 27 34 (34) (34) (34) (34) 39

Lenin, VI 1975, *Selected Works,* revised, vol. 1, Progress Publishers, Moscow.
19 28 57 60 76 89

-----1975, *Selected Works,* revised, vol. 2, Progress publishers, Moscow.
15 23 24 27 84 87 89 89 108

-----1975, *Selected Works,* revised, vol. 3, Progress Publishers, Moscow.
17 24 29 30 56 57 68 (68) 76 84 87 89 89 108

Lipsey, RG; Langeley, P & Mahoney, DM 1986, *Positive Economics for Australian Students,* 2nd edn, Weidenfeld and Nicolson, London.
62 127

McTaggart, Douglas; Findley, Christopher & Parkin, Michael 1992, *Economics,* Addison-Wesley Publishing Co, Sydney.
53 56 74 119 120 125

Marx, Karl 1954, *Capital,* vol. I: *The Process of Production of Capital,* translated from the third German edition by Samuel Moore and Edward Aveling and edited by Frederick Engels, Progress publishers, Moscow.
8 14 50 58 59 59 64 71 72 (72) 74 75 83 87 94 119

-----1956, *Capital,* vol. II: *The Process of Circulation of Capital,* translated from the German and edited by Frederick Engels, Progress Publishers, Moscow.
1 19 (19) 64 73

-----1959, *Capital,* vol. III: *The Process of Capitalist Production as a Whole,* translated from the German and edited by Frederick Engels, Progress publishers, Moscow.
10 52 55 63 67 72 72 73 74 83 104

-----1963, *Theories of Surplus Value,* part I, (Capital, vol. IV), translated by Emile Burns and edited by S Ryazanskaya, Progress Publishers, Moscow.
51 71 83 113

-----1968, *Theories of Surplus Value,* part II, (Capital, vol. IV), translated from the German and edited by S Ryazanskaya, Progress Publishers, Moscow.
72 118 119 (119) 119 119

-----1971, *Theories of Surplus Value,* part III, (Capital, vol. IV), translated from the German by Jack Cohen and SW Ryazanskaya and edited by SW Ryazanskaya and Richard Dixon, Progress Publishers, Moscow.
1 118 119 119 119

Marx, Karl & Engels, Frederick 1969, *Selected Works,* vol. 2, Progress Publishers, Moscow.

15 19 20 58 59 61 63 73 76 87 88 109 110

-----1970, *Selected Works,* vol. 3, Progress Publishers, Moscow.
52 53 65 68 (68) 80 86 (86) (86) 87

-----1989, *Selected Works,* revised edn, vol. 1, Progress Publishers, Moscow.
13 19 20 20 20 60 62 69 76 84 (84) (84) (84) 86 87 113

Mathias, P 1969, *The First Industrial Nation: An Economic History of Britain 1700-1914,* Methuen & Co Ltd, London.
8 14 56

Mercer, Derrik (editor-in-chief) 1996, *Chronicle of the World,* Dorling Kindersley, London.
13 25 48

Milston, Gwendda 1978, *A Short History of China,* Cassell Australia, Stanmore, NSW.
3 42 44

Montaigne, Michel de 1965, *The Complete Essays of Montaigne,* trans. DM Frame, Stanford University Press, California.
93

Murowchick, Robert E (ed.) 1994, *China: Ancient Culture, Modern Land,* Cradles of Civilization Series, Weldon Russell Pty Ltd, North Sydney.
123

Nove, A 1992, *An Economic History of the USSR 1917-1991,* 3rd edn, Penguin Books, Harmondsworth, England.
Reproduced by permission of Penguin Books Ltd.
19 24 31 (32) 32 (33) (33) 33 36 (36) 38 39 57 68 108 (109) 110

Randall, John Herman Jr 1976, *The Making of the Modern Mind,* Columbia University Press, New York.
14

Riasanovsky, Nicholas V 1977, *A History of Russia,* 3rd edn, Oxford University Press, New York.
18 (18) 25 26 28 28 29 33 34 39 (39) (39) 99 110 (110) (110) 110

Robbins, Lionel 1998, *A History of Economic Thought,* Princeton University Press, Princeton.
59 113

Roberts, JAG 1998, *Modern China: An Illustrated History,* Sutton Publishing Limited, Gloucester, Britain.
41 (41) (41) (41) 46 (46) (46) (46) (46) (46) (46) (46) (46) (47) (47) (47) (47) (47) (48)

Roebuck, Carl 1966, *The World of Ancient Times,* Charles Scribner's Sons, New York.
109

Roll, Eric 1961, *A History of Economic Thought,* Faber and Faber Ltd, London.
51 59 60 60 60 65 71 74 80 (80) (81) (81) 122

Rowse, AL 1979, *The Story of Britain,* Artus Publishing Co Ltd, London.
13

Samuelson, PA & Nordhause, WD 1985, *Economics,* 12th edn, Mcgraw-Hill, New York.
50

Smith, Adam 1991, *Wealth of Nations,* Great Minds Series, Prometheus Books, Buffalo, New York.
8 10 (10) 55 55 59 70 73 113 (113)

Spielvogel, Jackson J 1991, *Western Civilization,* West Publishing Co, St Paul.
13 (13) 78 (78) (78)

Walker, A 1978, *Marx: His Theory and Its Context,* Longman, London.
Reprinted by permission of Peters Fraser & Dunlop www.petersfraserdunlop.com on behalf of the Estate of Hilaire Belloc.
13 20 50 87 110

Wells, HG 1925, *The Outline of History,* revised edn, 2 vols, Cassell and Co Ltd, London.
6 7 17 57 70 78 89

Williams, Trevar I 1987, *The History of Invention: From Stone Axes to Silicon Chips,* Macdonald & Co Ltd, London.
6 (6) 7 8

Index

www.ingramcontent.com/pod-product-compliance
Lightning Source LLC
LaVergne TN
LVHW081150110826
845149LV00008B/1610